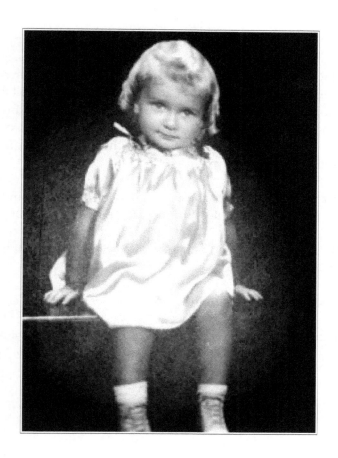

This book is dedicated to George and Bee Ullman's daughter

❧❧

Bunny

Published by:
Viale Industria Publicazioni
Torino, Italy
viplibri@libero.it
Copyright 2014

Original publication of *Valentino As I Knew Him,* by Macy-Masius, 1926
Second Edition by A.L. Burt, 1927.

ISBN: 978 8890 7063 63

In Deposito Legale presso SBN
http://www.sbn.it/opacsbn/opac/iccu/free.jsp
Opera protetta dalla legge del 22 Aprile 1941 n. 633 ("Protezione del diritto d'autore e di altri diritti connessi al suo esercizio") e successive modificazioni, e dal Titolo IX del Libro Quinto del Codice civile Italiano.

Cover Design by sepsispod@gmail.com

The S. George Ullman Memoir

◈◈

The Real Rudolph Valentino

by

The Man Who Knew Him Best

"...The truth is incontrovertible. Malice may attack it. Ignorance may deride it. But in the end, there it is."

Winston Churchill

A Table of Contents

Rudolph Valentino and George Ullman
on the set of
The Eagle, 1925

A Foreword

by

Evelyn Zumaya

"We (writers) must know that we can never escape the common misery and that our only justification, if indeed there is a justification, is to speak up, insofar as we can, for those who cannot do so."

Albert Camus

This past August thirteenth, I was privileged to enjoy a lunch with S. George Ullman's daughter, Bunny. Nearly twelve years had passed since I first visited this gracious woman in her scenic hilltop home. On that day, I came as a curious reporter working on a biography of Rudolph Valentino. This past August, I walked up the familiar winding path, past the holly bushes and many bird feeders, to be welcomed as a friend. As I sat with Bunny amid the fragrant blooms on her sunny patio, my thoughts wandered back to that first visit to her home. I could not help but feel humbled as I recollected the events awaiting me from that day forward. To encapsulate the saga that transpired after my first interview with Bunny would do little justice to the magnitude of this story. I will, however, in this Foreword, do my best to relate an overview of what became one of the most defining and arduous endeavors of my long life.

As Bunny and I discussed this publication, she reminded me that August thirteenth was her brother Bob's birthday. At the mention of his name, I felt every one of the many years since my last interview with her brother. For Bob played a critical role in my research and read a final draft of my book, which I titled, *Affairs Valentino* just a few weeks before he passed away in 2005. Bob worked diligently assisting me in my efforts to ensure his father's legacy be reported truthfully and based upon factual documentation. In gratitude for his contributions, I dedicated the book to his memory.

From 1923 to 1926, Bob and Bunny's father, George Ullman held the position of silent film icon Rudolph Valentino's closest friend, mentor and business manager. After Valentino's death in 1926, he was appointed executor of the movie star's estate. I was well aware of Ullman's prominent role in Valentino's story and for this reason I made locating his surviving relatives an early objective in my Valentino research .

I began my search for Ullman's family in 2002, as I hoped they could direct me to any archives which might provide me with details of Ullman's tenure as Rudolph Valentino's business manager and executor. At that time, I had no idea just how much I would discover nor the controversy I would instigate in revealing these discoveries.

Within a few weeks I was in contact with George Ullman's grandson. He directed me to Ullman's surviving children; Bunny, then seventy-four years old and her older brother Bob, who at seventy-nine, was quite ill. George Ullman's grandson also informed me that his father, Ullman's oldest son Dan, passed away some years earlier.

I forwarded a letter of introduction to Bob and Bunny Ullman and within a few days I received a telephone call from Bob. During our first conversation, he said that he welcomed an opportunity to discuss his father's story with me as no one in the Ullman family had ever been contacted regarding their father's association with Rudolph Valentino. I made plans to travel to interview him in person. Meanwhile, I placed a telephone call to his sister Bunny and I was able to meet with her within a few days. During the first of many interviews with Bunny, she presented me with a cache of unpublished documents and photographs relating to her father and Rudolph Valentino.

Within the next week, I conducted my first interview with Bob Ullman and he shared his collection of family photographs and documents. He also had many questions for me regarding his father's tenure as Valentino's executor. This was a subject of particular interest to Bob, as his father told him little about his thirty year involvement in the contentious settlement of Valentino's estate. Bob made it clear to me how profoundly his father's legal travails as Valentino's executor affected the Ullman household. I knew this was a subject receiving scant coverage in publications on Valentino and it was, at that time, a subject I had yet to research thoroughly. I soon realized that investigating Valentino's "after-life" would undoubtedly reveal a great deal about his business affairs as well as his affiliation with Ullman.

During my first interview with Bob Ullman, we also discussed a campaign to disparage his father's memory conducted primarily by a few members of Valentino's inner circle, including Valentino's brother. Bob felt their animosity was in response to their resentment of his father's closeness to Valentino during the star's life and because of his authority over his post-mortem affairs. As a result of this resentment, Bob felt his father was victimized by years of allegations which were never substantiated by any factual documentation. He said this frustration was shared by the entire Ullman family and was exacerbated when his father denied opportunities to defend himself publicly against the uncorroborated, denigrating reports.

I assured Bob I would ascertain the truth about his father's performance as Valentino's executor and make this my research priority. Bob encouraged me to begin my research in the Los Angeles County Hall of Records where I could review Valentino's case file of probate records housed in that facility. These documents, he said, would reveal the facts of his father's true story.

Without a doubt, the most important item in the treasure trove presented to me by Bob and Bunny Ullman during these initial interviews was their father's unpublished memoir. Prior to his death in 1975, George Ullman wrote this frank memoir revealing his behind-the-scenes life with Rudolph Valentino. I add that by the time I began my interviews with the Ullmans, I had read nearly every published word about Valentino. So as I read Ullman's memoir for the first time, I was riveted by a wealth of new and personal anecdotes. The more I read, the more I realized that Ullman's tales of life with "Rudy" were drastically altering the currently held version of the star's character and his life story.

In his memoir, Ullman delved into many aspects of Valentino's life which had never been mentioned in any publication to date. For example, some of these subjects included the negotiation of Valentino's second contract with United Artists, Valentino's propensity to gamble and the existence of several press agents who were employed full-time by Valentino to prevent news of some of his unsavory behavior from ever reaching his adoring public. Other more cryptic mentions included Ullman's opinion that Valentino's brother, Alberto's attorneys were funded by United Artists and details of the decades long collection process held against him by Alberto Valentino.

Consequently, while I continued interviewing Bob and Bunny Ullman, I followed the clues provided to me in the memoir and embarked upon a campaign to locate more supportive documents and other archives in order to fact-check and substantiate Ullman's claims. By the time I began my vetting of the Ullman memoir, I had been researching and writing about Rudolph Valentino for a few years and believed I was nearing completion of my work. However, the revelations contained within Ullman's memoir and my subsequent discoveries were of such significance, I was compelled to rethink, rewrite and begin my work on Valentino anew.

I noticed the memoir opened with excerpts from a book Ullman published in 1926, titled, *Valentino As I Knew Him*. According to Bob and Bunny Ullman, their mother, Bee, told them that their father wrote *Valentino As I Knew Him* in the weeks just after Rudolph Valentino's sudden death in New York City on August 23, 1926. He penned his manuscript as a sort of personal eulogy while on board Valentino's funeral train traveling home to California with an entourage of loved ones and press.

Ullman was still grieving the loss of his dear friend, Rudy at the time and consequently his final 1926 manuscript was not only a biographical narrative but an intimate account of Valentino's last hours of life. As Ullman kept vigil by Valentino's deathbed and witnessed his death, he felt compelled to share some appropriate details with the movie star's public. To quote the 1970 memoir and Ullman's reason for writing *Valentino As I Knew Him* in 1926:

"....In the year that Rudy passed away I wrote a book---rather hurriedly I'm afraid, so that the many thousands of his admirers could have at least an honest, although brief biography quickly because I knew that a great amount of fiction and inaccurate accounts would soon be published, which indeed did happen. "

Since that time, erroneous reports have surfaced that Ullman's 1926, *Valentino as I Knew Him* was ghostwritten. Several prominent experts on Valentino have even made this inaccurate claim. I state with all authority that George Ullman wrote *Valentino As I Knew Him* in 1926. His friends and his wife Bee, recall seeing him working on this book while on the funeral train riding to California. Many pages of the original manuscript, in Ullman's handwriting, are still in existence.

It is also worthy of note to compare the stylistic composition of Ullman's 1926, *Valentino As I Knew Him* with his 1970, memoir. His characteristic construction of short paragraphs, consisting of long, single sentences stands as one example of his unique writing style. This is consistently apparent in both *Valentino As I Knew Him* and the 1970, memoir. *Valentino As I Knew Him* did receive editorial embellishments before publication while the 1970, memoir exists solely as Ullman's unedited working draft. Despite this, readers will readily observe the familiar phrasing, compositional and grammatical quirks of George Ullman in both works. Additionally, his free-flowing writing style in the 1970, memoir is the same style evident in *Valentino As I Knew Him,* as he writes with little emphasis upon the chronological order of his narrative.

The final manuscript of his 1926, *Valentino As I Knew Him* was readied for publication with the editorial assistance and expertise of Los Angeles writer, Lillian Bell and Raymond Fager, a clerk and typist employed by Rudolph Valentino Productions. George Ullman's *Valentino as I Knew Him* was first published in October of 1926 by Macy-Masius and second and third editions were released in 1927 by the publisher, A.L. Burt. I have included a *New York Times* review of the First Edition in this publication.

It was over four decades later, in the 1970's, when Ullman began writing his memoir, initially as an apparent rewrite of his original publication, *Valentino As I Knew Him.* He soon abandoned this direction to write instead a sequence of anecdotes and personal memories.

Although Ullman has been accused of writing his 1970's memoir to exploit Rudolph Valentino, this is a false statement. Ullman was in failing health at the time and his children recall how they encouraged him to pen his memoirs about his life with Rudy; as Bunny Ullman said, "More to give him something to do".

As Ullman completed the handwritten pages of his memoir, his children delivered them to a typist. I learned from Bunny Ullman this past August, that her father recorded some of the memoir on a reel to reel tape recorder. She recalled that a portion of those tapes included her father swearing in frustration as he tried to figure out how to work the tape recorder.

I received Ullman's copy of his unpublished 1970, memoir as a stack of loose, yellowing pages; some faded and others barely readable. Tucked within these pages, Ullman included a copy of his original managerial contract signed with Valentino in 1923, a personal letter he received from Valentino's attending physician at the time of his death and an article referring to the creation of a childrens ward in Valentino's honor in a London hospital. It was nearly impossible for me to accept that this remarkable document had remained unpublished and largely forgotten for thirty years after Ullman's death.

Throughout this phase of my research, my primary focus was always the recovery of Rudolph Valentino's probate court records as it was critical I verify the truth about George Ullman's tenure as executor with facts. Bob Ullman was adamant that without this documentation anything I wrote about this subject would just be more surmise and speculation. My search for these records would span more than one year. But on May 3rd, 2004, I was informed by the Los Angeles County

Clerk that the entire case file of Rudolph Valentino's Probate records was not available for public review as it was missing from its lawful location. I was, however, after another lengthy search, able to locate certified copies of these missing records. The story of their recovery and significance is explained in George Ullman's biography in this book and revealed in comprehensive detail in *Affairs Valentino*.

I state here, after years of analysis of these documents, that contrary to the reports continuing to plague Ullman's legacy, he was completely exonerated by the court and found not guilty of any fraud or mismanagement of the Rudolph Valentino estate. A thorough court audit found his book keeping to be in impeccable order. I will say that thankfully, due to the recovery of these valuable court records and the first accurate telling of his story in *Affairs Valentino*, the falsifications about Ullman are waning. This said, I believe, after a decade researching this story, that one of the reasons Rudolph Valentino's probate court records were stolen was to suppress the truth about George Ullman. Furthermore, I feel that the concerted effort by a determined few to impugn Ullman was the reason why the very existence of his 1970, memoir was also suppressed.

I came to this conclusion after learning that there is allegedly at least one other copy of Ullman's unpublished memoir in circulation. This was revealed to me while I was being interviewed for an article with the *Los Angeles Times* about my work on Valentino. The reporter interviewed the Valentino family spokeswoman and then called me to tell me that she informed him she had read the Ullman memoir. Both I and the Ullman family were stunned to learn this as they previously knew of no other copies available. I state here, for the record, that all other copies are unauthorized by the Ullman estate.

Again, it was only after intense analysis of the minute details of the recovered court records, that I understood why there are such strong, emotional reactions to the subject of George Ullman. I also developed my theories as to how another copy might have been procured and if this was so, why the information contained within the memoir was suppressed for decades. This silence by others, allegedly in possession of this bootleg copy is not golden. These key individuals, outwardly representing Valentino's legacy, claim to have had access to this memoir for years, yet have never issued a single mention of its existence in any book or publication on Rudolph Valentino. Furthermore, Ullman's anecdotes were never related until I brought them forward. Indeed, I wondered how all of Ullman's colorful new Valentino lore escaped decades of Valentino biographers and his thriving fan base's knowledge.

If these individuals claiming to have had access to a bootleg copy of the Ullman memoir were being truthful, I ask why they suppressed the fact this document existed and why they did not share the contents with Valentino's public. If they had come across a copy of the memoir, then I ask why they did not notify the Ullman estate of their possession of this important document.

Despite what became mounting opposition to my work on Ullman from these determined few, I forged forward to write as accurate an account of his life and his affiliation with Rudolph Valentino as possible. I will admit that I faced a difficult task of organizing and writing a tale that spanned some one hundred years and involved a complex account of unforgivable betrayals, high-stakes courtroom dramas, ruthless power plays and a rash of individuals still conspiring to prevent the truth from ever being revealed. These various story lines, along with the righting of the wrongful and continuing campaign of denigration levied against George Ullman comprised the basis for my new telling of Valentino's story.

I add here that I had been under attack from Ullman's detractors for two years prior to the publication of *Affairs Valentino* in 2011. With the publication of the First Edition of my book, I came under further intense and withering attack from its day one. This opposition continues as of this writing.

Today these Valentino fundamentalists, (referring to the definition of fundamentalist as one adhering to an ancient doctrine of belief) purport the studio-generated and fictional versions of Valentino's life and perpetuate their historical inaccuracies regarding Ullman despite the existence of publicly available court evidence and documented truths. In my opinion these few comprise Valentino memorabilia collectors and Valentino biographers who parrot the misinformation as they are unwilling to break rank from the Valentino family's officially issued and "approved" versions of this story. It is lamentable, in light of the evidence I brought forth, to realize that these few not only control Valentino's legacy but are the same few who have perpetuated the falsehoods about Ullman for decades.

The many misconceptions they have perpetuated throughout the years include the allegation that Ullman plotted to break up

Valentino's marriage. This is false. They have reported that he negotiated a contract for Valentino with United Artists that specifically mentioned Valentino's wife, Natacha Rambova's exclusion from any role in her husband's films. This is false. They have even reported that Ullman contributed to Valentino's death. This is a ludicrously false claim. I address these and many more falsehoods about Ullman in *Affairs Valentino*.

Both of George Ullman's manuscripts, his book first published in 1926, *Valentino as I Knew Him* and his 1970, memoir are included in their entirety in this volume. I have included additional materials relevant to this story; photographs, personal documents of Ullman and the entire Court of Appeals Exoneration. I also point out the following to readers as they consider the fascinating comparison of both documents.

In his 1926, *Valentino As I Knew Him*, George Ullman created a textbook example of his finest advertising "speak", crafted during the years he was employed as Valentino's business manager. I would not say he misrepresented Valentino in his first book, but rather he omitted elements to stay the course as point man in his efforts to groom the further marketing of Rudolph Valentino. As readers study the differences between both works, they will note Ullman expanded his story considerably in his 1970, memoir.

Additionally, documents I subsequently discovered upon the direction of the memoir such as the court documents, court testimony and the book keeping of Valentino's business and personal accounts further contributed to the verification of Ullman's revelations which he did not include in the 1926, *Valentino As I Knew Him*. I cite only two examples of many to illustrate this point.

In the 1926, *Valentino As I Knew Him*, Ullman described the scene at the train station and the last kiss of Rudolph Valentino and his wife Natacha Rambova as they initiated a "marital separation". It was revealed in the 1970, memoir and supported by the court records that a great deal more took place before that last kiss at the train station. In fact, Valentino established his new production company that day with the purpose of eliminating his wife's role in his business affairs.

Also, the near exclusion of any mention of Valentino's godfather, Frank Mennillo in the 1926, *Valentino As I Knew Him*, is further evidence of the adherence to the marketable version of Valentino's story. Court records and again the 1970, memoir, revealed Mennillo's integral role in Valentino's life.

It is best to appreciate *Valentino As I Knew Him* by considering the date it was published and the daunting task facing George Ullman at the time of his writing. It is my opinion that the 1926 work stands as a powerful, effusive advertising tour de force by Rudolph Valentino's business manager who, at that time, was very much still hard at work polishing Rudolph Valentino's brilliant public image.

For when Ullman wrote *Valentino As I Knew Him* in 1926, he faced the challenging task of marketing Valentino's last movie, *The Son of the Sheik,* released just prior to the star's death. Ullman also had no choice but to market Valentino and his films, in order to clear the heavily-indebted estate. For this reason, in *Valentino As I Knew Him,* Ullman adheres largely to the studio-generated version of Valentino's life; a story which Ullman himself, at times, personally crafted for public consumption.

As a final consideration, I add that before George Ullman became Rudolph Valentino's manager, he studied Industrial Engineering. I comment on this as I feel this academic discipline formed the basis for Ullman's success as Valentino's manager and provided him with the ability to endure the events that transpired following Valentino's death. I personally feel that if it were not for Ullman's clever promotions and hard work in the days and months after Valentino's death, the star might not today be enjoying the degree of international popularity that currently envelopes his legacy. There is no doubt that Ullman's study of Industrial Engineering taught him well how to optimize his efforts in synthesizing the disparate aspects of Valentino's businesses and analyzing the statistical results of his work. His scientific application in utilizing these key aspects of Industrial Engineering, resulted in his meticulous book keeping and expertise in sales and public relations. In this effort he forged his own iconic legacy as Valentino's manager. Ullman's broad understanding of the market in which Valentino was employed and his ability to assimilate the principles of corporate management with celebrity management were practical applications he utilized which were decades ahead of his time.

In light of the events transpiring in George Ullman's life during the nearly fifty year time span between the writing of his first publication in 1926 and his memoir in the 1970's, I feel Ullman demonstrated remarkable restraint in his latter memoir. His dignified literary demeanor stands as proof of his enduring affection and respect for his friend Rudolph Valentino.

After an exhaustive analysis of this wealth of newly-discovered documentation, I am able to say without reservation that George Ullman was a man of high integrity and an honest businessman. Anyone seeking to fact-check the supporting documentation upon which I make this statement may reference case number 83678 in The Los Angeles County Hall of Records and the case of "S. George Ullman v. Alberto Guglielmi Et Al, Respondents", in The Hastings Law Library/California Appeals Court Library in San Francisco, California.

Although a contract was signed between the Ullmans and myself in 2005, granting me permission to issue this publication, a great deal has transpired in the meanwhile. Despite the interminable delays, I am happy at last to see this project realized and to have the Ullman estate's authorization for this continued effort to ensure George Ullman receive the praise he has always deserved.

I was sad to say good bye to Bunny Ullman after our lunch this past August. For I live a world away and was not sure when I would venture back for my next visit. Before we parted I asked her if she would choose a photograph of her father for the cover of this book. With a nod of agreement, she perused the several I had chosen as candidates before making her decision saying, "This one looks most like him". She then walked with me to my car where we snapped a photo of us together and said our good bye.

Despite the years of opposition to my work as I brought forth George Ullman's inspiring story, I here present first the 1970, *S. George Ullman Memoir* and then the 1926, classic, *Valentino As I Knew Him*. These lost chapters in Hollywood's history are not only an important addition to my process of disclosing the source materials I referenced in telling this story in *Affairs Valentino*, but as testament to a great man, George Ullman. And now....he will, at long last, have his own say.

Respectfully,

Evelyn Zumaya
Turin
September 2014

The S. George Ullman Memoir

Please Note: The passages in Italic in this memoir denote text previously published in George Ullman's, 1926 publication, *Valentino As I Knew Him*.

Rudolph Valentino died more than forty-six years ago. Yet now, as in previous years, there has been a resurgence of interest in his life and work; his last two pictures are being exhibited in various theaters in the U.S and in foreign lands. Always, there are capacity audiences. There are still numerous requests for any photographs and for any personal belongings that he might have touched. There is no explanation for this phenomenon and it is truly the only time in history that interest such as this has ever been manifested for any person throughout such a long period of time.

Certainly not many of his adult admirers at the time of his death are still living. So it must be that today's fans are the children and possibly the grandchildren of those who were adults in 1926.

In the year that Rudy passed away I wrote a book---rather hurriedly I'm afraid, so that the many thousands of his admirers could have at least an honest, although brief biography quickly because I knew that a great amount of fiction and inaccurate accounts would soon be published, which indeed did happen. In the writing of my book *Valentino As I Knew Him*, it was necessary to omit many pertinent observations because there were then many living persons who might have felt aggrieved. Now however, I believe that only a few people remain, so that I am able to reveal many true incidents concerning Valentino which I had to repress before.

During these intervening years practically all of my memoranda and papers have disappeared. Most have been stolen from my offices. Pictures and other things were lost when a large wicker trunk was stolen from the basement of my home. So I must largely depend on my memory and some research to write an authentic and comprehensive review of Valentino's life, incorporating facts hitherto not revealed.

❧

Rudolph Valentino's struggle for success was not less than that of almost all the greats of industry or art or literature and a brief review of his early years in America might be interesting to those who have not read or known of it before. Rudy arrived in New York two days before Christmas in 1913.

Young Valentino, when he set sail, knew not a single word of English; on the way over, he made every effort to pick up a few words. As they sailed into the harbor and he caught his first view of the New York sky line, he asked a young Italian friend where to go when he landed, and was told of an Italian place, Giolitto's, on West 49*th* Street.

The gay life in Paris, along with its many disasters, had taught Rudy the one thing which he now found needful, and that was to dance. From some South American friends of his he had learned the tango, so that, when his money gave out in America, and he had tried many forms of work, failing gloriously in most of them, his thoughts turned to the one thing he could do well, namely, dance.

With this in mind, he applied first to the manager of a restaurant where he had formerly appeared as a guest. Here he did so well that it was not long before one of his admirers mentioned him to Bonnie Glass, and brought about an introduction. She was then in need of a dancing partner to take the place of Clifton Webb. She invited Rudy to her hotel the next afternoon and, after the first tryout, Miss Glass engaged him at a salary of fifty dollars per week.

Later, in San Francisco, he applied to Major Manchester, Commander of the British Recruiting Station but was told that he could not possibly pass the examination, and would only be sent back at his own expense. He had intended going to Canada to try to make the Royal Flying Corps.

Valentino and Bonnie Glass played their engagement at the Palace Theater and made a tour of the larger eastern cities. Then Bonnie opened the Chez-Fisher on 55*th* Street, which was very exclusive yet popular with the best people. Here they danced until she married Ben Ali Haggin and retired.

Joan Sawyer then engaged Valentino to dance with her during a vaudeville tour. Afterwards they appeared at the Woodmansten Inn.

Although, as the world knows, Valentino was such a success as a dancer that he could have made dancing his career and doubtless a fortune at it, nevertheless he disliked it with his whole soul when it was placed on a commercial basis, and longed to get away from it as a profession.

Deep down in his heart was always the thought that, since he had made his one success in Italy at an agricultural college, he should do something worth-wile with the knowledge thus acquired at such cost.

Hearing that California offered great opportunities, the wonders of that golden country being dinned in his ears, he joined a musical comedy called the Masked Model, because this was going to the coast. His salary was seventy-five dollars per week and traveling expenses.

In San Francisco he played with Richard Carl in Nobody Home. Shortly after this he met Norman Kerry, who was the business representative for his wealthy father, but who disliked the whole thing so much that he was thinking of going into pictures, and suggested this to Rudy. Having nothing in particular which appealed to him more, Rudy was agreeable, and set his heart on getting into Los Angeles.

But how? As usual he was out of money. He himself said he never could save, and I, as his business manager, know that this was no lie.

The transportation problem to Los Angeles was answered by an invitation from the late Frank Carter, husband of Marilyn Miller, who suggested that Rudy go with the "Passing Show", in which Al Jolson was starring.

"Join us," he said. "We are doing one night stands to Los Angeles and there is always an extra berth on our train."

Al Jolson, being consulted, was also very friendly and confirmed the invitation, thus giving Valentino his trip to Los Angeles free.

Rudy told me that on this trip Frank Carter would not let him spend a nickel of his little hoard of money, insisting that he would need every penny of it when he got to Hollywood. This generosity on the part of Frank Carter established him as a prince in the estimation of Valentino, for appreciation was certainly one of Rudy's most notable qualities.

He was enormously pleased that Norman Kerry met him at the station, and, in spite of Rudy's protests that he could not afford it, insisted that he put up at the Hotel Alexandria, then the best in town, and start out by making a good impression.

It is a fortunate thing that the poor boy knew nothing of what awaited him. Having achieved some note as a dancer, a little more as an actor, and having made some new and influential friends in the profession, he doubtless felt that all he had to do was to utilize a few introductions and thus be started on his career.

But Hollywood is terra incognita to one and all. The profession of motion pictures is strewn with the failures of those great in the professional, theatrical, literary and dramatic world.

Literally scores of artists, great in their own field, have come to Hollywood intent upon cashing in on reputations already secure in the East, and even in Europe, and have crashed to failure because the requirements of motion pictures were such that they could not qualify.

7

To succeed one must think in pictures, and this many are unable to do. Furthermore, all the large producing companies have an already filled staff of men and women whose past experience has made them valuable, so that it must indeed be an outstanding figure or presence which can get by the Cerberus who guards the entrance to these studios.

Plainly speaking, it is a case of supply and demand; and there is always an over supply on account of the fact that Hollywood is the Mecca of all artists who hope, through the magic of pictures, to obtain a wider field for their talents.

Valentino's first job in motion pictures was an extra, for which he received the munificent sum of five dollars a day, when he worked, and this was not continuously. Thus his stay at the Hotel Alexandria was dramatically short.

Valentino was always very grateful to Emmett Flynn, who was the first director to employ him. The picture was "Alimony", starring Josephine Whittel, who was then the wife of Robert Warwick. It is a noteworthy fact that working in this same picture, also as an extra, was a young girl named Alice Taffe. Later you saw her on the screen as Alice Terry in "The Four Horsemen of the Apocalypse". Thus these two untried young actors reached fame at a single bound, in and through the same vehicle.

The author of "Alimony" was Hayden Talbot, and one day Norman Kerry introduced Rudy to him. Valentino told me that Talbot had not noticed him among the extras but immediately upon meeting him said:

"You are a great type for a story I have in mind. If I ever write it and it is produced, you will get the part."

Rudy thanked him, but it was so much like other Hollywood promises that he wisely thought no more about it.

Naturally, after having secured the attention of Emmett Flynn, Rudy was very hopeful. He had earned his first real money in pictures. He felt so sure the way had opened that it was difficult for him to understand his inability to get constant work.

In company with thousands of others he tramped from studio to studio, besieging doorkeepers and casting directors and meeting with an indifference which breaks the heart of all except the stout of soul. He did not realize that, being so unmistakably foreign in type, he did not even fit into the ordinary extra class, which comprised mostly American types. Thus Valentino started with an even greater handicap than most beginners.

His money being gone, Rudy was forced to appeal to the generosity of Norman Kerry, who very willingly staked him; and he took a small apartment at Grand Avenue and Fifth Street.

It is interesting to think what might have been the result had Valentino not possessed a friend at this crucial time who was able and willing to give him the necessary financial assistance to keep going. Some are not so fortunate, and fall by the wayside or return home in despair, so that it is in reality largely due to the big-heartedness of Norman Kerry that Valentino reached a fame far surpassing that of his benefactor; who never, however, had the smallness to feel or exhibit the slightest jealousy but openly rejoice in his friend's success.

About this time Baron Long opened the Watts Tavern, a roadhouse on the outskirts of Los Angeles. He offered Rudy thirty-five dollars a week to dance there. As this meant eating regularly, Valentino was glad to accept this offer, and, as the tavern was a rendezvous for film people, Rudy had the secret hope in some way to attract the attention of a director, and go back to pictures.

His dancing partner was Marjorie Tain, who afterwards was featured in "Christie Comedies".

Nothing in pictures came of this engagement, but Rudy did meet some very fine people from Pasadena, who suggested that the Hotel Maryland, one of Pasadena's most exclusive hotels, might be able to utilize his services as a dancer.

He followed up on this suggestion, and the Maryland engaged him for one exhibition on Thanksgiving Day, when he danced with Katherine Phelps. They were so well received in their dance that when the proprietor, Mr. Linnard, returned from the East, he offered Valentino a permanent engagement. But the terms were so small that Valentino could not afford to accept them.

By a curious turn of fate, the very day that Rudy turned down the Hotel Maryland offer he accidentally met Emmet Flynn on the street. Flynn seized Rudy by the arm and told him that the story Hayden Talbot had written with Valentino in mind was about to be produced. Flynn urged Rudy to go at once to see Mr. Maxwell, the supervisor of productions.

Wildly elated, Rudy flew to the studio as on wings. He found the part to be that of a heavy, and Italian Count.

"Will you play the part for fifty dollars a week?" asked Mr. Maxwell.

Would he? With his usual hopefulness, Valentino imagined that this was the big chance which would lead straight on to fame. But, just here, the *jinx blotted out his star momentarily. There was a fight over the negative. The camera men had not been paid and they had obtained a lien on the film, thus tying up the picture. Later it was released and advertised in this wise:*

RUDOLPH VALENTINO

IN

THE MARRIED VIRGIN

&vx&

Having thus unconsciously starred in his first part, although there was no intention of conferring such honors upon him when the picture was made, he naturally looked for a continuation of his good luck. But there was another long period of inactivity; in spite of his most personal efforts, he could get nothing.

This astonished Valentino, who was not then inured to the vicissitudes of a movie career. He did not know that he might star in half a dozen pictures, and then suddenly find his services unnecessary.

Once more Emmet Flynn came to his rescue. Flynn, possessing finer feelings than some, rather hesitated to offer Valentino the part of an extra after he had played a lead but he finally ventured.

"Would you be willing to play the part of an Italian Bowery tough?" he asked.

"I will play anything!" cried Rudy, who was then only too happy to get the seven-fifty a day to which extras had then been increased.

Rudy afterwards told me, almost with tears in his eyes, that Emmett Flynn kept him on the payroll during the entire production, although he did not work every day. Valentino never forgot a kindness.

About this time, Valentino caught the attention of Henry Otto, a director for Fox, who surprised upon Rudy's face one of those inimitable expressions which were afterwards to make him famous. Otto tried to impress upon the Fox Company the value of his new find, but he failed.

Just here Mae Murray, and her then husband, Bob Leonard, whom Valentino had known in New York, came prominently into his life.

One day, on passing through their set, Rudy called out a gay "Hello" to Bob Leonard. His gallant bearing caught the attention of the artistic Mae Murray and, a few hours later, Rudy received, by telephone, an offer of the role of leading man in "The Big Little Person", to play opposite Miss Murray.

It seemed that they had been searching for the right type to play this part, and Rudy had happened to walk on at the crucial moment. This fitted in excellently with Valentino's belief in his star of destiny.

It is impossible to describe the transport of happiness into which this plunged the volatile young Italian. Rudy was almost beside himself with joy, as Mae Murray was then at the height of her youthful fame, and to be selected to play opposite her was like receiving the right hand of fellowship from the gods.

Little did Miss Murray, being a modest person, imagine to what heights she had raised the handsome boy. But this was indeed the first chance that Rudolph Valentino had had in a real picture. That he was afterwards starred in that picture with the horrible name, "The Married Virgin", was due to the fame he had achieved between the filming of the picture and its release.

But with Mae Murray he was an honest-to-goodness leading man, and that he put his best efforts into her picture goes without saying.

He retained her friendship to the very end, for when, after divorcing Bob Leonard, she married Prince Mdivani, she invited Valentino and Pola Negri to be her attendants at her wedding, which was a secret one.

Bob Leonard remained Valentino's friend, and when he could no longer get Rudy into pictures he was directing, he recommended the young fellow to Paul Powell, who was about to direct Carmel Meyers in "A Society Sensation". Valentino landed the part in his first interview with the manager, at a salary of one hundred and twenty-five per week. Rudy told me that Paul Powell was the first to say:

"Stick to it, and you will some day make a name for yourself."

This munificent salary so went to the head of the youthful leading man that he went out and bought a used Mercer for seven hundred and fifty dollars, for which he agreed to pay a hundred down and fifty a month. But it cost him about twice that much to keep it in repair, so that, when it was finally taken away from him, because he failed to keep up the payments, he was rather glad to let it go.

Paul Powell liked Valentino so much in "A Society Sensation" that he engaged him for his next production, "All Night", and was also instrumental in getting Rudy a raise to a hundred and fifty a week.

It was about this time that an epidemic of Spanish influenza broke out, closing all the studios and taking the last chance from Valentino to get work. He resisted the disease for some time, but finally came down with it and, although he had it in a severe form, he refused to have doctors or to take medicine, because he declared he believed in neither.

Bryan Foy, one of the thirteen Foys, children of the famous Eddie Foy, about this time became Rudy's roommate, and he has told me that even at this time Valentino possessed the aristocratic bearing and grandiloquent manners which later were a part of his fame. Bryan also said that Rudy would starve in order to buy suitable clothes for his parts, being even at this time always meticulously dressed.

Earl Williams, then at the height of his fame, offered Valentino a part in "Rogue's Romance", in which Rudy had to do an Apache dance. James Young was directing, and, since he had the sense to see that Valentino knew what he was about, he allowed the boy to stage the dance just as he pleased, with the result that it was a great success.

So much so, in fact, that Valentino got the idea of some day starring in the part of an Apache. This remained with him to such an extent that when he signed his last contract, under which he had a voice in the selection of his plays, he asked to have an Apache story written for him, which was done. Since this story was written entirely around Valentino's personality, the idea was very pleasing to him. It had been returned to the authors for some minor changes when he went east on our last trip. When Valentino was taken to the hospital and his recovery was expected by all, the authors planned to send the story east by the hand of Pola Negri, who was to have read it aloud to him during his expected convalescence.

Death put an end to these plans, as to many others.

James Young took a great fancy to Valentino. Having been a well-known actor of Shakespeare, and being a man of vision as well as of artistic ability, he saw the possibilities in this as yet unknown actor. It is my opinion that had not James Young had such tragic experiences in his life, he would have become one of the greatest directors in the motion picture industry. But his sensitiveness led him to take things too much to heart.

Valentino sensed this appreciation and idolized his director. Mr. Young once said to him:

"Rudy, you ought to be a great actor some day, for you have more ability than most."

These words put fresh courage unto the young man's heart and Rudy told me later that many times, when he was discouraged and was wondering if fame would always remain just beyond his grasp, these words kept coming back to him, and he would say to himself," I must have the stuff, I must! For Mr. Young is a great artist and knows ability when he sees it."

12

Tomas Ince was Valentino's next employer. Although his salary was but seventy-five dollars a week, the money was so welcome at the time that it seemed a fortune.

Rudy's next call was from D.W. Griffith, and he owed this to another letter from Paul Powell. Griffith was starring Dorothy Gish in "Out of Luck", and Valentino was engaged for the heavy.

Again when Mr. Griffith presented "The Greatest Thing in Life" at The Auditorium in Los Angeles, Valentino was engaged to dance with Carol Dempster in the prologue. This, at a hundred dollars a week, occupied Valentino for about three months, and earned him so much recognition from the public that, when "Scarlet Days" was shown at The Grauman Theater, he was also a dancer in the prologue.

It was through Douglas Gerrard that he began to have a part in the social life in Hollywood. Gerrard was a director, and entertained much at The Los Angeles Athletic Club. It was at one of these parties that Valentino met Pauline Frederick, and it was at a party at Pauline Frederick's that Valentino met Jean Acker, his first wife.

It was a case of love at first sight, and they were married almost immediately. Valentino was then working in "Once To Every Woman", starring Dorothy Phillips. His marriage to Jean Acker lasted but a short time, yet in spite of the fact that they were divorced, they remained friends, each always saying kindly and appreciative things about the other. Indeed, I may say that the grief of Jean Acker, when it was known that Valentino was doomed, was one of the most genuine things I have ever witnessed. Feeling that the end was so near, and knowing that Rudy's last wishes would have been even more kindly than those which he always manifested, I allowed Jean Acker to come to his bedside. He was unconscious and knew no one.

She had been his companion on many occasions during this last visit to New York, and I realized that there was a growing friendliness between them such as often remarked with those who are about to die. Thus Jean Acker was the last woman to see Rudolph Valentino in life.

Three other pictures came in rapid succession to Valentino. "Passion's Playground", starring Katherine MacDonald, in which he played the part of a brother to Norman Kerry, then as a heavy in "The Great Moment", starring Margaret Namara, and again in "The Fog", with Eugene O'Brien.

Imagine the surprise of Valentino when, after he had played these small parts, he was called upon to play the part of Julio in "The Four Horsemen of the Apocalypse".

In my opinion June Mathis should sit forever in the seats of the mighty for having had the vision to see Rudolph Valentino, first as the young South American tango dancer, then as the young soldier in the battle of Armageddon. She visualized him in the part so clearly that she fought for his appointment and won over all her opponents. Too much credit cannot be given to June Mathis for thus drawing back the velvet curtain for Rudolph Valentino in his Great Adventure, his ceaseless quest for undying romance.

To Rex Ingram, super-director, whose artistry has just won for him international recognition, in the presentation of the Cross of The Legion of Honor for his accuracy and poesy in depicting French history, should go unstinted praise in the handling of that difficult novel of Ibanez. The haunting figure or Rudolph Valentino as Julio, lonely even when among the wheat fields of his South American ranch, lonely even in the drawing room of Paris when he struggled with the great problems of where his loyalty and allegiance lay, loneliest of all when in the trenches and on the battle fields of France he was alone with his God, was the one outstanding memory which world audiences carried with them from the countless theaters in which this marvelous picture was displayed.

Fifty years from now those who saw this picture in their youth will tell of it to little children, and old men sitting in their clubs, watching the smoke spiral upwards from their cigars, will hark back to the haunting sweetness and forever loneliness of that wistful young figure, whose beauty they were never able to forget.

To say that Rudolph Valentino was made by "The Four Horsemen of the Apocalypse" is to state the case too mildly. Rather was Vincente Ibanez made in pictures by Rudolph Valentino. For then, and not until then, was created the vogue for his books, for pictures. And I venture to say that this novel of "The Four Horsemen" later sold by the hundred thousand because of the association of Rudolph Valentino with the character of Julio.

I myself had read the novel before the picture was produced. It made upon me no particular impression, any more than can be said of any thrilling novel of its type. Yet when I read it again, after I had seen the picture, I wept over the tragic story of Julio, because to my mind he was Rudolph Valentino.

When the picture was planned, the part of Julio was not intended to outshine the others. Neither was it planned to be an all star production, but merely a super-picture, with every part adequately taken. But when the first rushes of Julio were viewed in the projection room, both June Mathis and Rex Ingram were swept off their feet, and, seeing the possibilities which might come from featuring Julio, they began at once to build up the part, literally molding the character of Julio to fit the haunting individuality of Rudolph Valentino.

I think that never before in the history of motion pictures has such a thing been so conspicuously done; a great tribute to the budding genius of Valentino.

After this he played with Alice Lake in "Uncharted Seas". Then Armand with Nazimova in "Camille".

It is amusing now to relate that Rudy got only three hundred fifty dollars a week during all three of these pictures, and that when, after "The Four Horsemen" was released, he asked for a raise of fifty dollars a week, he was told that Metro did not feel that he was worth it, nor could they afford it.

A peculiar thing about Hollywood is that it does not at once realize the success of its pictures abroad. A preview here, a short run there, is all that Hollywood knows of its greatest successes, so that Valentino was long in discovering the tremendous hit he was making in the East.

Valentino's first work for Famous Players-Lasky Corporation not only marked an increase in salary to five hundred a week, it gave him great satisfaction to work for that firm, which he regarded as the finest in the motion picture industry.

The filming of "The Sheik", with Agnes Ayres as his leading woman, gave happiness to all concerned, inasmuch as they believed that they were filming a masterpiece.

The sale of the book, by E.M. Hull, an English author, so totally unknown that it was months before the public discovered that its writer was a woman, had reached such proportions that not to have read "The Sheik" placed one in the moron class; and the enormous success of the picture is too well known to need comment.

At an increase to seven hundred a week, Valentino then made "Moran of the Lady Letty", starring Dorothy Dalton, and, in order to obtain the offer of Famous Players-Lasky of one thousand dollars a week to play the lead in "Beyond the Rocks", Valentino gave the company an option on his services. Trouble began to brew with work on "Blood and Sand". Rudy understood that he was to have George Fitzmaurice as the director of the picture, and that the picture was to be made in Spain. Whether his contract failed to call for this, or whether he was assured by some one not in authority to believe that these conditions would be carried out, has never been satisfactorily settled; but there is no doubt in my mind that Rudy was perfectly sincere in thinking that he had been badly treated when, with another director, the picture was made in Hollywood.

It is a strange commentary on the character of Valentino, that, notwithstanding the artistic picture which Fred Niblo produced and its box office success, Rudy still clung to the idea that he had cause for grievance.

The fact remains, however, that beyond expressing himself with Italian volubility to all who would lend an ear to his alleged injustice, Valentino was too much of an artist to let his inner dissatisfaction interfere with his work. It is well known that he threw himself into the production of "Blood and Sand" with all the enthusiasm and energy of which he was capable. It was the comment of Charlie Chaplin, after the death of Valentino, that he considered Valentino's acting in "Blood and Sand" as the greatest achievement of his career.

"Blood and Sand" was followed by "The Young Rajah", which, although a vivid and colorful production gorgeously costumed and staged, was lacking in dramatic interest and was, on the whole, an inferior production. This Valentino resented, in the whole-hearted manner of the true artist which Valentino undoubtedly was.

Although he was getting a thousand dollars a week, the highest that he had yet received, the habit of some companies, of producing one or more great pictures to be followed by inferior films which Rudy called "cheaters" thus mulcting the public on the reputation of previous successes, was extremely reprehensible to him and filled him with fury. And the mounting trouble between Valentino and Famous Player-Lasky, he always declared, was because they did this, and made him the goat.

In the speeches which Valentino made while on his dancing tour with Natacha Rambova, which I shall explain further in detail a little later along in this narrative, he invariably made the statement that the quarrel with Famous Players-Lasky which resulted in their obtaining an injunction to prevent him from appearing on stage or screen for a long period, was a penalty he gladly paid in order to keep faith with his public. He openly accused Famous Players-Lasky of carrying out the nefarious practice of producing "cheaters" with every star they had under contract.

He also knew that if this practice had been kept up with him, his career would not be that continuously cumulative achievement which he so

16

ardently hoped it would be. And he openly attributed the unnecessarily short-lived careers of other stars on other companies to this dishonest and short-sighted policy.

How much of truth there was in these contentions of Valentino I myself am no judge. I set myself up as no arbiter. I am only trying to outline, in the simplest way possible, the real Valentino as he appeared to me during the all too short years in which I was privileged to know him.

But this I can truly state without fear of contradiction. Rudolph Valentino paid dearly and willingly for his determination to do what he could to elevate stars in the motion picture industry to what he considered was their proper and rightful status. He always declared that no one knew so well as the star himself or herself in what sort of story he or she could best shine.

Furthermore, he contended most of all for the rights of stars to keep faith with their public, and not be exploited for the benefit of the producers regardless of the artistic careers of their stars.

In my opinion a grave injustice was done Valentino by his own attorney, who, in filing his answer in the law suit brought by Famous Players against Valentino for alleged breach of contract, laid stress on the lack of proper dressing room accommodations, as if this constituted the main count of his grievance. This gave Famous Players attorneys a marvelous opening, of which they were swift to avail themselves. They played up what they were pleased to term Valentino's temperamental nature and hysterical demands, thus giving the public an entirely unfair and unjust picture of an earnest young actor whose sacrifices for his art entailed discomfort, ignominy, poverty and false representation in the press. Whereas I maintain that Rudolph Valentino was the only star in the entire motion picture industry who was willing to starve for an ideal.

His was an isolated example of the determination of all true artists to force justice and to maintain high ideals of dramatic art. These, when called en masse, constituted the actor's strike, famous in history, which resulted in the formation of that tremendous organization called Equity.

I must tell about the manner in which I met Valentino and the commencement of our association. Early in 1918, I had become interested in a then new science called "Industrial Engineering." I attended New York University at night for over three years in the study of this subject. It is the use of studies and methods to reduce the time of operations in industries, the creating of new techniques in operations in business and, among other things, to prepare and install systems of accounting and to suggest other developments which would help businesses function more smoothly and more profitably.

Late in 1922, I was engaged by a firm named Mineralava, Inc. because they were in financial difficulties, even though their sales were very satisfactory. They manufactured a beauty clay which was being sold to barber shops, beauty parlors, and, to some extent, to department stores. As usual I began a complete survey of their operations and soon discovered that they were spending almost as much on advertising as their gross amount of sales! It was obvious that any prolonged method such as this would soon bankrupt the business if this practice was not halted.

The directors of the company and I had long conferences for the purpose of finding some substitute to replace the large advertising expense and yet keep the business at a high level. A unique idea came to me in a few days. The plan had never been used before and it was received with some misgivings by the firm's directors.

My plan was to find out some important personality to appear in selected cities throughout the U.S., in each city a beauty contest would be conducted by the celebrity, after which he or she would make a short speech about the efficacy of the Mineralava Beauty Clay to a captive audience.

An acquaintance of mine to whom I told the Mineralava beauty contest idea called my attention to an actor who had been placed under injunction by the Paramount Pictures Corporation for refusing to abide by the terms of his contract with them. From newspaper files, I found the history of the case of Rudolph Valentino and Paramount and the name of Valentino's New York lawyer, Arthur Butler Grahm.

The directors of the beauty clay company had by this time engaged me to develop the beauty contest idea, so I proceeded to attack the first problem, that of securing the services of a known personality. I admit that it was with some misgivings that I called upon Valentino's lawyer and presented my proposition. Mr. Grahm told me that by an injunction against Valentino obtained by Paramount Pictures he was legally prohibited from working for any theatrical or motion picture firm until his contract with Paramount had been fulfilled or settled!

Valentino had been out of work for some months because of the injunction obtained by the Paramount Pictures Corporation and apparently Mr. Grahm was too busy with other matters to attempt any settlement with them. I had prepared a preliminary plan for our venture and convinced Mr. Grahm that Valentino would not be violating the injunction if he did not act or appear on a stage. He agreed, especially after I told him of the financial benefits to Valentino.

The terms I offered were as follows: Rudolph Valentino and a female partner of his selection would appear in the various cities we would select, in each of which he would 1) dance the tango, which he had made famous in his starring picture, "The Four Horsemen" 2) help select the beauty contest winner and the winners in a dancing contest 3) award the prizes and 4) deliver a speech about the merits of the Mineralava product. I had to offer, what was then, and even now would be, a prodigious salary and other inducements so that Valentino could not refuse. His attorney, of course, strongly urged him to accept. The salary and other benefits offered were as follows:

Valentino was to receive $7000 weekly for his and his partner's appearances. They would live in a private railroad car during the tour. There would be a chef and steward aboard and all expenses would be paid by the Mineralava Company. I counted upon his personal drawing power, of course, to more than offset the high cost of this unusual plan and I was not wrong! In fact, in many cities where the show was held, more than $5000 was paid by the attending audiences for the one night's performance!

I arranged the scheduled cities, engaged the private railroad car and made all conceivable plans so that the proposed tour would proceed smoothly and safely. I had also engaged the personnel, an advance man who would arrange for publicity in each city in advance of the train's arrival, two men for duties in the halls or armories or coliseums where Valentino was to appear and a man with the experience to see that the schedules were kept and in general to supervise the tours. But this man proved inadequate.

At the last moment, everybody concerned was reluctant to start the tour unless someone close to the project went along, at least in the beginning. So, I was it!

With only about six hours for preparation I arranged matters in my office and in my home and caught the 20th Century Limited out of

New York to Chicago where I was to meet Rudolph Valentino and his wife, Natacha.

I shall never forget my first meeting with them. The "Colonial" was the private railroad car which had recently been used by the King of Belgium when he made his historic tour of the United States. When I entered the car at the depot in Chicago, there, leaning against the wall of the dining-living room was one of the handsomest men I had ever seen and a beautiful young woman standing next to him. This was Natacha, Rudy's second wife. I noticed her classic beauty and her becoming outfit. Later I learned that she was the envy of many of the Hollywood stars because of her self-designed clothes and the fine materials she always had the couturiers use.

My first impression was that Valentino appeared to be belligerent, but we shook hands and spoke of my trip and then sat down and began to know each other. Rudy had a fine speaking voice, warm and cultured and so had Natacha. Rudy had a slight Italian accent. He was well set up, weighing about 150 pounds and was 5'10" in height. Soon we were discussing their part in the new venture.

Incidentally this was on March 8, 1923, the day of their legal marriage which took place that morning in Crowne Point, Indiana. The year of their enforced "separation" had ended at midnight. They had been married one year before in Mexicali, Mexico contrary to the California law which prohibits marriage of either party until the interlocutory decree had been in effect for one year. Rudy had been divorced from Jean Acker in 1922, and with total disregard for the law in California and the advice of his friends, he and Natacha had blithely skipped to Mexico where they were married, following the divorce from Jean Acker, in a brief ceremony by a judge there. They then returned to Palm Springs, California.

I must pause here to describe the interior of the private car "Colonial". There was a living-dining room, nicely furnished, two bedrooms with brass beds and wardrobes and one compartment with regulation sleeping car bunks. There also were two full-sized showers. The bedroom I was to use was adjacent to the Valentino's room, and when Natacha's aunt, Mrs. Teresa Werner, joined us, she occupied the compartment. All of the meals were prepared by the chef (who was excellent) in the kitchen on the train. The kitchen had a coal burning stove and the meals were served by the steward. As the saying goes we lived "high on the hog". The cost of all this luxury was high. Each ten

20

days I had to pay the railroad company one thousand dollars for the food and help. Each time the private car was attached to a regular train for a move from one city to the next, I had to pay for twenty-five tickets, as if twenty-five people were aboard our car. At any rate no potentate could possible have lived in greater comfort on the road!

On March 9th, 1923 we set out for the first show which was to be given in an armory in Omaha, Nebraska. By the terms of the injunction, Rudy was not permitted to appear in any theater or on any stage, so he frequently had to perform in a boxing ring or on the floor of an armory, gymnasium or coliseum. If ever there were two "good sports" Rudy and Natacha were. Some conditions in the various places where they appeared would have been intolerable for almost any professional dancers, but they cheerfully accepted such things as warped and uneven floors and torn canvasses in the boxing rings in which they had to dance, and the very frequent absence of dressing rooms. They helped improvise screens of any kind so that they could change into their costumes.

When we arrived in Omaha, Nebraska, a real blizzard was in progress. I was much disturbed, of course, because I could hardly believe that people would be hardy enough to brave the elements to see an actor. How wrong I was! The armory floor was jammed with men and women and boys and girls. There were no chairs and the audience stood through the entire show, which lasted about two hours.

I forgot to mention that we had our own band of six musicians who traveled in a regular train to which our private car was attached.

The band played an introductory number and I stepped into the ring and introduced the performers. Then Rudy and Natacha were in the ring. He wore the costume of a gaucho and she a Spanish dancer's dress and shawl. Their first steps brought immense applause and when they completed the number the audience belonged to them!

After quieting the people I announced that the beauty contest was about to begin. The girls who were the contestants had been chosen before we arrived in a contest conducted by a local newspaper. The number of girls varied in each city, but here in Omaha there were twenty. They filed into the ring and paraded before Rudy and Natacha. Actually, Rudy did not select the winner. By their applause the audience itself selected her. The winning girl in each city received a set of beautiful dolls in the image of Rudy and Natacha in their dancing costumes. These were made by Sardieux in New York to whom we paid one hundred dollars for each pair. Each winner in the eighty seven cities where the contests were held was later to be brought to New York City to appear in the Madison Square Garden where the finals of the contest were to be held and the beauty queen would be chosen by a group of nationally known artists. This was the first time that any such contest was held anywhere and it required an enormous amount of planning and labor on my part to bring it to conclusion.

After the beauty contest in each city was completed, Rudy gave the short prepared speech about Mineralava and then he delivered a tirade against the Paramount Pictures Corporation and motion picture methods in general. This, I am sure, was Natacha's idea because she often spoke about the inefficiency of every facet of motion picture production methods.

When the dancing contest commenced there were so many contestants that there had to be several relays. Out of each group a winning couple was selected by audience applause. These interim winners later appeared again when the final winning couple was chosen by the audience. The winner received a large, handsome plated cup upon which was engraved "Winner of the Mineralava Dancing Contest."

In all, Valentino and company appeared in eighty-seven cities in the U.S. and Canada. Some of the experiences we had in the various cities were unbelievable! The frenzied women made all manner of attempts to get close to Rudy. It was frequently necessary to ask police protection to prevent bodily harm to him.

For example, in Salt Lake City, while the show was in progress, a pleasant husky man came to me and called my attention to one of the pretty girls ready to enter the beauty contest. I recognized him at once. He was Jack Dempsey, the heavyweight boxing champion, and this was his protégé. I introduced him to Rudy. His girl won. Rudy and Jack later became great friends in Hollywood.

I must return to the early days of the tour. The Valentinos and I were fast becoming good friends. They were delightful to be with and they were entirely co-operative and compliant with the many changes which had to be made in the daily routine. They began to talk about their personal problems often and in great detail. About four or five days after the tour began, Rudy said to me, "George, why don't you be my manager after this tour is over?" I'm afraid that I was a little undiplomatic when I said to him, "You haven't much to manage, have you?" In short, I declined the offer and he said, "You will be my manager some day, I'm sure." Long afterwards, I learned that the Valentinos were in frequent communication with a lady named Cora McGeachy, who almost daily sent them automatic writings she received and wrote while in a trance. It was her letters with predictions from "Black Feather" and "Mesolope" who were supposed to be his astral guides, that gave Rudy and Natacha the confidence they needed.

There are groups of Valentino worshippers all over the world who claim that Rudy is in direct touch with them through their chosen psychics or mediums. All allege deep psychological messages from Rudy, or through him by various entities. Books have been written divulging these profound messages and quotations. I have received many dozens of letters from writers who were "instructed" to send messages to me, but cannot honestly say that any of these were recognizable or important.

I know how great was Rudy's and Natacha's belief in all psychic matters and how often they would believe that an event was a "demonstration". There probably was something akin to superstition in their acceptance of all the advice given in the automatic writings of Cora McGeachy, some of which were not in their best interests. But I never heard either of them complain when the McGeachy transcriptions proved faulty or incorrect. Their contact with Cora ended when they decided to part.

Cora was occasionally employed by Universal Studios in North Hollywood as an assistant designer of women's styles. She was also a musician and had composed many songs, none of which, unfortunately, received recognition. Another talent of hers was to paint. She created many landscapes and seascapes, some of which were bought by friends.

∂ৡৎ

In Paris, the Valentinos were interviewed by a reporter, who, in general really resembled Rudy. They were so enthused over their discovery that they persuaded this young man to accompany them to New York (at their expense of course), and had him as a guest in their Park Avenue apartment. Rudy actually insisted that Andre Devan be given a small part in the *Monsieur Beaucaire* picture, but, without any training or ability, his screen debut didn't develop. But, what did develop was that Devan ran up large bills for dental work and purchases and even borrowed five hundred dollars from one of our friends. All of this came to light after Andre suddenly decided to return to Paris without more than a perfunctory farewell to Rudy and Natacha. Later I sent him a statement of his indebtedness to Rudy, but his reply, written in French, was to the effect that Rudy had interrupted his newspaper career and that he held him responsible for his time lost! This is just one other example of the manner in which Rudy and Natacha spent their money on a whim.

After Rudy died, Natacha wrote a book based upon messages received from Rudy through a psychic. These messages were almost entirely general in substance and how much was in fact "received" or how much was invented, we will never know.

Many years later, in 1965, Mrs. Lynn Russell, quite evidently a dedicated spiritualist, wrote a book that was published in London, under the title, "The Voice of Valentino." These revelations came through a medium whose name was Leslie Flint. Here, again, are profound utterances, through the voice of Mr. Flint, by Rudy, describing in detail the events in his Heavenly Home and his constant contacts with departed spirits of persons from Hollywood and everywhere imaginable, including his meetings with historical personalities almost as far back as the beginning of the world!

I will not dispute with Mr. Flint or Mrs. Russell any of the advices and revelations allegedly from Valentino's spirit world because I have no reason to do so. My only reservation is that nowhere in all the messages in this book of one hundred and eighty-eight pages are any quotations or references to events that I personally could recognize either in style or substance relative to discussions Rudy and

I had through the many hours we spent together or of events which only he and I knew.

Recently, a former journalist in Washington, whose name is Ruth Montgomery, wrote a book in which she quoted words of wisdom, descriptive of life after death, all dictated to her and typed by her on an electric typewriter through her gift of automatic writing. She also received information that Rudy was alive again, happily married and living in Paris. Here again I dislike to question the validity of this and hope that the statement about Rudy's matrimonial bliss is factual. I would love to hear from him.

While in New York, the Valentinos and my wife and I attended several séances in the home of Victor Miller, a dealer in antiques and from whom Rudy bought many rare pieces.

The séances there were attended by a large group of spiritualistic mediums of both sexes and the principal quest was for materialism, that is, the visual appearance of departed persons.

The sessions were held in a large darkened room and each of those in attendance, in their own method, invoked a spirit to materialize. Frequently one or more of the guests would loudly claim that they were seeing a form and the others would welcome the manifestation. Unfortunately, I couldn't see anything.

After each of the prolonged sessions, Mr. Miller provided a splendid French dinner with appropriate wines. All prepared, he said, by himself!

❧❧

We had gotten to the point where Rudy asked me to look at his accounts and letters from his lawyer in New York. I was appalled to see that Mr. Grahm, his lawyer, was taking $2500 out of each weekly $7000 check from my company as a retainer fee for himself. From the remainder, Mr. Grahm detailed payments of debts allegedly owed by the Valentinos. Rudy was practically broke again. It was then I decided that Valentino needed someone to protect his interests and that I would gamble my future to do this for him. But I did not tell him at this time. It is difficult even now to understand the reason for my decision. But Rudy's magnetic personality and graciousness and yes, helplessness, were certainly contributing factors.

There were many unusual occurrences during the Mineralava tour even beyond the daily manifestations of the women and girls. For example, in Atlanta, Georgia, I had arranged to have two performances, one in the later afternoon for the white people and the other in the evening for blacks. I was standing near the box office when a neatly dressed, aristocratic appearing white woman approached me and firmly suggested that I call off the evening show for the blacks. I was probably naïve and said that I could see no reason to give up the added income until she said, "Did you ever hear of the Ku Klux Klan?" Then I realized that Rudy and Natcha could be endangered. So I did cancel the evening show and got out of Atlanta as quickly as possible after the matinee performance.

From time to time my wife joined us at different stops and the Valentinos turned on their charms for her. She was overwhelmed by their attentions and friendliness.

When we were in Rochester, Minnesota, we met Dr. Walter Mayo, who invited us to accompany him to tour the large insane asylum there. We, Natacha, Rudy and I, without much thought, agreed to go with him. It was a sad visit. In one section were the men, some young and others old, unhappy, despondent souls. We spoke to several of them and each had a fanciful message they wished to have delivered to someone or anyone. Dr. Mayo told us that these were the non-violent inmates, all incurable.

Then we went to the women's section. The word "bedlam" is the only description I can make. Here were dozens of females shrieking and shaking the steel doors trying to get to Rudy. I don't believe they knew who he was but he was handsome and well groomed. We were happy to get out of there quickly.

One of our stops was in Montreal, Canada. There was, if possible, even greater enthusiasm there than in the U.S. In making his speech about the beauty clay and about motion pictures, Rudy realized that many in the audience probably did not understand English, so, after the English version he smoothly switched to the same speech but in perfect French. The effect was unbelievable because quite evidently the largest portion of the audience was French-Canadian! One woman came to me and, showing me a five hundred dollar banknote said that she would give it to me if Rudy would visit her in her hotel room! I didn't tell him but I am sure he would not have gone there especially so because Natacha was with us!

While arranging the schedule of the cities we were to appear in, Rudy told me that he could not go to Los Angeles or Hollywood. He feared arrest, he said, because of several judgments held against him. I assured him that none of these judgments were in the least based upon criminal offenses. They were simply for several debts he had made and had been unable to pay. But I agreed that it was better to avoid any possibility that might delay our scheduled tours.

We were in Vancouver, Washington, the last city in the U.S. before crossing a bridge into Vancouver, British Columbia. Our train was stopped and an American officer came aboard our train. He told me in no uncertain terms that no one should bring any whiskey or other alcoholic beverages to the train purchased in Vancouver. He threatened to put our car on a siding if he found any upon our return and that we would be held until the case was heard in the Federal Court. This was heard by Rudy and Natacha and the other occupants of our car.

The usual performance and as always the audience was enchanted by the Valentino's dancing and Rudy's talk. Always, after each performance, I checked the box office receipts and took the money to a telegraph office. Then sent it by wire to the bank account of the Mineralava Company in New York City. This operation took about an hour after which I returned to the train to plan the next move for the following day's performance.

On this evening, when I returned to the train, there was an unmistakable air of excitement but Rudy denied that anything was amiss. When I entered my room I noticed several wooden cases under my bed and I knew then what had been taking place while I was absent. There was simply nothing I could do to rectify what had been done. Rudy had ordered several cases of whiskey, liquors and wines brought aboard and stacked then under his bed, my bed and under the floor boards in the hall of the train. I told everyone to stay in their sleeping quarters and told Rudy not to open his door should the customs man board the train in the morning.

Sure enough, quite early in the morning, I heard a loud voice shouting in the kitchen. It was the officer. I opened my door, pretending to have a bad hangover and yelled at the top of my lungs for them to stop the noise. The officer came to my door holding three almost empty bottles and said, "I warned you! This will cost you thirty dollars!" I pretended to be angry with the chef and steward and said I would take it out of their pay. I gave the officer the thirty dollars and with great relief saw him swing off the train and signal for us to go ahead.

Had the officer found the hidden cases he could have caused us great expense and perhaps my arrest. But Rudy, even though he was always supplied with any kind of drinks he wanted, couldn't resist the impulse to gamble on his luck.

One of the last cities in which we held a show was in Atlantic City, New Jersey. The armory there was packed at 7:30 p.m. but Valentino had not arrived. He had gone to New York City with Natacha the day before and I had spoken with him from Atlantic City to remind him to be on time for the show. He said that Natacha didn't feel well but was sure that she would be with him and that they would arrive at 7 p.m. Now it was eight o'clock and there was no sign of Rudy. I tried to reach him by phone but received no answer.

It can well be imagined how great my concern was, particularly because a sheriff had placed himself next to me and told me that he would wait only a little while longer and then arrest me for fraud!

Just about nine o'clock, when I had almost called off the show, Rudy arrived with a substitute dancer. He was badly shaken himself but started to get ready to go on. I appeared on the platform and told the audience of Rudy's and Natacha's difficulties and offered any patron the return of their admittance price if they cared to leave because Natacha wasn't going to appear.

Not one person moved and I started the show. As usual, Rudy captivated the audience but I was almost a wreck!

During this travel period I learned much about Rudy's and Natacha's character and beliefs. They were ardent believers in the occult and had attended many séances in Cora McGeachey's home in Brooklyn, New York. In fact, almost all of their decisions were made after receiving the automatic writings from Cora.

Prior to coming to Pittsburgh, Pa. a hotel keeper wired me to request a performance in the hotel ballroom. He sent a payment of one thousand dollars as a gesture to insure his seriousness. Later I learned that he had sent out elaborate invitations to several hundred persons in

Pittsburgh requesting their presence at the price of $5.00 for each admission.

Since this stop didn't interfere with our schedule, I accepted his offer and we subsequently arrived in the ballroom of the hotel. There were only about thirty people assembled so, after a reasonable wait, I gave him back his deposit and we left without giving a show.

There were, of course, many incidents during the tour which were unpleasant and disheartening. In Duluth, Minnesota, when I went to the ticket office to check the receipts against the number of tickets sold, the light suddenly was extinguished and when it came on again, there was a stack of currency, amounting to one thousand dollars missing. I knew that the cashier hadn't taken it. The only other person having access to the money was the visiting president of Mineralava Company. He knew that I knew that he had filched the package but he made a great show of searching for it, even going to the cashier's hotel room with me to look through drawers and baggage.

In Cinncinati, there were more than six thousand persons gathered in the Coliseum to see and hear Rudy and Natacha. From this city alone Mineralava Company received more than twelve thousand dollars.

It should be noted that in the days and nights of the tour I carried large sums of money through the streets to the telegraph offices in the various towns where the shows were held, but not once was there any attempt to molest me nor any attempt of a hold up. I walked alone, unharmed, to and from the train, to the telegraph and to the theater. There were few hippies or gangsters in those days.

At the end of the long and arduous tour of eighty-eight cities, we returned to New York so that I could begin the preparation of the final beauty contest which was to be held in Madison Square Garden, at that time the largest auditorium in the East, with a seating capacity of about twelve thousand.

As we stepped off the train I said to Rudy, "I have decided to undertake your management, if you still want me to do so," and he said, "I knew you would, Black Feather told me!" He and Natacha agreed to abide by my decisions at all times and, to a large degree, they did.

The next day we met in Mr. Max Steuer's law offices where a short contract between Rudy and myself was prepared and signed. At Rudy's insistence they also signed a document giving me full power of attorney which authorized me to sign any documents in their name, make any deal and generally conduct all their affairs in their names.

I became busy working on the plans for the final beauty contest, which included arrangements for the transportation of the contestants from their homes to New York and their hotel reservations and chaperones for each of them while there. There were dozens of details involved to insure the safety and comfort of the girls and plans for their entertainment while away from their homes.

The railroad executives were most cooperative. I did not want to send the winning beauty contestants either the money or the tickets for their railroad fare, simply because I thought that some of the girls might use the money (or convert the tickets) and fail to appear in New York City at the required date. So I arranged with the various railroad executives to allow the conductors on the trains to accept the girl's signatures in lieu of cash or tickets. All of the girls got to New York in time.

I had made arrangements with a large automobile agency to provide cars so that the girls and their chaperones could visit some interesting land marks in New York City, and actually, there was a parade by these autos from lower Manhattan up to Fifth Avenue to 59th Street and then the return to the various hotels where the girls were housed.

Later the whole group was sent by train to Washington, D.C. where President Coolidge shook hands with each of them.

I must mention here that my wife, Beatrice, was in over all charge of the housing for the girls, the selection of the chaperones and maintenance of discipline throughout. It is a tribute to her energy and diplomacy that there wasn't one single disrupting influence during the entire week that the young beauty contestants were in her care, although many men made valiant attempts to date the girls, many of whom were not reluctant to carry on!

The final appearance of the beauty contestants was an incredible example of the need for perfect preparedness and attention to the most minute details.

The Madison Square Garden seats were entirely filled. The judges were in one section but not distinguishable from the rest of the audience. This event was the first of any kind of national beauty contest and the pattern was followed by other beauty contests during subsequent years.

The girls paraded across the stage several times and each time some of the girls were eliminated by the judges. Finally, there were ten girls left and (with the audiences help) the judges selected the winner —the girl from Toronto, Canada!

It is interesting to relate that many years later I was at the Farmers Market in Hollywood with my wife. We stopped at a booth where chickens were displayed. The lady behind the counter said to me, "Aren't you Mr. Ullman?" I said that I was and she identified herself as the beauty contest winner—the girl from Toronto!

About this time a man named J.D. Williams came to my office. Until a few months before coming to see me, he had been the sales manager for Warner Features. He was known throughout the industry as an enterprising executive and, so far as I could find out, he was a competent and hard working individual. He told me that he had resigned from Warner Features in order to enter the production and distribution field as head of his own company. He said that he had formed a new firm called Ritz-Carlton Productions, Inc. and that he wanted to sign Rudolph Valentino to a two picture contract to take effect after the Paramount contract with Rudy had been fulfilled or settled, whenever that would be.

To show his good faith, I asked him to pay Rudy the sum of $25,000 as an inducement for us to agree to such a contract. All of the conditions which we had been fighting for were to be incorporated into this contract, including entire control of every phase of production, the selection of stories, writers and directors and the cutting, editing and casting. This contract was soon written and signed and the payment made.

I must truthfully note that Rudy and Natacha were vehement in voicing their praises for my "sagacity" but told me that they had known from his spiritual guide that a deal would occur by which they would receive a large sum of money.

Rudy, as usual, was without funds and this windfall was a great relief to him. I suggested that he use part of this money and go to

Europe with Natacha so that I could earnestly undertake the settlement of the contract with the Paramount Company. I did not know where Rudy had obtained sufficient funds to live on before his income from the Mineralava Company began. I found out when, after receiving this money from J.D. Williams, he asked me to come with him to the bank where he drew $11,000 in crisp $1000 bills from his account, we taxied to the Metro Goldwyn Building. He had me go with him to Mr. Joe Godsol's office. It was this man who had subsidized Rudy during his battle with Paramount by loaning him various sums during that period.

Rudy spread out the eleven one thousand dollar bills and expressed his gratitude for Mr. Godsol's faith in him. Godsol was too flabbergasted to speak because, I am sure, he never expected the return of his loans in one lump sum. To me, this was another exhibit of Rudy's character and honesty and made me more determined to bring this splendid young man the success he deserved.

So Rudy and Natacha happily sailed for Paris, vowing to be careful of their expenditures and to return as soon as I cabled him to do so.

Natacha's mother and step-father lived in a chateau in Juan les Pins in France. Rudy and Natacha thought that a visit there would be the ideal place to spend the honeymoon they didn't have when they were married. The chateau is a huge building with many surrounding acres. It was well staffed with many servants and ground keepers.

While the Valentinos were in France, I, acting under my power of attorney, discharged Rudy's lawyer (July 23rd). I demanded an accounting and the return of any and all of Rudy's assets. Mr. Graham thereupon sent his bill for an additional $27,000 for services presumably performed for Rudy. I sensed a difficult time so I again enlisted the help of Mr. Steuer, who by now knew the history of the Valentino-Graham relationship.

He spoke to Mr. Graham who threatened to release certain confidential information to the press unless he was paid. But when Mr. Steuer reminded him of the penalty for blackmail, Mr. Graham agreed to turn over all the papers and documents he had and to settle his claim for $10,000. Actually the important papers he had were mostly newspaper clippings of several episodes when Rudy first came to America, some of which referred to police matters for miscellaneous minor infractions during those early days.

The day I saw the Valentinos safely aboard I made an appointment to see Mr. Steuer, probably at that time the most prominent lawyer in New York. We discussed the method of approach to begin settlement negotiations with Paramount and decided that the direct approach was most desirable. Mr. Steuer was well acquainted with Paramount's attorney, Mr. Emil Ludwig. He had his secretary get Mr. Ludwig on the phone. Perhaps because the following events made such a vivid impression upon me I can quote the conversation verbatim.

Mr. Steuer, "How are you, Ludwig?" Then, "In my office now is Mr. George Ullman, the manager of Rudolph Valentino. I suggested that he meet with you to seek a solution to the contractual impasse." Then he turned to me and said, "Today?" And I said, "Sure. 4 p.m." This was convenient for Mr. Ludwig and at 4 o'clock that afternoon I was ushered into Mr. Ludwig's office in the Paramount Building.

Mr. Ludwig was a most cordial gentleman and, after some discussion, accepted my proposal that Rudy would star in two pictures for the company and that this would cancel the old contract under the terms of which he would have received only $1250 weekly. The terms I asked and to which Mr. Ludwig agreed were as follows. Rudy was to receive $6500 weekly plus living expenses of $500 weekly for himself and Natacha while in New York. This salary was to commence the day the first of the pictures began and continue until the second picture under the agreement was completed. Mr. Ludwig then phoned Mr. Jesse Lasky, the head of the Paramount Company and asked him to come to his office to give his approval of the arrangements.

When Mr. Lasky came to the office he was cool but friendly and after hearing the terms we had agreed upon, gave his consent. When he was leaving the office he turned and said to me, "I don't want anything to do with Valentino. You make the pictures!" And out he went. I turned to Mr. Ludwig and said, "That was just a figure of speech, I'm sure." "No," said Ludwig, "He means that!"

I told him that I did not know one single thing about the production of motion pictures and he blandly said, "You'll learn." He made the contract with the studio manager at the Paramount Studio in Astoria, Long Island and told him about the "new producer" and that I

33

was coming to see him the following day and asked that he assist me as much as possible.

The next day I was welcomed at the Long Island studio by a representative group of the studio personnel. When I met with the manager I told him bluntly that I hadn't the faintest idea how or where to begin the project. He told me that the first thing to do was to find a story or book acceptable to the company and Rudy!

❦

I remembered Rudy's enthusiasm about a book he had read while on tour. The title was "Monsieur Beaucaire" by Booth Tarkington. I asked how I went about securing the rights to this book if Rudy approved. He said, "The company will buy it!"

I cabled all these details to Rudy in Paris and received a cable from him in which he stated his gratitude for my efforts and his unqualified acceptance of the arrangements I had made. Then I formally requested that the studio purchase the motion picture rights of the book "Monsieur Beaucaire", which they did, paying the exorbitant price of $50,000 to the author.

I asked my "guide", "What next?" and he suggested that I must get a director and the screenplay writers. Of course I didn't know a director but remembered the name of Sidney Olcott on a picture I had recently seen. He had directed Miss Marion Davies in "Little Old New York" and I sensed the easy flow of the action. He told me that Olcott was under contract to the studio and would come from Hollywood to meet me, if I so desired. There were no transcontinental planes in those days, so I waited for a full week until Mr. Olcott arrived by train from Hollywood.

I only asked Mr. Olcott one question when I met him," What do you think of Rudolph Valentino?" His reply, "I think that he's a very talented young man, very much misunderstood! I like him!" He was my man then. He was assigned to direct "Monsieur Beaucaire" and our next stop was to find a writer suitable to write the screenplay for this kind of story. Mr. Olcott knew a writer, Forrest Halsey who lived in Brooklyn close to New York City. Soon Mr. Halsey was engaged and he and Olcott started to work on the screenplay. Each day or so they gave me the pages they had written. I'm certain more out of courtesy and custom than for any other reason. Invariably I agreed and only occasionally made a suggestion or two pertaining to the action.

I cabled Valentino then and asked him to return to prepare for the picture. In reply, he said that he wanted to have his own costumes made in Paris because they had the proper materials and specimens of the authentic costumes of the period. It took quite a bit of doing to get the studio heads to agree to this expense and delay, but they capitulated and gave their approval. I must say that these were probably the most gorgeous costumes ever made for motion pictures. The number of cables to and from the Valentinos was tremendous. Always in code, as it intrigued Rudy to play this game.

The Valentinos finally arrived in New York harbor and I met them on board the big ship. I was acquainted with the harbor master and through him I was able to get to the boat in a tug-boat while the liner was still in harbor.

I was genuinely happy to see these two people. They were relaxed and happy and overwhelming in their praises of my accomplishments. They again expressed their entire faith in my judgment and wisdom, etc. etc. Rudy asked me to carry his large camera.

I had reserved a suite for them at the Ritz-Carlton Hotel which at that time was one of the finest in New York or elsewhere.

When we got to his hotel suite, he took the camera from me and said," Do you know that you are a smuggler?" When I said, "No," he removed the lens from the camera and took out a large, brilliant unset diamond! I was aghast at his temerity and told him that I wanted to return to customs and declare the gem. He prevailed upon me not to do that and swore he would never, never do anything like that again. Of course, Rudy and Natacha had spent the Ritz-Carlton $25,000 and were practically out of money.

During the next couple of hours I acquainted the Valentinos with the terms of his adjusted contract and the development of the "Beaucaire" screenplay, part of which I gave him to read. He made a few suggestions but since there wasn't any dialogue the changes he saw were mostly in entrances and exits. Now Natacha read the script. She saw numerous things she thought should be changed and got quite excited about her ideas for the costumes of the other principal parts in the picture. She had in mind, of course, the casting of several of her Hollywood friends, but when I explained the expense and

35

difficulty in bringing them from Hollywood to Long Island where the picture was to be made, she saw the logic of my veto and graciously, for the time being, gave way.

Rudy and Natacha were extremely happy and wanted to celebrate his "victory." I bowed out because I had too many loose ends to bring together. As a start, however, Rudy ordered room service to bring up a pound can of Russian caviar, a delicacy he greatly enjoyed, which he proceeded to eat by large tablespoonfuls. On that week's hotel bill I discovered that this little luxury cost $100.

Rudy was complex. He would order and buy most extravagantly as long as he did not have to pay for anything with money out of his own pocket.

❧❧

One night Rudy and Natacha and I were walking along Park Avenue in New York City and sauntered into Grand Central Station. There was an elderly man sitting on a chair in front of a small display of fruit and Rudy picked out a plum and asked the man, "How much?" When the man said, "Ten cents.", Rudy put the plum back and said, "I won't pay ten cents for a prune," and angrily walked away. This was an entirely different side of Rudy which I hadn't seen before and, in a way, it saddened me. Natacha selected a bag full of fruit to bring to their apartment and I paid for it. Rudy fussed a bit but began to munch on the fruit as we walked to their home.

On the other hand, he was liberal in offering his cigarettes, (which cost 20 cents each) to anyone near when he opened his cigarette case to enjoy one himself. But he didn't pay for these since they arrived from London in quantity and were paid for by check. The brand was Abdullah #5.

Rudy seldom relaxed when in the company of others. Even with Natacha there seemed to be a reticence which may have been because she so dominated any discussion that he didn't want to start an argument with her.

With me, however, he was quite natural and would discuss any interesting subject he or I brought up, although his favorite subject was himself. He was concerned about his future, the thinning of his hair and his lack of education. He tried to learn from some text books I

36

got for him but his interest in abstract knowledge waned quickly and his attention reverted to books or plays related to motion pictures or history.

Soon the Valentinos met the director, Sidney Olcott, who was most gracious, especially with Natacha. She quickly took full advantage of his good disposition and, in her charming manner, told him her ideas about directing and casting and almost every facet of the forthcoming production.

Actually, all of the negotiations with the cast principals were done by myself and several times Natacha and I were on the verge of battle. For example, she wanted a certain actor for the part of king, but I wanted Lowell Sherman, a splendid legitimate actor then in a play in New York. Natacha was certain that he would refuse a relatively subordinate role, but I went to see Mr. Sherman in his stage dressing room and without much persuasion he gave his consent to appear at the studio when needed. Perhaps one of the reasons was that I told him that we could pay him $25,000 for his services. At that time this was a large sum for any supporting player.

Rudy had met an actress in the picture names Doris Kenyon. She was a beautiful blonde girl and a good actress. She evidently had been unemployed for some time and was happy to get the small part. She must have made a fine impression on Rudy because, when her engagement with us was nearly completed, he asked me, as a special favor to him, to try and get her a term contract with some major studio.

I was acquainted with the head of the MGM studio, Mr. Richard Rowland, and at lunch with him one day I made a deal for Miss Kenyon for a yearly contract with options, under the terms of which she would receive $500 weekly for the first full 52 weeks plus all expenses for her Mother and herself when she worked in Hollywood. I must note that her appreciation was noticeable by its absence. MGM loaned her for a picture at Warner Brothers Studio where she met Milton Sills whom she later married. After the first year at MGM her contract was not renewed. But in that first year she and her Mother took full advantage of the terms in the contract, which also included an automobile and chauffeur at her service. They traveled north and south and east in this luxurious auto while waiting for assignments by the studio.

After many difficulties the picture "Monsieur Beaucaire" was completed. Natacha caused considerable trouble by her interference with the director. She attended the showing of the previous day's filming (called rushes) in the studio projection room and, after about an hour there, she began to tell the cutter which scenes to keep and which scenes to remove and discard. This, at last was too much for Mr. Olcott, the director, to accept, so he withdrew his permission for her to attend these sessions.

This was the beginning of Natacha's attempts to dominate and control every facet of Rudy's work and this caused frequent quarrels between them. But Rudy always was won over to her way of thinking and he tried to intervene on her behalf whenever situations were not as she would have them.

The final editing of "Beaucaire" completed, the company rushed out prints to the exhibitors because Paramount hadn't had a successful picture in almost a year and they needed the money to continue operations.

For the record, the "Monsieur Beaucaire" picture cost was totaled at $562,000, which figure included the studio overhead for many preceding months as well as salaries paid to home office employees during that period. Much later I learned that this picture grossed more than five million dollars.

◈◈◈

Paramount owned a book "Rope's End" by George Barr McCutcheon. It was a meager story but the principal character was that of a young and vigorous Spaniard. Rudy liked the story and Forrest Halsey was again assigned to write the screenplay. A different director, Joseph Henaberry, was engaged to direct.

From the onset this picture was doomed! Natacha, with her new but limited knowledge of motion picture production, immediately assumed command over all preparation of the screenplay, the planning and building of the sets and the choice of cast and crew, much to the consternation of the studio heads and myself.

The studio issued an edict that Natacha was to be barred from the studio until the picture was completed. The result was much unhappiness for her and for Rudy. But she occupied herself by shopping and attending various auctions where she bought many valuable, illustrated books of various periods from many countries.

She was a real pigeon at the auctions, frequently bidding

38

against herself with complete disregard to the real value of the books she wanted. She rode around in the beautiful little Isotta Fraschini Cabriolet, one of the automobiles they had purchased in Italy, with a chauffeur driving. This was the only automobile of its kind in America. It was low and small. It had a seat in front for a chauffeur and a glass partition separated the one seat in the back for the passengers. Whenever it was seen it was admired by even the blasé New Yorkers.

All during the making of "Monsieur Beaucaire" and "Rope's End", Rudy was receiving the salary of $6500 weekly plus all living expenses. So they had no immediate concerns about money matters.

"Rope's End" was released under the title of "The Sainted Devil" and, as I anticipated, it didn't cause much excitement and box office returned weren't good.

Now that the Paramount obligations had been completed, Rudy's salary and his expenses were now his to pay.

❦

The Ritz-Carlton Picture Corporation, eager to attract attention to the company and to sell some of its stock, began urging us to get to Hollywood to prepare for the first Valentino picture under the optional contract they held upon Rudy's services. But Rudy was reluctant to go west until he felt assured that he would not encounter legal difficulties because of the outstanding judgments against him. So I went to Hollywood first to try to settle the judgments against him. It was my introduction to the movie capitol although I had twice before been to L.A., but for other interests.

My first visit was to Mr. W.I. Gilbert, a prominent Los Angeles lawyer, who had advised Rudy during his entanglement with Jean Acker. I then knew only a little of the Jean Acker matter because Rudy and Natacha were naturally reticent about it.

From Mr. Gilbert I learned the details of Rudy's marriage to Jean Acker. They are interesting enough to tell here. Jean Acker was a very ambitious and pretty young actress with not quite enough screen personality to warrant stardom, but she knew that to achieve the attention of the picture companies and the public she had to do something to attract notice to herself. In the files pertaining to the Jean Acker-Rudolph Valentino marriage debacle, the following is pertinent.

39

Shortly after Rudy completed the very successful "Four Horsemen of the Apocalypse", Jean Acker, his wife, sued him for separate maintenance. She charged that he had deserted her, had refused to live with her and refused to support her. She asked for $300 a week for herself and $1500 for attorney's fees. Jean had met Rudy before he became important to Hollywood and she simply set out to snare the young and rather unsophisticated actor into marriage. The truth about their separation after three days of marriage is that she had a physical problem which prohibited her from having sex relations and it was for this reason that they agreed to part.

By this time Rudy had become friendly with Natacha Rambova who was employed as a dress designer by the famous Nazimova who was then also a Metro Goldwyn Mayer star. Natacha advised and comforted Rudy, directed his relationship with the MGM star, to whom he was under weekly contract, and generally proceeded to tell him how to demand more money and attention from the studio executives.

It was during the filming of "Camille" that Natacha began to advise Rudy and to help him formulate his attitude in his relationship with the studio. She taught him to demand the attention she believed a star should have. She gave him lessons in make-up technique and generally molded him to her image of the man she decided to marry.

I cannot say that her interest in Rudy harmed him in the least, but he became so dependent upon her approval that he lost much of his original natural personality.

Jean Acker's attorney increased her demand for alimony now that Rudy's importance and income had increased. In November 1921, the lawsuit began. I will not publish the many false accusations made against Rudy by Miss Acker's lawyer. After several delays by the court, the presiding judge decided against Jean Acker and gave Rudy the divorce he had asked for in his cross complaint.

On May 12th, 1922, accompanied by friends, Rudy and Natacha left for Palm Springs, California, and the next morning the party drove to Mexicali, Mexico, where they were married at the home of the mayor. Their plans for a honeymoon were disrupted when a Los Angeles judge issued a statement that this marriage was invalid because Rudy had received only an interlocutory divorce decree, but not a final one, and that marriage within one year after the first decree constituted bigamy!

Natacha, after much persuasion, left for New York at once. The then district attorney of Los Angeles, Thomas Woolwine, perhaps eager for publicity for himself, since this was an election year, issued an order for Rudy's arrest.

Rudy went to the D.A.'s office to surrender himself and to plead guilty, because of ignorance of the California law, to the charge of bigamy. The bail was set at $10,000. Of course Rudy had no such sum, neither did Mr. Gilbert. So Rudy was put into a cell with assorted drunks, gamblers and petty thieves.

Actually the bail was put up by a star of the time, Thomas Meighan, who had never even met Rudy. Mr. Meighan had been visiting the San Francisco police chief, Dan O'Brien, when Rudy's friend, Douglas Gerrard, telephoned to Mr. O'Brien, who was his friend, and told him Rudy's predicament. When Meighan heard part of the conversation, he asked the chief," Is there some friend of yours in trouble?" O'Brien told him and Meighan promptly went to the bank and returned with a certified check for $10,000. So that is how Rudolph Valentino was released from jail.

When he later appeared for hearing on the charge of bigamy, he was able to prove, to the court's satisfaction, that his marriage to Natacha had not been consummated and he was cleared. The judge warned him that he must not remarry before the interlocutory decree became final. Rudy then went to New York, where he and Natacha set up separate homes.

Mr. Gilbert had in his files all of the judgments against Valentino. They consisted primarily of unpaid obligations such as unpaid bills on a home in Hollywood, balances due on repossessed automobiles, some personal loans he had neglected to pay and a few other minor issues. It did not take me long to call upon the judgment holders and settle with each of them for a portion of the judgment because most of these people had abandoned any hope of collecting anything at all!

While in Hollywood at this time I contracted for the studio space we would require at United Artists for the making of the first picture for the Ritz-Carlton firm. I also engaged a domestic couple to prepare the Valentino's Whitley Heights home for the return of Natacha and Rudy, found and rented a home for my family in Hollywood and then returned to New York.

Rudy had ordered three automobiles while in Europe. One was the small Isotta Fraschini Cabriolet which Natacha had used while in New York. It was a junior version of a limousine and cost $7000, a large Isotta Fraschini limousine for which he agreed to pay $12,000 and a sleek French roadster, a Voisin, grey with red upholstery, which cost $6000 in Paris. On March 9th, 1972 this Voisin roadster was sold at auction to Mr. J.B. Nethercut for the reported price of $22,000. The report stated that Mr. Nethercut was an antique car collector and the Voisin was then forty-nine years old. I sold the small Isotta in New York before the Valentinos returned to Los Angeles for the exact price Rudy paid for it, plus shipping charges. There wasn't any room at the Hollywood home for more than two cars.

The return to Hollywood was a big event. Our publicity man had extended himself to assure a large crowd to welcome the Valentinos. The trunks and luggage had been sent ahead. It is interesting to record that Natacha's luggage was at least five times that of Rudy's because, while in Paris she had come under the spell of Poiret, at that time the foremost designer of women's clothes. When she chose one garment she had it duplicated in five or six colors or combinations. She also purchased dozens of scarves and turbans from Poiret. Natacha was undoubtedly one of the best dressed women in New York and Hollywood. She had a beautiful figure and knew how best to show it. She never wore the short dresses which were the fashion in those days. She either wore long flowing dresses or Chinese silk pajamas. I later learned that, because of her former ballet and dancing activities, her legs and thighs had become rather thick and heavy.

My family and I left New York on a separate train because there were many personal things I had to attend to in order to settle my little family, which by now consisted of my wife and two little boys, Daniel and Robert. Daniel was six and Robert one year old when we arrived in Hollywood on November 24, 1924.

The Valentinos occupied their home in Whitley Heights in Hollywood. This was only about a ten minute drive to the studio. From its windows you could see the hills which form the Hollywood

Bowl and the electrically lighted cross over the famous theater where the Pilgrimage Play was presented each year.

It was a hillside home. The entrance hall led to the floor with the two bedrooms and two baths. The living room with its black marble floor was on the floor below. The color scheme was canary and silver. The exotic combination of colors throughout the house was Natacha's creation. There was a small dining room raised a few steps at the end of the living room. The furniture was red Chinese lacquer with black satin upholstery.

Midway in the living room was an enormous bay window above a deeply cushioned seat on which there was enough room for four or five persons to sit at ease. It was here that I spent many happy evenings with the Valentinos.

Few people know that Rudy was a poet and a philosopher. His book of poems entitled, "Day Dreams" was published both in America and in England and contained such gems of thought as:

A Baby's Skin
Three Generation of Kisses
You
Dust to Dust

Because of the childlike joy with which the Valentinos threw themselves into preparation for their first Christmas together in California, I almost came to think that they believed in Santa Claus.

Naturally I expected each to give a gift to the other, and a very handsome one. But I had no idea that I would be pulled hither and yon, called to confer secretly, first with one and then with the other, until my mind was in a whirl.

Considering the fact that serious differences between these two had begun to manifest themselves, this Christmas enthusiasm gave me great satisfaction. I could not believe that the trouble was basic when both husband and wife were perfectly serious and eager in their desire to please each other.

Receiving an imperative summons from Natacha to come at once because Rudy was out, I dashed up to the house, fearing the worst, only to find that I was to carry out for her an idea which has since caused more comment than any gift from a woman to the man she loved since the days of Cleopatra and Marc Antony. It was the famous platinum slave bracelet which the world has attributed as the gift from no less than a score of beautiful women, but which in reality was a Christmas present from his own wife, and was made to order from a design which she herself drew and gave to me to carry out.

For obvious reasons, I have kept silent when confronted with diverse rumors, but now that the world is learning for the first time the true Valentino in all his weaknesses, his strength, his fascination, and the respect he inspired among the men and women who knew him best, I am telling the truth about the famous slave bracelet.

It was given to Rudy by Natacha.

When newspaper writers, intent upon earning their salaries on space, discovered the innocent fact that Rudolph Valentino wore a slave bracelet, they worried over it as a dog worries a bone, dragging its description and their deductions concerning it from paragraph to paragraph, it is worthy of note that their jibes and insults never for one moment tempted Valentino to leave off wearing it. That this shows courage of a supreme order no man can deny, for fear of ridicule is an inherent quality in most mortals.

Calamities can be borne with more fortitude than ridicule, and severe pain with more equanimity than continuous gnat bites. But Valentino was superbly indifferent to both. When he set his feet on a certain path, he pursued it calmly to the end, fixing his mind upon his destination and disregarding both rocks and pebbles which might cause him to stumble. A quality of greatness, I call this serene, uplifted attitude.

Nor could a husband's fidelity to the gift of his wife, prepared with such loving care, be attributed to stubbornness. To my mind it is an insult to the quality of Rudy's love for Natacha to suggest such a thing. I am inclined to call it more a quality of faithfulness to memories of the greatest happiness which ever came into his life, that he persisted in wearing this much discussed slave bracelet, and wore it to his death.

The slave bracelet given Rudolph Valentino by Natacha Rambova rests with him in his tomb.

And the New York reporter who, in commenting on the unfortunate editorial published in a Chicago newspaper, quoted Rudy as saying, "Yes, I shall continue to wear this bracelet, as it was given to me by some one whom I dearly love," remarked that then Valentino looked thoughtfully down at the bracelet and off into space, caught, to my mind, more nearly the truth of Valentino's feelings in regard to the bracelet, than any writer who commented

44

upon it. *Every time that Rudy's eyes rested upon his slave bracelet, I believe that the image of his wife rose before his mental vision.*

Rudy's Christmas gift to Natacha had a history which can be duplicated in the memories of countless young couples.

This is the story of it.

Several years before, when Rudy and Natacha were engaged; and by the way, it was the year before his divorce from Jean Acker became final; they were looking at a watch in a downtown jewelry store. It was surrounded by diamonds, and embedded in a thinly cut moonstone. It could be worn as a locket or watch; but, at that time, the price of $2000 was more than Rudy could afford.

Natacha had been crazy about it and had always remembered it, once in a while referring to its chaste beauty.

Evidently Valentino had borne this in mind for, on another morning, I was hastily summoned to his bungalow dressing room. With suppressed excitement, he seized my arm and asked me if I remembered the times when Natacha had described this watch.

I did not, but said I did, for it seemed impossible in any way to dampen Rudy's ardor. Feverishly he gave me the name of the jeweler, refreshed my mind by a careful and minute description of the bauble, and urged me to go down that very moment and buy it if it was still obtainable.

I went to the bank and drew two one thousand dollar bills. One I placed in my wallet, and the other I held in my hand.

I had no difficulty in finding it, for the moment I began to describe the watch the salesman interrupted me, saying he knew exactly the one I meant.

Owing to the fact that it was still on their hands, I imagined they might be willing to take less than the $2000 price tag on the watch. I therefore laid the thousand dollar bill on the counter and offered to take the watch at that price.

After some demur, a few impassioned arguments, and the statement that at this price it was nothing short of a gift, I succeeded in purchasing the moonstone watch at exactly one-half that had been asked of the Valentinos some years before. Evidently the sight of a thousand dollar bill was too much for them.

On the way home I stopped at the bank, placed the remaining thousand dollar bill to Valentino's account and came home in triumph to my friend, who was delighted with a business ability which he never would have thought to emulate.

While driving along, with this precious jewel, in its white velvet box, safe in my pocket, I could not help thinking of the thousands of young people, either engaged or married, who window-shopped in their spare moments, and selected their heart's desires behind plate glass windows with an, "Oh, I wish we could afford that!" from the girl, followed by an equally impassioned, "Well, darling, just as soon as I get that raise from The Old Man, you shall have it."

Paralleled in ten thousand lesser ways was the window shopping of the Valentinos. Yet I dare say that just as much love and generosity were in their gifts to each other, as in the humblest lad's selection of a silver plated premium for his sweetheart, to be paid for by coupons.

From this time on, seeing that I was to partake of a Christmas the like of which I had not seen for twenty years, I threw myself into their plans with all the enthusiasm of which I was capable. Dark secrets were in the air every moment. Whenever one or the other would be alone I was sure to receive a summons for a conference, and, by their laughter and air of mystery, I rather imagined that I too was due for a surprise.

Now Christmas in California is a feature which I have never encountered elsewhere. What Californians call cold weather is about the climate we Easterners find in autumn, in what we call Indian summer, with the exception that, there having been no frost, autumn colors are lacking. I refer merely to the quality of the atmosphere, for that which meets the eye is very different.

The hills, green in summer, have now turned dun. The grass on the lawn is still green, the roses are still in bloom, and the flowering shrubs lend splotches of color to a landscape of beauty to be found nowhere else but the southlands of Europe.

The so-called rainy season has not yet begun, and Christmas may always be counted upon to be a day of fair weather.

Present giving on Christmas in California overflows the boundaries of families and spreads itself delightfully among friends and choice acquaintances. It is safe to say that on Christmas morning almost every one goes out for an hour or two to distribute gifts of remembrance in person. It reminded me more of the old-fashioned habit of New Year calls than anything I could remember.

On this particular Christmas, at six o'clock in the morning I was called from my bed by a frantic ringing of the telephone. Answering it, I found myself commanded after a cheery "Merry Christmas," to bring Mrs.

Ullman and my little boy, Danny, then about six years old, and come immediately to the Valentino home. It was Natacha's voice, and she told me explicitly not to stop for breakfast, but to come at once.

Scrambling into our clothes, we hurriedly obeyed. Our own excitement almost equaled that of our small boy, who was fairly dancing with impatience to get to his beloved "Uncle Rudy."

Upon our arrival there, not later than seven o'clock, we were met in the patio by Natacha, who halted us with a great air of mystery and would not permit us to enter.

When Natacha chose to exert herself, she could be the most entertaining and charming woman I have ever met, and she chose to exert herself that Christmas morning, when, without even a cup of coffee, we had dashed around to obey her summons. It was perhaps half an hour she held us there in the bright California sunshine, curbing our impatience with what grace we could. Then a wild shout of "All Ready!" was heard from within the house and, leading the way, Natacha hurried us down the stairs into the living room where a sight met our eyes to take the breath of grown-ups, let alone an impressionable child like Danny.

Covering the entire black marble floor of the great living room was a network of railroad tracks, tunnels, roundhouses, electric switches, freight cars, passenger cars, engines and what not, the whole appearing as a railway terminal in a great city might look to an aviator flying over it.

The cost of this extravagant toy I dared not estimate, and Natacha told us that all night, in fact until dawn, Rudy had spent his time setting up this toy, catching a terrible cold from sitting and crawling around the cold marble floor for so many hours!

But his joy in seeing the excitement of Danny as the mysterious electricity caused these tiny trains to move forward and back, to switch around, more than compensated Rudy for all his toil and trouble. Natacha jeered at him in a friendly way and declared that Rudy had set the toy up as much to enjoy himself as to please the child.

Possibly this was true, as I myself had guilty recollections of doing similar things in taking my small son to a circus I had a sneaking desire to see myself.

I was reminded also of Rudy's passion for machinery and his love for taking things apart "To see the wheels go wound," as Helen's babies used to say.

I remember that at one time he overhauled his expensive Voisin car with the help of his chauffeur, who was an expert mechanic, cleaned and oiled

47

every part, and put it back together again. This he did, I am persuaded, from an intense curiosity to see how the thing worked. He could not bear to be in ignorance of the source of its power, yet at the same time he had a mechanic's delight in tinkering and fooling with machinery.

Breakfast was rather a sketchy meal, for over in the corner, shrouded under sheets, stood what even Danny knew to be a Christmas tree. When this was unveiled, it turned out to be a very gorgeous thing, hung with many presents, not only for us, but for the friends that were expected to drop in during the day.

The night before, Natacha told us, she and Rudy had had a quarrel, and in the early morning they were hardly speaking. But I observed that the good cheer and friendliness engendered by the Christmas season had evidently completely wiped away all differences, and they were as tender and loving to each other as I had ever seen them.

After this, came the presentation of the Valentino gifts to each other. With real solemnity I saw Natacha place the now famous slave bracelet on Rudy's wrist, from which it was never removed, and witnessed the kiss of fervent gratitude for the symbol it expressed. He declared that he was the slave of her beauty and kindliness, and Natacha seemed to welcome the expressions of fervent gratitude which he uttered.

When she opened the white velvet case and saw the coveted jewel she uttered a cry of genuine pleasure and flung herself into his arms with the abandonment of love.

Rudy was enchanted by Natacha's delight. She immediately put the watch on and continued to admire it all day, and always, and the delight gave him a far greater pleasure than in any gift he could have received for himself. Nothing ever gave him such pleasure as to make his wife happy, and in this he exercised an ingenuity and persistence which made him one of the greatest lovers in real life.

❧

All of us settled down quickly and preparations were begun to film the first picture for The Ritz-Carlton firm.

One afternoon, on a whim, Rudy decided that he would like to visit the Coronado Beach Hotel. He couldn't be dissuaded and Natacha and my wife and I piled into his Voisin Roadster and in about three hours we were there. After dinner his real objective came to light. He wanted to go to Tia Juana, then a wide open gambling town in Mexico, but only about an hour's drive from the Coronado.

That's where we went again in Rudy's automobile. But by this time Rudy was a bit high on the few drinks we had had at the hotel and was a little belligerent and loud. A few more drinks and a few losses in the casino and we had all we could do to make him quiet down.

I warned him several times to keep his voice low because I noticed a Mexican policeman close by watching, and I told that to Rudy. He said something to the effect of, "To hell with the police." And the officer moved in and said, "What did you say?" I had a tight hold on Rudy now and whispered in his ear to shout, "Viva Mexican police!" which he did.

The policeman moved away and Rudy again became abusive so there was nothing I could do but to hit him in the jaw, not too hard but enough to partially sober him up. Natacha got some coffee and made him drink it. Then after a while, he agreed to let me drive back to the hotel. He was angry at me then but the following morning he sheepishly apologized and all was well again.

Natacha had been working with several writers on her original story she titled "The Hooded Falcon". It was an elaborate story about the Moors in the 16th century. Natacha had collected drawings and sketches of furniture and furnishings of this period and happily set about having the studio craftsmen design and make many of these carved pieces of furniture.

The costs began to mount tremendously. It was at this time that I learned that J.D. Williams had sold his contract with Rudy to Paramount Pictures Corporation, the firm that Rudy had vowed never to work for again. This clause was stipulated in the contract between Rudy and Ritz-Carlton.

There was the danger that Rudy would walk out of the contract if he found out about Williams' double cross, so I decided to withhold this news from him because a contract breach, no matter if warranted, at this time, would have harmed him greatly. I will not go into the things I said to Williams.

Also, at this time, Williams told me that by Paramount orders he had to close down further preparation for the making of "The Hooded Falcon."

Williams had gone to New York during this upheaval but soon returned with the motion picture rights to a moderately successful Broadway play named "Cobra." It was not the type of picture I wanted for Rudy, since it was a completely modern fiction story and the "Cobra" was a woman. But Williams had already bought it and Rudy had had a psychic message through Cora McGeachy that Black Feather, Rudy's guide, had communicated his wishes that Rudy should accept this story because it was right for him!

By this time the Valentinos had spent the money they had been receiving from the Ritz-Carlton company each week without any attempt to save any part of it. Nothing I said to them had any effect upon either of them to make them stop this manner of living. They had complete confidence in their continued prosperity so strongly because they believed the automatic writings from Cora McGeachy, which they received almost daily. These were always to the effect that very soon they would become very wealthy. Probably this caused their total disregard for money with which to purchase things for themselves.

᪥

The few years that Valentino lived in affluence, 1923-1926, in Hollywood were, in my opinion, much more glamorous than they were later on. Stars behaved like stars. Most of them were aware that they were continually being observed by the press and especially by the columnists—gossips who had their "spies" everywhere. In restaurants, the waiters and headwaiters, in hotels, the bell captains and the desk clerks, in steam rooms and even in gymnasiums there were alert people who sold tidbits of scandal to Louella Parsons, the Hearst News Syndicate's motion picture gossip columnist.

This woman had more power to make or unmake careers than almost any other single force at that time. Then came Hedda Hopper, another columnist for a different news syndicate. There were frequent verbal battles between these ladies whose prestige rose as more and more moral lapses were published under their bylines. It is lamentable that the stars and the studios found it practically a necessity to cater to them and often to present them with costly gifts.

In those days there were very few night clubs or exclusive restaurants. Almost all of the large dinners and parties were held in the homes of the prominent actors, actresses and directors. These were the days when prohibition was in effect and the hosts and hostesses vied with each other to offer the best wines and liquors from their own bootleggers. The quality was sometimes questionable, but the quantity never was. But the cost was great and the bootleggers became wealthy, if not worthy, citizens.

But, at that, almost all of the "parties" were formal and except for isolated instances, there were seldom scandals or indecencies for the columnists' edification.

Even during the daytime hours men and women wore conventional clothing and, in the evening, long dresses were in vogue.

Of course, there were a few notorious episodes during that period, such as the affairs of Charlie Chaplin and his child brides and the Roscoe Fatty Arbuckle case, the Mary Miles Minter scandal and the death of Wallace Reid, a Paramount star, from an overdose of morphine.

These events were blown up out of all proportion in the press throughout the country and Hollywood became the wicked city where no girl was safe. As may be expected, the promise of success and perhaps danger, lured young girls from all over the world to glamorous Hollywood. Some did succeed. Most returned to their homes after their resources had been consumed and others found employment in fields other than motion pictures.

Nevertheless, the studio chiefs decided to create a position for a "Czar" to censor screenplays and the social activities in this Hollywood "city of sin." They offered the job to Will Hays, then the Postmaster General of the United States, who had frequently declared that he would bar all salacious material from the mails. The salary he was offered was $100,000 annually and, of course, he accepted.

His influence was not enough to prevent some tragic events involving picture personalities, but, in fairness it must be said that these were long in the making before Mr. Hays took office as president of the Motion Picture Producers and Distributors of America, Inc.,which was formed by the heads of all the major companies.

Valentino's parties were small in comparison to the frequent invitational events that took place at Marion Davies large home on the beach in Malibu. There were often as many as one hundred guests, but no inkling of scandal was ever rumored, probably because of the influence of Mr. Hearst's gossip columnist, Louella Parsons, who gathered records for her own use to be released only if a guest questioned her demands at a future time.

These were the days when the studio heads really took charge of production matters. Men, such as Louis B. Mayer, Carl Laemmle, Irving Thalberg and others would not tolerate excessive spending or waste by any of the producers or directors they employed and without hesitation dismissed any employee who indulged in excesses. These rugged studio heads had achieved their prominence by hard work and careful expenditures and were able, if necessary, to undertake the completion of any pictures.

It was not the practice to allow stars to share in profits until I came along with the contract idea for Rudy. Much later there were similar contracts given to important stars. Now it seems to be quite the customary procedure for almost all stars, as well as some producers and directors, to accept percentages of profits or sometimes of the gross receipts of their pictures in lieu of their formerly high salaries.

But the glamour is gone. There are no longer any "super stars" whose personalities are comparable to the magnetism of Rudolph Valentino. Yet, he and I often walked along Fifth Avenue in New York and, if any person recognized him they didn't stop or stare! In an office or restaurant it was different. There, in any office we had to pass through, all work stopped and did not resume until he had left. The same in restaurants, excepting in Hollywood, where it was almost impossible for Rudy to have a quiet meal because of the embarrassing stares and often even approaches by women and girls under varying excuses. This, of course, caused some of the men diners to become disgruntled and on several occasions, he had to leave his table and the restaurant.

I have often been asked the question, "To what do you attribute Valentino's attraction to women?" My opinion is that they looked upon him as romance itself. More so because they never heard his voice and could imagine any sound they chose coming from the man on the screen. In other words, he could have been other than human because he spoke only with his eyes and body.

These were the days when almost all those actors and actresses who were in the higher earning brackets indulged in anything they desired. Then Hollywood was full of racketeers of every description and they were expert in relieving these gullible people of great amounts of money. There were the stock salesmen who, sometimes in collusion with people in the movies, were able to mingle with stars and executives and unload gold and oil and land shares in large amounts. There were only a small number of business managers and some of these, also, were involved in shady speculation deals.

I remember one such business manager who invested his client's money in building projects for which his father was the contractor. By a stroke of fortune the depression of the early 1920's ended and a boom in real estate occurred overnight resulting in large profits to the business manager and his clients.

Other business managers were not so lucky. They had invested in the securities of small businesses and the depression had forced many of these ventures into bankruptcy making their stocks worthless. I do not recall any public suit against these managers by their clients, but there were recriminations. On two occasions I had to intervene to recoup partial repayment from a manager on behalf of two of Rudy's friends.

Today the custom is quite different. The business managers usually put their clients on budgets and only in rare instances do they waver from the arrangements. Also, the large earning stars of today are much wiser than they were in the 1920s.

≈≈≈

Within a week after our arrival in Hollywood I received a section seating eight at the American Legion boxing stadium. My interest in boxing began many years before when I boxed professionally for about a year in New York City, and the stadium was a popular gathering place for the motion picture people.

Rudy and Natacha were avid fans and very frequently accompanied my wife and myself on Friday nights. It is amusing to look back and remember Rudy's loud enthusiasm when an Italian pugilist was in the ring. He yelled encouraging words in Italian while Lupe Velez, in a nearby box, yelled more loudly when a Mexican boxer was in the ring.

But Rudy and Natacha were attractions there. Natacha, always beautifully dressed with a turban around her hair, and Rudy, immaculate in the tweed knickers and English sport coat with the beret he wore to informal gatherings.

53

Of course, there were many who ridiculed Rudy's fastidiousness and especially his slave bracelet, but I believe that it was more from envy than anything else. But, if Rudy noticed anything, it certainly didn't effect him nor did he change his style. By today's standards, where men wear those outlandish shirts and chains and beads, he probably would be labeled a "square."

But Natacha was something else. She wore the long and fashionable dresses and the turban, which was a little unusual at the time, and presented a vision of charm and beauty.

Our company employed three publicity men, not for the usual purpose of creating sensational publicity for Rudy, but primarily to keep his name out of fan magazines and newspapers, because Rudy frequently got into some difficulties because of his reckless driving and because there were numerous attempts by love stricken women to get him into compromising situations and to then try to get their names in the press. These publicity men were chosen because of their connections with the magazines and newspapers and did, on several occasions, prevail upon their friends to "kill" false and planted stories.

For example, there was a pretty and young girl who, through various tricks, got into the studio and on the set almost daily. Wherever Rudy went this girl was near. I spoke to her as firmly as possible and she promised to stay away. But I saw her several times again and pointed her out to our watchman. It didn't make much difference until one evening she hid herself in his dressing room awaiting his return from the set. Luckily I came in with him but she set off a loud series of accusations against Rudy and threatened to expose him to the newspapers if she didn't get work in the picture. She actually did go to the newsroom at the "Times" office, but they had the foresight to check with our publicity department and obtaining the facts; they dropped the story.

Another time, Rudy was arrested for speeding after he had imbibed too liberally, and the policeman who had arrested Rudy said that he could smell liquor on Rudy's breath. But our attorney said that it might have been garlic he smelled and the complaint was dismissed. The reporters could have made a silly story of this, but here again, our publicity men persuaded the reporters to ignore the attorney's remark.

The picture "Cobra" was completed without much difficulty. The "Cobra" character was played by Nita Naldi, a very competent and co-operative actress and the picture cost did not exceed the budget. However, despite Rudy's immense popularity, the picture was not well received by his fans. They preferred to see him in period, or costume pictures instead of modern, conventional pictures.

During the making of "Cobra" I was asked by Mr. Joseph Schenck, one of the large independent producers in Hollywood, to see him to discuss a deal for Valentino to make two pictures for him and to be released by the United Artists Distributing Company.

We had several meetings but finally we agreed on a contract for Rudy which was radically different from any other contract he or anyone else had had up to this time. By its terms Rudy was to receive one hundred thousand dollars for each picture plus 50% of all profits. These profits were guaranteed by Mr. Schenck to amount to at least $50,000 for each picture. He was to be permitted to draw $10,000 weekly for 15 weeks during the production of each picture. Imagine this salary then when there weren't any income taxes.

Now I began paying off some of Valentino's debts. There were the three foreign automobiles and a second mortgage on the Whitley Heights home and the numerous bills for purchases in Europe and New York and in Hollywood. Also, he had agreed to purchase a large home in Beverly Hills because Natacha had wanted it. I made a very good deal with the realtor who had built and lived in this house. There were five and one-half acres adjoining the modern house which was set high on a hill top. There was also another building for servant's quarters. The price was $50,000.

Nowhere in all the world are grouped together such magnificent estates, so ideally situated as those owned by the movie colony surrounding "Falcon Lair" in Beverly Hills. Valentino's property, although comprising five and one half acres, was situated in the choicest part of Beverly Hills with a view excelled by no other estate.

While in Europe Rudy had, at various times with Natacha's able advice, made extensive purchases for the home they had one day hoped to acquire. From the apartment in New York and from the Whitley Heights home many antiques were now assembled. All of the furnishings and furniture were bought without regard to cost. But Natacha did not ever see the completed home nor did she ever live there.

In Seville, Spain, the Valentinos purchased among many other antiques, two great entrance doors for the Falcon Lair home. These were very old, probably from some castle and they were very costly. When these doors eventually arrived by boat in San Pedro, California, I was advised by the custom officials that the duty was in excess of $500. They totally ignored the fact that the doors were more than one hundred years old and therefore exempt from duty charges. So I had to prove to their satisfaction through verification from Seville the authenticity of my claim that the doors were really antiques.

The doors were finally put in place and they were still there when I last saw the Falcon Lair house.

Each door is framed by extended molding enclosing and recessing an upper and lower beautifully carved panel. When the doors were closed they form four centrally located framed carvings, adjoining and bordered on the top by two sculptured grotesque dragons facing a winged cherub head. The two upper principal panels are scenic carvings of Roman horsemen in combat in the foreground, with castles and an execution scene against the landscaped background. All beautifully carved and sculptured in high relief.

The reception hall had a beautiful French Gothic wainscot seat of the early 15th century interestingly carved with Gothic tracery and centered by shields with crests and crowns. There were also two Florentine Savonarola chairs, 16th century, and a wrought iron floor lamp. Some of the collection of antique shields and armor were on the walls.

Rudy, with characteristic energy proceeded to have many changes made. Possibly these ideas were given him by Pola Negri, by then almost his constant companion, who also didn't have much respect for money, especially if it was not her own!

Rudy had an underground tunnel passageway built between the servant's quarters and the main house, this probably to avoid the use of the main front entrance by the servants. This was constructed at an additional great cost. Added to this there appeared to be some danger of the house slipping down the hill, especially during heavy rains. So there was nothing else to do except have a steel reinforced retaining wall built completely around the rear of the house. These little changes cost more than $40,000 of Rudy's money.

The house had three bedrooms and baths and a study, living room, a family room and, of course, a large new kitchen. There was also another home close to the big house, for the use of the help.

Now Natacha had a new toy. She went about purchasing period furniture for every room and velvet draperies throughout. Only a few articles of furniture were moved from the Whitley Heights home including their bedroom set, a very modern group painted in black and silver and a nice contrast to the austere 17th century furniture in the other rooms.

During their visits to Paris and Spain, Rudy and Natacha had purchased several paintings at high prices which were later sold at the auction of Rudy's effects after his death. Among the paintings the Valentinos purchased abroad were two by Alonzo-Sanchez-Coello (16th Century) of the Duke and Duchess of Savoy. These were excellent examples of the artist's work worthy of museum ownership.

Then there was a painting by Jacob Roberts called Il Tintoretta, also created in the 16th century, a portrait of Elizabeth Foscari. This was elaborately and delicately done with the subject wearing pearls, gold bracelets and a chain girdle of gold.

There were several small paintings on wood panels from the 15th and 16th century and five water colors by Gustave Klimt which were beautiful and fantastic.

If I remember correctly, there were thirty-two fine paintings purchased with great discrimination at very high price. I believe most of this art was acquired at the auction by dealers for a fraction of their value.

Rudy and Natacha gathered numerous tapestries from all corners of the world. There were too many to enumerate here but some were purchased at the auction and later, when the Bank of America became the estate administrator, these valuable works of art, as well as most of Rudy's armament collection, were practically given away to speed the close of the estate.

A description of some of the antique guns and swords might be interesting because all of them were collector's pieces and even now may be in various museums here and abroad.

There was an Italian Wheel Lock rifle with gold inlaid Persian-Arab design. The stock was elaborately inlaid with bone with Renaissance scrolls and grotesque figures and animals. It was inscribed with the maker's name "Valadin-Sonday-Zella" and dated 1684.

There were several old Persian-Arab flint lock guns, some of the stocks overlaid with mother of pearl and studded with rubies and turquoises.

In the collection there were also several sets of dueling pistols, a dagger-pistol, the handle set with diamonds and rapiers, swords, maces and daggers from the 15th to the 17th century.

Prince Trobetskoy, a famous European sculptor and a close friend of Rudy's had modeled Rudy's hand in sculptured white carrara marble, because he was so impressed by the unusual and complex qualities in the hand. He presented this to Rudy in Paris.

There were numerous French, Italian and Arabic tapestries among which were an unusual 18th century Hispano-Arab with metallic gold and silver threads and nine by ten feet; a valuable gold embroidered cashmere brocade solid with pure silver washed in gold with a red and blue ground; a large Persian hanging with variegated circular and geometrical designs, circles of yellow centered by a star design and heavy black conventional designs finely embroidered on a brilliant crimson background. The size was nine feet by seven feet, six inches.

There were many more beautiful tapestries and hangings, hopefully now in appreciative hands.

Rudy had acquired some fifty-seven pieces of jewelry which included rings in platinum settings and with various precious stones, some of which were very valuable. These were offered for sale at the auction, but the bidding was sparse and unrealistic, so Rudy's brother Alberto, removed the jewel case and took possession of it all!

It might be interesting to describe some of the furniture in the Falcon Lair home. Here are a few examples:

In the dining room there were two cabinets. One from the later 15th century, finely carved with foliated Cathedral Gothic tracery. Flanking the doors were Gothic columns supporting sculptured figures of saints in niche-like frames.

The other was a Licurian walnut cabinet, rectangular in shape. The doors were carved in relief with heraldic knights of the Crusade in armor. Practically all the surfaces were carved with knights in combat with castles in the background.

There was a magnificent Gothic arm chair, 15th century, arms and back beautifully carved and a French throne chair covered with fine red Genovese velvet and embroidered with heavy appliqué. On the back was a royal crest with the date 1508.

There was a beautiful old Vargueno desk, Spanish 16th century. The drawers and doors were faced with elaborately carved and columned ivory panels depicting medieval scenes with figures in relief.

Tables, lamps and chairs, all antiques were in excellent condition.

Rudy's bedroom was, in contrast, entirely modern but unusual and custom built. The bed was six feet wide and seven feet long. It had a low rounded head board, no foot board. It was massive, but relieved by rounded corners and edges, beautifully enameled in deep blue with massive gilded ball feet.

There were two dressers with the same general design as the bed (one dresser was equipped with a perfume burner in the center of the top and heated by an electric light beneath.)

Two bedside cabinets in the same massive design and enameled in orange, three small round pedestal tables, an overstuffed settee, black sateen and an upholstered arm chair with circular back and sides, also covered with black sateen.

There were objects of art, too numerous to mention, among which were two silver knights on horses in full armor with ivory faces and seven silver knights, also in full armor with ivory faces embellished in gold and mounted on silver bases, these were thirteen inches high.

Lest the reader question the reason for my frequent references to the Valentinos' extravagances, here is a portion of a statement given to the reporters by Natacha's mother upon their visit to the Hudnut home in France.

"While in Seville, Rudy wished to present us each with a lovely old Spanish shawl. Directly beside the gates leading to the Alcazar was an antique dealer who possessed the most wonderful collection of antique shawls in Spain. It was while looking over these treasures that Natacha was struck by a brilliant idea. Why not buy the most beautiful of this collection and sell them for big profits to the smart of 5th Avenue shops? So glowingly did the children present their wonderful schemes that I, hypnotized by their enthusiasm always became converted to them.

Rudy, being so well known in the picture world, was never able to hide his identity for long, and the Valentino name, regarded as a dollar sign, often caused extra prices to be added to purchases. Time after time, when ten percent had been judiciously tacked on by some shrewd dealer, after long dickerings, this same ten percent was taken off as though a great favor was being granted to the famous screen artist.

Rudy and Natacha selected the most beautiful specimens of the collection and the bill only came to a modest sum of $10,000! These shawls were shipped to America in bond. Needless to say, none of them were ever sold, but these generous children gave away many to their friends. I, myself, am the proud possessor of three of the choicest. We were all very much interested in antiques, lovely old furniture, etc. Some of Rudy's handsomest pieces of armor and many of Natacha's most beautiful and valuable old ivories were found here in Seville. They also bought a number of other things, amongst which were a superb pair of Renaissance doors, a Gothic chair and two very wonderful Gothic chests. If I am not mistaken, all of these objects of art are now in Rudy's Hollywood home."

Mrs. Hudnut also wrote me on several occasions urging me to try to curtail Natacha's and Rudy's reckless spending, but I had to tell her that I had tried my best to teach them some idea of economy and that they had faithfully promised to abide by my advice. Nevertheless, whenever something caught their fancy, they did not hesitate to buy it, regardless of value or cost, much as a king and queen would act, I presume.

Just about this time Mr. Schenck told me that he had heard disquieting reports about Natacha's interference with production matters on the Ritz-Carlton picture and that he couldn't gamble on production costs increasing because anyone caused delays or dissension. I assured him that he need not have any concern because I had talked with Natacha and that she understood the fact that she was jeopardizing Rudy's career.

The first picture under this new contract would be"The Eagle" based upon a story entitled Dubrovsky by Alexander Pushkin. The writing of the screenplay, much interfered with by Natacha in her home, caused problems for me and of course, the writers. But Natacha's guile and diplomacy were such that Mr. Schenck never was aware of the cause for the delay in the completion of the screenplay.

Now came the matter of choosing the director and the cast. I must say that Natacha did not interfere with me in my search for a director and, after interviewing several prominent directors, I decided to try to engage Clarence Brown, a young, intelligent man who had directed several good pictures for other studios.

An amusing side note about the preliminary discussions pertaining to Mr. Brown took place when I asked him to see me in my office to discuss the salary for his work in directing "The Eagle." Instead of Mr. Brown appearing, he sent his wife "Ona" to make the deal with me. She didn't waste much time, and after a few perfunctory remarks said, "He will not accept this job unless he gets paid his regular salary of $2500 each week."

Of course I knew from Universal Studio, where he was just finishing a picture, that he was receiving $2000 weekly. I said to Mrs. Brown, I don't want to pay Mr. Brown $2500 a week. I want to pay him $5000 each week for five weeks." Even she could not find words to thank me and rushed away to tell her husband of her astuteness. Actually, we had allowed $75,000 in the budget for a director and I had interviewed several of the important motion picture directors in Hollywood, but Brown had that youthful enthusiasm I thought our director needed to inspire Rudy and the cast. The picture was completed in about six weeks but did not achieve critical acclaim nor box office success compared with some of Rudy's other pictures.

Natacha accused me of "selling out" to Joe Schenck and demanded that she be included in some executive capacity in the production of "The Eagle". She found much fault with the screenplay and stormed into Mr. Schenck's office to voice her dissatisfaction. The result was that Mr. Schenck sent me a note in which he stipulated that Natacha was not to have access to the stages, the cutting rooms, or in any manner to interfere with the production of "The Eagle" or the writing of the screenplay.

It can well be imagined the effect upon Natacha and Rudy as well. They drove to Palm Springs without telling me. I thought that she soon would realize that Rudy had to accept Schenck's ultimatum since they were again heavily in debt and, in the event of contract termination, they would be almost in the same straits as they were when they were first married. All they had now was a lot of furniture, books, clothes and some jewelry and the cars—but no money.

After two days passed I received an urgent phone call from Rudy begging me to rush to Palm Springs because Natacha was still inconsolable and would not even speak to him. I, at once, drove down to Palm Springs in a driving rain. It was a little more than three hours when I reached Palm Springs where the sun was shining and the weather beautiful. Rudy had rented a horse and was somewhere in the desert when I reached their rooms in Dr. White's guest house.

Natacha put on a great act. She would prove to all the "so and sos" in the picture industry that she had more knowledge about story and picture values than anyone there. She would produce a picture of her own! Her original story and screenplay made under her entire personal supervision. Naturally, I inquired as to what she would use for money to finance such a project, but she brushed this aside as unimportant. I cannot repeat her language because it could not be printed, but I was amazed that such words could emerge from her really pretty mouth.

Rudy returned then. He looked haggard and depressed. I am certain that he had heard, even in greater detail, Natacha's plans and her inflexibility. He asked me how we could possibly finance a project such as this and I had to tell him the truth that we would have to secure a bank loan for as much as possible based upon the Schenck contract, but that I doubted that even as much as $25,000 could be raised. Natacha almost shrieked that she didn't need as much as $25,000 because she would do so much of the work herself and was sure she could get a cast at minimum salaries.

I explained the need of obtaining a distribution contract before production began and that I would try my best to get such a contract for her. Now she was all light and sunshine so I left them, taking with me a copy of the story outline and proposed cast. She had a rather unusual story premise: a comedy based upon women's torture in the beauty parlors. The title of her story was "What Price Beauty?"

I tried as hard as I did, but I couldn't get one offer for distribution from any legitimate company. The best I could get were promises of immediate consideration when "What Price Beauty" was completed. So I most reluctantly arranged for preliminary financing by borrowing sums from various banks, guaranteeing the loans with my own and Rudy's endorsements.

Natacha began development and preparation of her brain child. She engaged a writer and director and other key men and women, such as wardrobe mistress, set designer, cameraman and other artisans, and by working all the days and much of the nights, finally was ready to cast the picture. She did get a splendid group of actors and actresses, among which were Nita Naldi, Pierre Gendron (they were both in Rudy's picture "Cobra"), Myrna Loy and a number of others for the smaller parts. The sets were straight from authentic beauty parlors. She was truly an excellent designer of sets and furniture.

The story was very funny but, as most of Natacha's ideas were, years ahead of its time.

❦

Just about this time the Valentinos invited a Spanish portrait painter that they had met in Seville, Spain, to come to Hollywood as their guest. His name was Beltram Masses, who was, while not a renowned artist, a skilled salesman and good company. Rudy introduced him to many notables in the film colony. He did a few portraits, among which was that of Marion Davies, for which he received $5000. He painted two larger than life sized portraits of Rudy, one as a gaucho and one as the Eagle. They weren't really masterpieces.

Masses' presence in the house was good company for Rudy since Natacha was at the studio on her picture almost all day and,

63

many times, a good part of the night, busy, she said, editing and cutting her completed picture. Masses, unaccustomed to wives such as Natacha, was suspicious of her outside activities and persuaded Rudy to have her shadowed for a few days. He told Rudy that if nothing was amiss there certainly wouldn't be any harm, but if there was, then Rudy should know about it. As soon as these reports began to come in, Rudy's friend Beltram Masses left Rudy's home and returned to Spain!

Rudy insisted that I engage a detective agency to follow Natacha day and night for a few days and to give me their daily reports which he wanted to see as soon as I received them. It is difficult, even now, to reconcile the events which were reported, with the almost childlike behavior of Natacha in her daily life. When she was not sulking or angry she was buoyant and happy and occasionally even thoughtful of others.

The first report dated July 17, 1925, cast some suspicion on Natacha's actions during the previous day. The report stated that she had parked her car in a parking lot and gone off in another car driven by a man. The next day's report was the same but included the information that they had driven to a house in Sherman Oaks, California, which they entered and remained from 1:15 p.m. until 4:15 p.m. There were more reports of subsequent meetings between Natacha and this man whose identity I know but will not divulge. He was married and the father of four children.

Rudy, of course, was aware of these meetings because he insisted upon receiving the detective's reports. One morning at about 2 a.m. he phoned me at my home and said, "She isn't home yet and when she gets here I'm going to kill her!"

I begged him to do nothing until I got there. I hurriedly put on a pair of knickers, tennis shoes and a sweater, dashed to my car and drove as quickly as possible to Valentino's home. There I saw Rudy walking up and down in front of the house with a revolver in his hand. He was really distraught, but I persuaded him to give me the gun and to wait inside the house until Natacha returned. She drove up to the house at about 3 a.m. and upon seeing me she said, "Aren't you the country gentleman?" and laughingly entered her house.

I was right behind her when I saw Rudy coming down the steps from the bed room with another pistol in his hand! I had to act fast and rough to get the gun away from him. When he came into the living room he shouted, "Where have you been", and she said, "I was having great trouble matching some frames in a scene." He leaped at her and backhanded her across her mouth shouting, "You dirty liar."

Natacha didn't cry although her lip was swelling. She sat stoically just glaring at Rudy who had to be restrained from attacking her again.

Rudy told her that he was going to divorce her, he named her paramour and told her some of the things he read in the reports from the detective agency. All the while she was silent and apparently unrepentant.

I then asked them both if they wanted to be alone, but both Rudy and Natacha wouldn't consider that and began to discuss the matter of a divorce. She seemed more anxious than he, I presume, of the indignity of the hard slap, but we did begin to talk of division of properties. At about four a.m. I left for my home. Before going, I took Rudy aside and told him not to occupy the bed with Natacha but to sleep on the couch in the living room, which he promised he would do.

I went home and prepared a brief property settlement agreement and, without any sleep at all, drove to the Valentino house. There they were, having a cozy breakfast together and apparently the best of friends. Rudy told me that they had reconciled after I left early that morning. She had explained to him that she did not have an affair with this man and that the reason for the meetings was only that she had tried to help him with his marital problems! It was a bold bluff but it worked with Rudy, for a time, at least.

The shadow of Natacha's indiscretion appeared every now and then and try as they both did, it seemed inevitable that a breach was soon to be. So it wasn't too much of a surprise to me when Rudy told me that they had decided to separate. Always the gentleman, he agreed that she should get the divorce decree in Paris and gave his word that this would not in any way reflect upon Natacha.

Their parting was publicized as a "Marital Vacation" although we knew that it would end in divorce.

Natacha and her aunt, Teresa Werner, a typical old "auntie" type, entrained for New York. I was on the same train since I had some important business to take care of in New York and I actually hoped that I could find some idea that might heal the breach between Rudy and Natacha. I knew that Rudy would have been willing to have her with him again.

I remember that one day I went to Rudy's bungalow on the United Artists' lot and there was Natacha blithely writing some changes she wanted to make in the picture she had just completed. I stood in front of her and simply said, "Why? Almost every woman in the world would like to have Rudy as her lover—yet you—" She began a tirade directed at Rudy and myself for not holding off signing the contract with Mr. Schenck until she had been included in some executive capacity.

I patiently explained to her all of the difficulty I had to obtain the unusual contract for Rudy in which, for the first time in any contract thus far given to stars, had received a percentage of profits with a specified guarantee as to the minimum profits he would receive as his share. Natacha just stared at me while I went on to point out to her the many extravagances she and Rudy had gone in for and, because of these debts, it was imperative that Rudy had to work.

As diplomatically as I could I enumerated the reasons that Mr. Schenck had insisted upon the clause which barred her from any participation in the pictures, but I wasn't sure that she paid any attention because she made no comment whatsoever, so it was not possible for me to know whether or not my lecture made any impression upon her. Subsequent events proved that it had not.

ॐ

When we arrived in New York City, Natacha and her aunt proceeded to the apartment at 270 Park Avenue, which she and Rudy had maintained for more than a year. I went to The Ambassador Hotel.

There were letters almost daily between Natacha and Rudy, none of which were conciliatory. There seemed slight chance of any change.

After a few days, Natacha asked me to arrange passage for her on a liner going to Paris. She said that she wanted to be with her mother and her step-father, Richard Hudnut, at their home in Juan les Pins.

The Hudnuts had frequently, in letters, expressed their love for Rudy, and he for them. On one occasion, as a gift, he had the Welte Mignon piano manufacturer ship them a large player piano, a duplicate of the one he had bought for Natacha. Perhaps here I should mention that Natacha was born to Mr. and Mrs. O'Shaugnessy in Salt Lake City. Her father, who was a retired soldier, died when she was very young. Her mother then married a man named DeWolfe in San Francisco. She soon divorced Mr. DeWolfe and married Mr. Hudnut.

He was somewhat older than Natacha's mother but he was very wealthy. Natacha didn't stay with them long for when she was seventeen years old she left their home and soon after went to Russia to study ballet. She became the pupil of Theodore Kosloff, a famous dancer and teacher. While Natacha didn't become an outstanding ballerina, the training and discipline gave her the grace and strength which enabled her to withstand many rigors and hardships in her intensive search for recognition in artistic fields.

Kosloff it was who persuaded her to change her name from Winifred O'Shaughnessy to Natacha Rambova and she used this name for the remainder of her life.

When Natacha arrived at her mother's chateau she must have described Rudy as an ogre and a beast, because soon very abusive letters began to come to Rudy, which, of course, pained him deeply. He wrote to them to try to explain some of the causes of the rift between Natacha and himself, but he never mentioned the real cause for their separation.

After Natacha's departure, Rudy threw himself into social activities. He again invited the men who were his friends in his early Hollywood days and he had many female companions. One was Pola Negri. He had been intrigued by her for quite a while and soon he and she were together to the exclusion of almost all other girls. Pola lived in a large rented house in Beverly Hills and Rudy spent much of his free time there and she at Falcon Lair.

The "romance" between Rudy and Pola Negri was not as great as Pola later professed it to be. They did spend much time together, of course, but Rudy actually had no intention of marrying Pola or anyone else!

Frequently, Rudy and Vilma Banky and my wife and I occupied a box at a boxing stadium in Hollywood called "The

American Legion Stadium." Rudy was acquainted with quite a few of the professional boxers and was most enthusiastic about this sport. He enjoyed the exercise of boxing and he and I often engaged in short bouts. I had to be very wary because he could hit real hard when he wanted to.

One time he and I went to the boxing matches alone in his car. As we emerged after the events he saw Mae Murray walking toward the parking lot. He invited her into his car and hugged and kissed her passionately and then drove off with her leaving me there without transportation. But I couldn't blame him!

Rudy spent many afternoons with my sons. He was very fond of them and they of him. It is now and was then a sad thought that he had had no children of his own. His entire life would have been happier. But Natacha, with her fierce determination to find success for herself, would not consider the idea of having a baby, believing that such a responsibility would tie her down. But she said that it was because of Rudy that she didn't want a child because it might be damaging to his career.

Almost weekly Rudy received letters from his brother Alberto in Italy, inevitably pleading for money, which Rudy, reluctantly, occasionally asked me to send him. Rudy also kept up the support of Natacha's aunt who lived in a small house in Hollywood. I am mentioning this only to point out the constant drain on Rudy's finances.

Another costly plaything Rudy purchased was a thirty-two foot Fellowcraft yacht propelled by gasoline engines. He loved this little boat and took great pride keeping it in good condition. He insisted upon polishing the metal, swabbing the deck and cooking the meals in the galley when he entertained guests on board.

My wife and I made many trips with him to Catalina and along the coast. On one such occasion while in the middle of the channel the engines failed and we just drifted until daylight when we were sighted and towed to port. It was a rather terrifying experience because we had no lights or power throughout the night.

Rudy and a friend, Manuel Reachi, who was a Mexican "diplomat" in Hollywood, decided to go to Paris to attempt a reconciliation with Natacha, they said, but I found out later that the trip was promoted by Reachi so that they both could have a good time to try and forget Natacha. All at Rudy's expense, of course.

Rudy always had yearned for a collection of ancient armor and on this jaunt he purchased many such swords, rapiers and pistols. He also bought many from an antique dealer in New York, whose name was Victor Miller. Rudy studied the place of origin of each piece and, when available, the names and histories of the original owners. He had an extensive and valuable collection of books and manuscripts in French, Spanish and Italian through which he searched each time he bought a new weapon.

When Valentino returned from the European trip he brought his older brother, Alberto and Alberto's wife and son Jean from Italy to live with him at his new home in Beverly Hills, "Falcon Lair." This was the home he and Natacha had wanted so much before their separation.

Rudy brought his family because he was lonely and depressed. He thought that having his immediate family with him would bring him some comfort. He greatly regretted this later because soon the brother and wife created difficulties with the housekeeper and the servants. Alberto even went so far as to ask Rudy to have locks placed on the refrigerator doors so that the help would not eat the same food that he did!

There were numerous quarrels between Rudy and Alberto during the family visit and I know that these quarrels definitely ruined Rudy's last few weeks at Falcon Lair.

About this time, I persuaded Mr. Schenck to buy the rights to a new book "The Son of the Sheik" by the same author who had written "The Sheik," Rudy's very successful picture made by Paramount. I conducted the negotiations with the author, Mrs. Hull, and after the purchase had been completed gave the news to Rudy. Now I had to get Rudy's picture into production and Rudy reported for the first day of camera work for the picture "The Son of the Sheik."

During the making of the "Son of the Sheik" many of Rudy's innate characteristics became apparent. It was he who persuaded Agnes Ayres, the young and beautiful actress who starred with him in the original "Sheik" to appear in this new picture in the character role of the Sheik's mother. The makeup and her delineation of the part were excellent. Rudy, of course, also played the part of the old Sheik and his portrayal gave an inkling of what he could have portrayed in parts of older characters which he hoped to do later in his career. Such as Cesare Borgia, Christopher Columbus, American Indians and mostly that of an Apache Chief.

The United Artists Company through Mr. Schenck asked Rudy to make personal appearances at various theaters in several large cities where "The Eagle" was being exhibited, to help boost the box office receipts which had been disappointing to the theater owners and to United Artists. Again I arranged these appearances and accompanied him to some large cities where, as usual, he created much excitement and brought large, enthusiastic audiences to the theaters.

About this time Rudy decided that Alberto and his family should return to Italy. He telephoned to Alberto and told him this decision. I made railroad and steamship reservations so that Alberto's departure from New York would coincide with our appearances in that city. My wife had come to New York from Hollywood.

We went to the pier in New York harbor to see Alberto and his family off. He came to me and said that Rudy had refused to give him any money and asked me to lend him some. I didn't have much money so I asked my wife to give him a hundred dollars, which she did. Of course she never got it back.

So there we were at the pier, Rudy waving to Alberto on the deck and when the boat started to move Rudy said (and I can never forget this) "There he goes. I hope I never see him again." Sadly enough, he never did because he didn't live very long after this.

Rudy's contract with Joseph Schenck and United Artists had now been completed and he was again an artist out of work. As usual, he had no money and his debts amounted to over $100,000. Many of the creditors were becoming anxious because it soon became known that Rudy's income had stopped.

᪥

It was at this time that a prominent banker suggested to Rudy that he should negotiate a loan from a finance company in order to consolidate his debts as much as possible. The finance company he recommended was the Cinema Finance Corporation, the only local finance company who would loan money to actors. Rudy pledged all of his possessions as collateral for a loan of $100,000 for one year at seven percent interest.

Upon receipt of the loan from Cinema Finance Corporation I paid off many of the accumulated debts but it left Rudy without much money of his own.

Now I had to find another contract quickly because Rudy's manner of living hadn't changed.

I approached several studio heads such as Mr. William Fox, president of Fox Films and Mr. Carl Laemmle, the president of Universal Pictures Corporation.

When I stated the financial arrangements I wanted for Valentino, Mr. Fox asked me whether I had seen his very successful picture "The Iron Horse". When I said that I had, he asked me "What do you think it cost?" I said I believed that it had cost about $800,000 and he said, "It cost $35,000 in its entirety." And that was the end of our discussion for I had told him that Rudy had to get $150,000 plus a percentage for himself alone.

Mr. Laemmle asked me to meet him in The Ambassador Hotel in downtown Los Angeles early one morning. When I mentioned terms he bluntly told me that such a deal was impossible for his company, because the amount I asked was the most they ever spent for an entire picture!

I had purposely avoided seeing Mr. Schenck, hoping for an approach from him. I almost had decided to speak with him the following day to discuss further productions with Valentino to be released by United Artists. But that evening I received a phone call from Mr. Schenck's assistant who asked me to see Mr. Schenck the following day to discuss a deal for more pictures starring Rudy.

I met with John Considine, Mr. Schenck's assistant and Mr. Schenck at the appointed time and we began to discuss the new contract.

There wasn't a chance, said Schenck, to renew the contract under the old terms because the grosses of the last picture didn't warrant that large payment to Rudy. I proposed an arrangement. That Rudy would accept $6500 weekly from the start of the contract until two pictures were completed plus 25% of the profit of both pictures. Mr. Schenck flatly turned this down and said that he would get back to me with an alternative offer. I used the customary ploy and told him that I had other offers and that he should not delay his decision.

Then I drove to see Rudy who was then at Pola Negri's home and, after relating the meeting with Schenck, actually commanded him not to talk to Schenck or Considine or anyone else if they should happen to phone him directly.

Just as I was about to have dinner at my home, Considine phoned me and said sadly that Mr. Schenck had rejected my proposition and that the best deal he would agree to was $3500 weekly plus only 10% of the profits. I told him that I knew for certain that Rudy would not accept such a deal but that in fairness I would discuss the deal with Rudy and phone him later that evening. I again went to Pola's house and told him of the offer and that I had rejected it outright. Pola very urgently told Rudy to accept. She said that it was more than she was earning and that he might be out of work for a long time. His reply to her was another indication of his confidence in me. He said," That is entirely up to George and he will decide what to do!"

I returned to my home and phoned Considine, saying that Rudy wouldn't budge from my offer of $6500 weekly plus 25% of the profits, and that Rudy was offended at their offer, etc. Considine told me that Mr. Schenck was even at this time in touch with another star, Gloria Swanson. And I told him to tell Mr. Schenck that I wished him all the good luck in the world.

With a very heavy heart I tried to have some dinner but could not eat. I felt sure that Considine or Schenck would come back with another offer and, sure enough, at about ten o'clock that same night, Considine phoned and said "I think he's crazy but Mr. Schenck said that we would accept your terms for the new contract." We agreed that salary would commence immediately upon signing.

I hurried back to see Rudy at Pola's house and the picture that I saw I shall never forget. They evidently had been quarreling ever since I left. He was pacing the living room and she was going up the stairs. When I told him the good news he looked up at Pola and said "You bitch!" and abruptly left the house with me.

After several offers and rejections, Schenck finally came upon a play, then on Broadway, called "The Firebrand" which was based upon the life of Benvenuto Cellini. It was a very dramatic play about the famous Italian sculptor who in his own life had been much of a daredevil and was much beloved by many women. The costumes of the period were very colorful. There was a lot of action such as in Rudy's most successful pictures. The writing of the screenplay got under way with many conferences between the writers and Rudy and myself.

When the principal part of the screenplay was acceptable to us, Mr. Schenck asked Rudy once again to make personal appearances in several large cities to bolster the sagging box office receipts in the theaters where "The Eagle" was being shown.

So off again, we went East after appearing in San Francisco. Here Mayor Rolph invited us to his residence for tea and as we were leaving he gave Rudy a beautiful water spaniel, black and silky. Rudy wanted to take this puppy with him, but the oppressive heat in New York and in the train was bad for the little dog, so I arranged to have the puppy shipped home to Los Angeles to be held until we returned. Soon after Rudy died, I returned this little dog to Mayor Rolph who said he would cherish it in Rudy's memory.

Valentino loved all animals. He owned many fine dogs; one a black Doberman Pincher "Kabar" was his almost constant companion on his auto trips and on the set and even sometimes in the evening. He trained this big dog to obey the command "attack" and the animal certainly obeyed. Rudy spoke to Kabar only in French and the dog understood him only. Others might have talked to the dog and perhaps alienated part of his affection if he could understand English and was approachable by others. Another dog he owned was a very large wolfhound. So big, in fact, that when he stood on his hind legs, he was a head taller than most men. The other two were a formidable looking but most gentle English bull dog and the little water spaniel which was a gift from Mayor Rolph.

Rudy had his stable of horses and, as I stated before, he had stables for four built near the Falcon Lair home. In this stable Rudy had installed all the known appurtenances for the comfort and convenience of these animals. There also was a "tack" room in which the extra saddles and bridles and blankets were kept, always in perfect order and cleanliness.

In his spare time he rode each of these horses almost daily up trails and firebreak roads but very seldom on the bridle paths in Beverly Hills.

We arrived in Chicago and the United Artists publicity man met us. He had a clipping from *The Chicago Tribune* which was so virulent that it was a great shock to Rudy. That which follows is exactly what occurred that day and I set forth these things now because of the effect upon Rudy. I believe that he grieved more about this editorial than about anything that had happened to him before and in fact was on his mind when he was later in the hospital during his last illness.

Although we were in Chicago only between trains, we went to The Blackstone Hotel. Here I was handed the now famous editorial which originally appeared in *The Chicago Tribune*. Since this scurrilous attack embittered the last days of Rudolph Valentino, killing his usual joy in living and causing him more mental anguish than any other article ever written about him, I quote the infamous anonymous attack, which I recognized as coming from the same poison pen which earlier in the year had, without cause and without reason, attacked my friend.

" PINK POWDER PUFFS"

"A new public ballroom was opened on the north side a few days ago, a truly handsome place and apparently well run. The pleasant impression lasts until one steps into the men's washroom and finds there on the wall a contraption of glass tubes and levers and a slot for the insertion of a coin. The glass tubes contain a fluffy pink solid, and beneath them one reads an amazing legend which runs something like this: "Insert coin. Hold personal puff beneath the tube. Then pull the lever."

A powder vending machine! In a men's washroom! Homo Americanus! Why didn't some one quietly drown Rudolph Guglielmi, alias Valentino, years ago?

And was the pink powder machine pulled from the wall or ignored? It was not. It was used. We personally saw two "men" - as young lady contributors to the Voice of the People are wont to describe the breed – step up, insert coin, hold kerchief beneath the spout, pull the lever, then take the pretty pink stuff and put it on their cheeks in front of the mirror.

Another member of this department, one of the most benevolent men on earth, burst raging into the office the other day because he had seen a young "man" combing his pomaded hair in the elevator. But we claim our pink powder story beats all this hollow.

It is time for a matriarchy if the male of the species allows such things to persist. Better a rule by masculine women than by effeminate men. Man began to slip, we are beginning to believe, when he discarded the straight razor for the safety pattern. We shall not be surprised when we hear that the safety razor has given way to the depilatory.

Who or what is to blame is what puzzles us. Is this degeneration into effeminacy a cognate reaction with pacifism to the virilities and realities of war? Are pink powder and parlor pinks in any way related? How does one reconcile masculine costumes, sheiks, floppy pants, and slave bracelets with a disregard for law and an aptitude for crime more in keeping with the frontier of half a century ago than a twentieth-century metropolis?

Do women like the type of "men" who pats pink powder on his face in a public washroom and arranges his coiffure in a public elevator? Do women at heart belong to the Wilsonian era of "I Didn't Raise My Boy to Be a Soldier?" What has become of the old "caveman" line?

It is a strange social phenomenon and one that is running its course not only here in America but in Europe as well. Chicago may have its powder puffs; London has its dancing men and Paris its gigolos. Down with Decatur; up with Elinor Glyn. Hollywood is the national school of masculinity. Rudy, the beautiful gardener's boy, is the prototype of the American male. Hell's Bells. Oh, Sugar. "

As I read this cowardly and yellow attack my countenance must have changed, for Rudy, watching me, immediately asked what was wrong. If he had not caught me in the act of reading it, I think that I never would have allowed him to see it, so profoundly do I regret the irritation and saddening effect it had upon him. He took the screed from my reluctant fingers, read it: instantly I realized how deeply he was moved. His face paled, his eyes blazed and his muscles stiffened.

I shared his anger, for it seemed to me then, and I have never changed my opinion, that not in all my experience with anonymous attacks in print had I ever read one in which the name of an honest gentleman had been dragged in the mud in so causeless a manner.

What, I ask you, had the installation of a powdering machine in any public bathroom in Chicago to do with a dignified actor in New York and Hollywood? Had Valentino made dancing his profession, I grant you there might have been some reason for this envious attack. But I have related in this volume how sincerely Valentino disliked the profession of dancing and what grave sacrifices he made both financially and otherwise in repudiating the career of a dancer and suffering the privations necessary to become an actor in motion pictures.

In running over in my mind the characters he portrayed on the screen in recent years, I mention "Monsieur Beaucaire", "Cobra", "The Sainted Devil", "The Four Horsemen", "The Sheik" and "The Son of the Sheik". And I ask the public to tell me if in any of these super pictures Valentino assumed a character which would connect him in any way with the sort of effeminate man who would resort to a pink powder puff.

For myself, I answer emphatically that there is no connection whatsoever; and I agreed with my friend that no one, unless he were animated by personal jealously of the exalted position Valentino enjoyed in the estimation of the American public, could have written so impudent an attack upon a gentleman. I purposely make use of the term impudent, because an inferior can be impudent only to his superior.

Wounded to the soul by the implication that his ancestry had been common, whereas the world knows that marriage between the daughter of a surgeon and an Italian calvalry officer constitute honorable parentage for offspring, to say the least, Valentino prepared at once to avenge the insult offered.

Summoning the representative of The Tribune's powerful and greatly feared rival The Chicago Herald-Examiner, Valentino handed to him for publication the following:

"July 19th, 1926

To The Man (?) Who Wrote The Editorial Headed "Pink Powder Puffs" in Sunday's "Tribune" :

The above mentioned editorial is at least the second scurrilous attack you have made upon me, my race, and my father's name.

You slur my Italian ancestry; you cast ridicule upon my Italian name; you cast doubt upon my manhood.

I call you, in return, a contemptible coward and to prove which of us is a better man, I challenge you to a personal test. This is not a challenge to a duel in the generally accepted sense – that would be illegal. But in Illinois boxing is legal, so is wrestling. I, therefore, defy you to meet me in the boxing or wrestling arena to prove, in typically American fashion (for I am an American citizen) , which of us is more a man. I prefer this test of honor to be private, so I may give you the beating you deserve, and because I want to make it absolutely plain that this challenge is not for purposes of publicity. I am handing copies of this to the newspapers simply because I doubt that any one so cowardly as to write about me as you have would respond to a defy unless forced by the press to do so. I do not know who you are or how big you are but this challenge stands if you are as big as Jack Dempsey.

I will meet you immediately or give you a reasonable time in which to prepare, for I assume that your muscles must be flabby and weak, judging by your cowardly mentality and that you will have to replace the vitriol in your veins for red blood – if there be a place in such a body as yours for red blood and manly muscle.

I want to make it plain that I hold no grievance against the *Chicago Tribune*, although it seems a mistake to let a cowardly writer use its valuable columns as this "man" does. My fight is personal – with the poison-pen writer of editorials that stoops to racial and personal prejudice. The *Tribune* through Miss Mae Tinee, has treated me and my work kindly and at times very favorably. I welcome criticism of my work as an actor – but I will resent with every muscle of my body attacks upon my manhood and ancestry.

Hoping I will have the opportunity to demonstrate to you that the wrist under a slave bracelet may snap a real fist into your sagging jaw and that I may teach you respect of a man even though he happens to prefer to keep his face clean, I remain with

Utter Contempt,
RUDOLPH VALENTINO

P.S. I will return to Chicago within ten days. You may send your answer to me in New York, care of United Artists Corp., 729 7th Ave. "

The publication of this challenge, which was originally in The Herald-Examiner, was flashed immediately over wires and cables to the four corners of the earth, and the furious discussion which resulted is of too recent date to need comment.

While we were on the train going from Chicago to New York I asked Rudy, as soon as he had had time to cool down and think coherently, for this attack had thrown him into a rage so abysmal that his whole being was disorganized:

"What are you going to do if you find that this editor is seven feet tall and twice your weight?"

To which he replied:

"What would be the difference? If I am licked by a more powerful man that will be no disgrace and at any rate I'll show him that I am no pink powder puff."

That unhappy epithet, pink powder puff, stuck in Rudy's craw. During the few short weeks between the time it was applied to him by this antagonist who was too cowardly to make himself known, and Valentino's untimely death, Rudy repeated the words more times than I heard him utter any other phrase in all the years that I knew him.

He would repeat them seemingly in agony of soul, as if fearful that, in the minds of some who did not know him, the thought of effeminacy might stick. Whereas I, as his friend, make the statement that no cowboy on the Western plains nor athlete from the Marines could boast a more powerful physique than that of Valentino, nor more truly possess the right to the title of he-man.

Having given for two weeks or more, the opportunity to the anonymous writer of the before quoted "pink powder puff" insult, Valentino then issued the following statement, which he gave to the press, the only paper in Chicago which failed to quote it being The Tribune, a thing, of course, which it could not very well afford to do, since it had been the source of the attack.

" It is evident you cannot make a coward fight any more than you can draw blood out of a turnip. The heroic silence of the writer who chose to attack me without any provocation in the *Chicago Tribune*

leaves no doubt as to the total absence of manliness in his whole makeup.

I feel I have been vindicated because I consider his silence as a tacit retraction, and an admission which I am forced to accept even though it is not entirely to my liking.

The newspaper men and women whom it has been my privilege to know briefly or for a longer time have been so absolutely fair and so loyal to their profession and their publications, that I need hardly say how conspicuous is this exception to the newspaper profession. "

I want it understood that the vehemence with which I denounce the anonymous writer of this cowardly attack upon my friend is not based so much upon what the article contained as upon the deep hurt it gave Rudy, embittering as it did the last days of his life and, in my opinion, hastening his death.

Who knows but that, in those last days when he was conscious, able to think and undisturbed by visitors, his mind might not have dwelt on his inability to avenge the insult and that, had his last hours been more free from anxiety, his power to cope with the inroads of the septic poisoning might have been increased, and possibly his life spared.

This will always be a moot question with me. And with others who have not been slow to express a similar opinion. For this reason, to the day of my death, this question will be unanswered.

It is only fair to say that the last paragraph in Valentino's statement, quoted above, is absolutely true. The United Artists as well as Mr. Valentino himself subscribed to press clipping bureaus, by means of which we were informed of practically everything printed about our stars. And I reiterate that never before has anything come to our attention so bitterly worded, so personal, so far-fetched and entirely uncalled for as The Chicago Tribune's editorial.

We went on to Pittsburgh and Philadelphia and then to Atlantic City where, after the usual onslaught of the fanatic women, I noticed that his color wasn't good. He looked haggard and exhausted. I wanted to get a doctor then but he said that he was just tired and felt certain that a good night's rest would be all he needed. I recall that he took a large dose of bicarbonate of soda before retiring. He slept soundly and appeared refreshed and cheerful at breakfast.

Rudy smoked many cigarettes each day, perhaps as many as one hundred. He preferred the Turkish blend and we imported the "Abdullah" cigarettes from London in fifty-two boxes each containing one hundred cigarettes! At that time there was no agitation about smoking as there is now, but perhaps his smoking did weaken his heart and lungs.

Another import was his shaving soap from London. It came in polished wooden bowls and was a small luxury he enjoyed using.

Valentino was next to appear in New York City. The reception at The Strand Theatre there was just as overwhelming as it had been in the other cities and Rudy was having a social whirl at parties given by Barclay Warburton and others. He seldom came back to The Ambassador Hotel where we had a suite of rooms until the early morning hours. His bedroom was at one end of the living room and my wife's and my bedroom at the other end, so, of course, we knew the time of his arrival.

On Sunday morning, August 15th, 1926, my wife and I were having breakfast in the living room of the suite when Rudy came in. He looked awful but said that he would join us in a few minutes. We heard a loud groan from Rudy's room and went in to see him. He said he had a stomach ache and knew what would help it. He then poured almost a full glass of brandy and quickly drank it and said he felt much better. He got into his bed and said that he wanted to sleep all day because he had a big date that night.

Mrs. Ullman and I left our room to visit nearby friends and on the way out we asked the telephone operator not to put through any calls to the room until we returned.

At about four o'clock that afternoon we returned to the hotel and heard loud groans from Rudy's room. Rudy was in severe pain in the region of his stomach, so I phoned to the desk to ask for the hotel physician. There was a doctor whose home was across the street from the hotel and I asked the clerk to get him up to the room as quickly as possible. Dr. Paul Durham arrived in a few minutes and his first diagnosis was that Rudy was suffering from a perforated ulcer.

Dr. Durham wasn't certain that his diagnosis was entirely correct and phoned Dr. C.K. Manning to examine Rudy at the hotel to confirm his findings. When Dr. Manning arrived he advised Rudy's immediate removal by ambulance to The Polyclinic Hospital. Dr. Harold D. Meeker, a prominent surgeon, was called and he advised immediate surgery. Preparations were made and Dr. Meeker performed the surgery at 6 o'clock in the evening on Sunday. Dr. Battey, the senior Polyclinic physician was his assistant.

When Rudy was brought down to his hospital room he was still under the anesthetic. I asked Dr. Meeker whether Rudy was in any grave danger. He told me that gangrene had set in at the place of incision of the ulcer but that he thought that he had been able to excise the gangrene. Again I asked him what the chances of Rudy's survival were and he said, "About 50-50." That was a great blow to me to be sure.

I went about getting the best nurses Dr. Battey recommended and placed two guards to keep all visitors away from the room.

The newspaper reporters were already assembled in a private room on the lower floor of the hospital and I went to them and gave them a condensed review of the surgery and the time of Rudy's probable stay at the hospital. Each day more press and magazine representatives congregated in the hospital room assigned to them and several times each day I visited with them and gave them details of Rudy's condition and other information to enable them to write their stories. My main reason for my efforts to keep the press interested was that for the first four days of Valentino's illness I felt certain that he would recover but that the time for his convalescence might be fairly long.

At one time I asked Rudy whether I should send for his brother and he said, "By no means. Just please cable him that I am indisposed and that I will soon be up and around."

As I wrote before, these are almost deathbed words of my friend and I would not distort them by so much as a misplaced word and I quote only those which are necessary to this narration.

Rudy asked for no one and slept almost all the time. He said that he felt no pain and only expressed himself as being "so tired."

The newscasters and writers, at my request, frequently made the announcement that no one was permitted to see Valentino, but despite this, people continuously tried, by every conceivable ruse, to gain admittance to the hospital and even to the corridor near the room where Rudy was fighting for his life.

Thousands of telegrams, letters and religious medals began to arrive for Rudy. Flowers arrived by the truckloads. I told Rudy about these things whenever I could and he asked me to have the flowers distributed to the free wards in the hospital.

He also asked me to let him have a hand mirror. His illness had left him so thin that I tried to avoid getting one for him, but he said "Ok, let me have it! I only want to see what I look like when I am sick, so that if I ever have to play that kind of part I will know how to put on my make up."

He was definitely on the road to recovery on Sunday morning at one thirty when Mrs. Ullman and I left him. Neither the nurses or doctors had expressed any anxiety about his condition.

Nevertheless, I was uneasy. I do not say that I had a premonition, but after I had taken my wife to the hotel, where I shaved and showered, instead of going to bed, I returned to the hospital, arriving there about five o'clock Sunday morning.

It was still dark and the night nurses were on duty. Rudy was asleep. I read his chart, and, to my consternation, saw that both his pulse and respiration were much more rapid than when I saw him earlier. I immediately phoned the four physicians to come at once, which they did.

A little before seven o'clock Rudy awakened and said, "I feel fine now. The pain is gone. All I can feel is the place where they made the incision. Perhaps on Monday Mr. Schenck and Norma can come for a visit. Later on perhaps I can go back to the hotel and rest there."

The doctors examined Rudy and then held a consultation which lasted about an hour. One of the doctors, Dr. Durham, urgently suggested blood transfusions, but the others disagreed.

At about 8 o'clock that morning I went into what I thought was an empty hospital room, to try and rest awhile. In one of the beds I saw Dr. Durham, the man who first examined Rudy at the hotel. He was lying on his back listening to his own heart and then sternly demanded that I get to bed at once because my heart was in very bad shape. Without thinking much about it, I said, "I think you're crazy." And I left the room. I said this without meaning it, of course, but a month or so after Valentino's death, I learned that Dr. Durham was actually confined in a Texas home for mental patients!

While I was in the corridor near Rudy's room, a priest told me that he wanted to see Rudy. I thought Rudy might be alarmed if he saw a priest at this time, so I refused to permit the priest access to Rudy. He frowned and looking down at me said, "If he should die without the last rites, it will be upon your head!" I mention these things only to show the strain upon me at this time.

The doctors, at my request, had canceled all their other appointments and stood by to try anything that might get Rudy past the crisis. They issued hourly bulletins and, in silence, crowds began to gather in the street, for word of hope, which never came.

Early on Monday morning when I went again to his bedside, I saw that he was sinking rapidly. His fever had increased and his pulse was very rapid.

Realizing that were he able to ask he would probably want to see a priest, now I called Father Leonard, with whom I had spoken several times during the past previous days. He was pastor of a church called the "Actor's Church" on West 47th Street.

Father Leonard soon arrived and went alone into Rudy's room where he remained for some time. When he came out his face was uplifted. Later when I saw Rudy I was sure that I had done the right thing because he appeared calm and peaceful.

Mr. and Mrs. Joseph Schenck came to visit Rudy and he spoke with them quite normally, inquiring about their health and the health of Norma's sister, Connie Talmadge.

I sent for an old friend of Rudy's, an Italian gentleman named Frank Menillo, because I thought Rudy might want to say something to him in his native language. But he spoke in English and said, "Thank you, Frank, I'll be well soon."

Early next morning when I again went to his room, he called me by name in a voice so much stronger that I was greatly encouraged, until he said, "Wasn't it an awful thing that we were lost in the woods last night?" I was too shocked to answer and just stood next to his bed and stroked his head. He looked up at me and said, "On the one hand, you don't appreciate the humor of that, do you?" I tried to smile and said, "Sure I do, Rudy, sure I do."

Fearing to excite him and hoping that he might fall asleep again I turned to pull down the blinds, for the sun was rising. I turned at the sound of his voice. He waved a feeble hand and with a smile just touching his lips he said, "Don't pull down the blinds. I feel fine. I want the sunlight to greet me!"

These were the last intelligible words he spoke. Hurriedly I brought Frank Menillo and an Italian priest into the room. I thought that Rudy might say something in his native tongue to a confessor, but Rudy was already in coma and muttered only one word in Italian, which I thought was, "Madre."

At 12:10 p.m. on Monday, August 23rd, 1926, Rudolph Valentino was dead; age, thirty-one years.

Now, despite the anguish which I suffered, I had to undertake the harsh duties connected with death.

I first phoned The Frank Campbell Undertakers and requested that someone come to the hospital to see me. Then I went down to the room where the now somewhat bored newsmen were assembled and without any preamble simply extended my arms and said, "He's dead!"

The effect was like that of a bomb shell. The men and women almost catapulted from their chairs and rushed to get to phones anywhere they could be found. I believe that the impact of the unexpected announcement upon them resulted in the banner headlines which appeared that afternoon and next day in every newspaper in the U.S. and foreign countries.

I was standing on the steps of the hospital waiting for the man from Frank Campbell funeral parlor to arrive when Mr. Schenck came to me and said, "George, this might not be the right time to say this, but I'd be happy to have you join my organization, if you would consider it." While I hadn't had time to think of my own future activities, I had received no fewer than thirty-three offers of positions in as many varied industries. But I liked Mr. Schenck and his rough exterior and I said to him "Yes! I would be glad to be associated with you and as soon as I possibly can after I have completed my work for Valentino." I mention this here because of Mr. Schenck's later behavior.

I knew at this time that I had an enormous task ahead of me after Rudy had been laid to rest. Mr. Schenck actually offered me a job with him supposing that I would hypothecate Rudy's percentage of the two last pictures in return for his offer. He sent a man to see me in my office after I had begun to work on the estate, who obligingly suggested that I arrange with the court to sell Rudy's share to Schenck for a comparatively small price. Of course I wouldn't agree to this and Schenck's agreement for my services never materialized.

Now, Mr. Campbell himself appeared and commenced selling his coffins. I told him that I would discuss that with him at his office but that I wanted to arrange to have Rudy's body removed as quickly and as quietly as possible to his establishment. Within thirty minutes his men arrived and I watched them place poor Rudy's body in a large wicker basket and into the rear elevator to the street.

I went to Frank Campbell's office and he very seriously tried to have me order a silver coffin costing $30,000. It was only proper, said he, that a man of such distinction should have the finest casket available. I didn't agree, but finally chose one which was priced at $4000, probably four times its true value. Here I must dispute other reports by writers who contend that Mr. Campbell did not want any money for the funeral expenses. That is incorrect and untrue.

Of course I cabled Alberto in Italy and phoned Pola Negri in Hollywood. She had been giving interviews in Hollywood to reporters avowing her great loss and grief upon Rudy's death. I knew that I should not have Rudy's body moved from Campbell's until the brother arrived.

I had arranged for the harrowing experience of allowing the public to view Rudy in his coffin at Campbell's. It is now an almost unbelievable segment of my life in the days the public were first admitted. I thought that I had anticipated eventualities by having a dozen New York foot policemen under a sergeant and several policemen on horseback near Campbell's entrance when the first group of visitors arrived at about 7 o'clock in the morning. But the crowd quickly grew to almost riot proportion and more and more police had to be called upon to try to keep order. The lines extended five blocks north of the Campbell entrance and a drizzle of rain had begun to fall. This did not discourage the mob and there was a great deal of pushing and shoving along the line. It was extremely difficult to keep some semblance of order inside the Campbell establishment and I was constantly concerned lest some one might desecrate the body of Valentino in the Gold Room.

85

I had been coming and going by a hidden side entrance of the building, and late in the evening, when I was walking along the line of people waiting for their turn to reach the entrance, I saw several men and women selling hot dogs and other food and trinkets every fifty feet or so. I went to Mr. Campbell and told him to close the doors now and not to admit any more viewers. Outside the crowd then became really unruly! They crowded against the two policemen on their mounts and shoved them against the large plate glass window of Campbell's until it broke. The horses, becoming frightened, jumped about and injured quite a few in the crowd.

Around the world, newspapers reported several suicides by young women, many holding pictures of Valentino in their hands or the walls in their homes covered with newspaper photographs of Rudy in various costumes. I am sure that this was greatly exaggerated, but it provided sensational reading for the public.

I received word that Alberto, Rudy's brother was sailing and would arrive in about a week. He had never met Mr. Schenck or any other important person in this country but out of respect for Rudy's family I didn't want to arrange for funeral services until Alberto arrived. I did, however, try to arrange for the mass at the St. Patrick's Cathedral, the largest and best known Catholic church in New York, but they refused to permit this, giving the reason that Rudy's life had not been exemplary, that he had been divorced and lived in sin! So I again approached Father Leonard at the St. Malachy's church, who, without any hesitation, agreed to conduct the mass for Rudy and to co-operate fully with our arrangements.

❦

Alberto arrived on September 1st and I again obtained permission from the Harbor Master to meet the Homeric in mid-harbor by getting there in a tugboat.

When I got to the upper deck, Alberto rushed to meet me. He said, "I am so very sorry. I will take his place." This jolted me, of course, for several reasons.

Alberto had practically no resemblance at all to Rudy and, in fact was not physically, nor in any other manner, qualified to ever be considered for any screen appearance. I said this to him because I was so affronted by his egotism, but he either didn't understand me or didn't want to, for his next question to me there on the deck of the Homeric was, "How big is the estate?" Up to this time I hadn't thought of anything other than that Rudy should have a decent burial, so I turned away from Alberto saying, "I haven't any idea."

In a taxicab we drove to Campbell's funeral parlor and I escorted Alberto to the room where they had taken Rudy's body. Alberto just looked at Rudy briefly and was ready to depart.

The next day Pola Negri arrived by train from Hollywood. Mrs. Ullman and I met her and her secretary at the station and escorted them to Campbell's where she just briefly looked at Rudy's body and attempted to faint, but there weren't any reporters or cameramen around at this time.

Somewhere, probably in The Ambassador Hotel, a man approached Pola and said that he had been appointed by the Campbell establishment to be available to her if she should require medical attention. He gave his name as Dr. Sterling Wyman and later on she introduced him to me as her physician. Neither his bearing or her conversation marked him as a professional man but I didn't question him then because I had many more important matters to attend to.

It is amusing to relate the identity of this "Dr. Wyman" and his unusual gift of mimicry. I shall do so in a later chapter.

The day of the church service arrived. Pola with her secretary, Miss Hein, rode to the church with Mrs. Ullman and myself. There, at the curb, near the entrance was a hospital ambulance brought there, I was told, by Pola Negri's "physician" who said he feared that his patient might have to be hospitalized because of the emotional strain.

The poor overtaxed police officers again performed almost miraculous feats in keeping the curious and morbid crowd away from the church and keeping lanes open for the invited congregation. The services were beautifully conducted by Father Leonard and there were no unusual incidents during the time in church.

The return trip to Hollywood was quickly arranged. Only Pola and Miss Hein, her secretary, James Quirk, the editor of Photoplay magazine and a good friend to both Rudy and myself, Alberto and Mrs. Ullman and I were on this special train, which had a baggage section where Rudy's coffin was placed. There was also a space for a cook and steward and small kitchen. Grief stricken Pola ate like a starved person. She said that the emotion made her hungry.

The train made frequent stops at depots across the country. Often there were large crowds gathered quietly; men removed their hats and many touched the sides of the train in reverence. Flowers were delivered to the steward who placed them near the coffin. Pola often stood in the vestibule and appeared almost to faint. James Quirk became annoyed after a few of these exhibitions and said to her, after looking at a small gathering at one of the depots, "Not enough people to faint for. You might as well stay here!"

But I must return to some events before we entrained for Hollywood. An Italian from Brooklyn got in touch with Alberto and said that he was sure that Rudy had been murdered. Alberto, with some help, got in touch with the precinct police sergeant who relayed the message to the New York District Attorney. He phoned me at The Ambassador Hotel and read to me the statement Alberto had made and asked me," What about it?" I simply suggested that he speak with Dr. Meeker, who performed the surgery on Rudy and to ask for the complete medical report. He thanked me and that was the last I heard from him.

Of course there were many publicity seekers with conjectures and reports which some newspapers allowed to appear in various of their editions, but there were no other official inquiries.

Just to record the actual report from the Dr. Meeker, here is his letter describing the surgery he performed:

(This is included in the "Documents" section, p. 267-268)

By this time I had begun to suspect "Dr. S. Wyman" and asked a reporter friend to check his background. I would not permit Wyman to accompany us to Hollywood, even though Miss Negri requested it. I was hardly surprised when, shortly after my return to Hollywood, I read dispatches quoting New York papers. In the *New York Times* the headline stated "Dr. Wyman exposed as ex-convict", "Man Who Took Active Part in Valentino Rites Identified as Impersonator", "Wyman Served Term for Wearing Naval Uniform as Escort to Princess Fatima at White House." Further, the papers reported that "Dr." Wyman had graduated from public school #18 and E High School in Brooklyn. He had received a degree in political science from a small collage in Charleston, North Carolina. He next enrolled in a "diploma factory" in Washington where he bought a medical degree for $25. The Dean and

President of this institute had later been sent to a Federal penitentiary for using the mails to defraud!

Wyman repeatedly alleged that I was his close friend, which of course was untrue. Pola Negri introduced him to me when she arrived in New York for the funeral.

Not many months later Sterling Wyman was shot to death during a robbery attempt in the lobby of a small hotel in New York City where he was employed as a night clerk.

On the train bearing Rudy's body (and the few of us in another section) I worked on the plans for the next grim event, the funeral service in the Church of the Good Shepherd in Beverly Hills and the placing of the casket in a crypt in the Hollywood Cemetery.

June Mathis, the famous scenarist and long Rudy's mentor, had, in a telegram to me while I was still in New York, offered one of her family crypts in the Hollywood Cemetery as a temporary place to keep Rudy's coffin until we could make other arrangements.

Invitations to the church services had been mailed by my secretary at my request to the many people who composed the Hollywood professionals. Due to this foresight, very few incidents occurred that the competent Beverly Hills police didn't promptly control. The services were brief and solemn and then the coffin was brought to the Hollywood Cemetery where Rudy rests even to this day.

The day following Rudy's interment, I went to my office in the United Artists Studio to begin the arduous task of settling Rudy's affairs. A lawyer named Raymond Stewart had drawn up Valentino's will probably at a time shortly following his divorce from Natacha. Mr. Stewart brought the will to me and I, believing that Rudy's friend and lawyer should file it, arranged to meet with W.I. Gilbert to attend this function.

By the terms of the will, which I had not seen before, Rudy's brother Alberto was to receive one third, his sister one third and the other third was bequested to Mrs. Teresa Werner, Natacha's aunt. It specifically cut off Natacha with a bequest of one dollar. I do believe that Rudy left the one third to Natacha's aunt knowing that, if there was any estate, she would give her share to Natacha.

89

I was named executor and general manager, I presume, because Rudy knew I was aware of the heap of debts he had accumulated and didn't want to worry about these things, even after death. I am sure that the will was not drawn with any anticipation of death. He simply followed Mr. Stewart's suggestion to have his will made out.

Alberto began to become annoying almost at once. He wanted to be the executor of the will and resented my appointment. He rented a bungalow on the grounds of the Ambassador Hotel on Wilshire Blvd. in Hollywood at a monthly rental of $750. He installed himself in "star" fashion, with Rudy's dog Kabar and, eventually, female companionship. He had meals from the hotel kitchen brought in and ordered quantities of wines and liquors. He didn't have any money of his own and every purchase was on credit which he obtained because of his anticipated inheritance.

I explained to him in the simplest words I could think of that, at the moment, there wasn't any money in the estate and told him the plan I had for increasing the grosses of Rudy's last two pictures, "The Eagle" and "The Son of the Sheik," but that the initial cost of the plan had to be born by myself. The idea was simply to select a list of fans who had written intelligent letters to Rudy during the past year and address them in letters from me suggesting that they could keep Valentino's name alive by forming groups who would insist that their local exhibitors run these pictures periodically and that they would attend these showings in groups. I mailed 50,000 letters all personally signed by myself.

The result was better than I anticipated for, all over the United States and Canada and Europe, Valentino Memorial Clubs were formed for the purpose I suggested. Some of these clubs are still in existence, but the origin of the idea has been forgotten. At any rate, these activities were quite productive and United Artists had to send out a great number of new motion picture prints to the theaters.

I asked Alberto to change his manner of living until some of Rudy's assets could be liquidated, but he took offense at that and went to a Los Angeles attorney, apparently at Pola's suggestion, and Milton Cohen became his legal representative.

The terms of Rudy's will were published soon after it was filed. It was brief and simple.

Soon after he had become Alberto's lawyer, Mr. Cohen asked me to advance $5000 to Alberto because some creditors were demanding payment of their long overdue bills. Reluctantly, I did advance this sum to Alberto through his lawyer, taking the sum from the money I had set aside to pay some of Rudy's old obligations.

I should have then realized that I would only have trouble and aggravation in the handling of the estate and immediately turned everything over to the court to administer, but I was too idealistic to let the world know that Rudy had no real assets but actually owed over $235,000 for money borrowed from the Cinema Finance Corporation, $100,000 and interest, second mortgages on two homes and dozens of debts both here and in New York and London. He had ordered some forty suits in London, shoes in dozen lots, several dozen shirts and other wearing apparel, none of which he got to wear. These were taken by his brother after Rudy died.

As soon as I could, I repaid the Cinema Finance Corporation because they held a trust deed as collateral under which they could, if they wished to, foreclose on every single asset Rudy had when he died. The amount paid to them was $108,750.

I had, during the years of management of Rudy's affairs paid all accounts and transacted all business within the framework of a corporation call Rudolph Valentino Productions, Inc. After discussing the matter with Mr. Gilbert, the estate lawyer, he definitely agreed that it was proper to continue to do so. I continued to process all transactions in this manner. For this reason I did not ask for the court's permission to invest some of the revenue in loans to banks and others at legal interest, all of which were repaid, including a loan of $22,000, I had made to Mae Murray.

Rudy's sister, Maria, wrote to me and asked me to advance money against her share to Frank Menillo to invest for her in his tomato packing plant. Later, the court, upon Alberto's legal representatives' arguments, held me responsible for all advances made without the court's approval, including the money I had advanced to Alberto himself, the salary I drew as treasurer and secretary of the corporation and for the payments I had made to creditors.

Since the premium paid for the Schenck policy was charged as a production cost, I felt justified in claiming 25% of the payment

91

Schenck received after Rudy's death as part of the profits due the Valentino estate, and it was in need of money to meet obligations.

Mr. Schenck and his lawyers strongly objected to the claim and there were many meetings between these people and myself. In the end, I was successful in acquiring the estate's share but it practically alienated Joseph Schenck's friendship as I discovered a year later.

Schenck had made a verbal contract with me to join his company when I had settled Rudy's complex estate. He made the commitment directly after Rudy's death, actually on the steps of the hospital. I accepted Schenck's offer and rejected at least a dozen other firms who sought my services. But a year later, when I notified Schenck that I was free, he asked me to see him in New York for conferences. When I did go to his New York offices, Schenck protested that his business was in Hollywood and that he would meet me there. He never did, and now, looking backward, I can partially understand his attitude although I told him candidly that my allegiance was to Rudy until I completed what I thought to be my duty.

More than this, I know that Schenck advised and partially financed Rudy's brother in Alberto's attempts to discredit me and my handling of Rudy's estate.

No one can possibly understand the persistent attacks upon my integrity and judgment in the handling of Rudy's estate brought by Rudy's brother, Alberto. As I stated elsewhere, I suspected that Joe Schenck, in retaliation for my insistence that he pay to the estate certain moneys he had acquired through his contractual relations with Valentino, actually financed Alberto's legal fees in his efforts to discover anything amiss in my administration. There were charges of various kinds brought by prominent Hollywood attorneys, but none were successful excepting for abstract claims that were only temporarily assessed by a judge here. Upon appeal the California Supreme Court reversed all assessments and in their decision, which was printed in The Hollywood Reporter, this court actually complimented me upon my efforts, one judge adding that he hoped to find someone like me to administer his estate when he died!

All of these court actions had to be defended and the legal fees I had to pay were considerable. Not only the cost of the trials but the time and effort I had to waste during these years was so great that it very seriously interfered with the development of my future career.

Actually all of Alberto's attacks upon me netted him nothing at all, for, when I resigned as executor, the remainder of Rudy's estate was assigned by the court to The Bank of America, who literally gave the remaining properties away to anyone wanting these things. Once such "sale" I recall. The bank "sold" all of the remaining armor to a man for one thousand dollars. The actual cost and value was more than $20,000!

At the time of the signing of the contract between Valentino and Joseph Schenck, a life insurance policy on Rudy's life was written with the corporation as beneficiary. The amount was $150,000. A most complete test of Rudy's physical condition was made at this time by the physicians from the insurance company. I remember that at this time the broker suggested that I also should insure Rudy with myself as beneficiary, but I didn't take his advice.

The decision against me was an incredible miscarriage of the law and the court of appeals in San Francisco reversed the probate court ruling and the presiding judge criticized the probate judge and complimented me upon creating something out of nothing.

But Alberto through new lawyers brought another suit which resulted in a judgment against me for an enormous amount. I never did find out how Alberto got prominent attorneys to represent him during the years of his attacks upon me. The judgment was later settled by a payment of $2500 to Alberto's son, Jean.

⋘⋙

Much as I dislike the idea of a public auction of Valentino's personal belongings, I had no other choice, because there was no other way to dispose of the hundreds of items he and his wife had collected---some still unpaid in Spain and London and Paris and here in the United States. I engaged a responsible and well known Los Angeles auctioneer, A.H. Weil. We prepared an elaborate catalogue with Rudy's photograph on the fly leaf. The cost of this catalogue was defrayed by its sale for $2.00 each to those attending the auction.

The days of the auction and the agony of seeing all the things Rudy had collected sold to anyone who bid the highest, were almost unbearable. Many of the better pieces were sold for rather high prices. The books, especially the art works acquired by Natacha and Rudy at great expense were not even bid on. But the auction in total brought in a gross amount of $94,000 from which, of course, the auctioneer received the customary fee for himself and his staff. He made several attempts to create interest in the many jewelry pieces collected by Rudy but there were no reasonable bids and Alberto took the case containing the jewels. He also took all of the clothing and accessories which were enough in quantity and quality to provide for his sartorial needs for very many years.

The harassment by Alberto and his legal representatives eventually compelled me to resign as administrator and to turn all of the Valentino assets over to the court. But before doing this I undertook to contest claims of the U.S. Treasury Department for delinquent taxes assessed against Valentino for several years before his death and other taxes levied against the estate. This was a difficult task and I had to carry the case to the last court of appeals in Washington to prove that the large assessment against Rudy was improper. They ruled in my favor.

I persuaded Mr. Schenck to try spot releases of "What Price Beauty", Natacha's brain child, so that he could determine whether he wanted to release the picture generally throughout the U.S. These showings were not received well enough, in his judgment, to warrant the cost of prints and advertising for a general release. I did finally get a release agreement from Pathe but all they ever returned to me were monthly bills for additional prints they said they needed. In about a year these bills stopped coming. When I asked for the return of the negative I was told that it had been destroyed!

Pola Negri filed an action against the Valentino estate in the probate court for the sum of $15,000 plus interest. She had loaned this sum to Rudy for some obscure purpose. The court approved this claim and I issued a check to her.

Since this is an entirely honest account of the last days of Rudolph Valentino, I think that I should mention his "great romance" with Pola Negri. The "romance" between Rudy and Pola Negri was not as great as Pola later professed it to be. They did spend some time together, of course, but Rudy actually had no intention of marrying Pola or anyone else! They did have several telephone conversations while he was at The Ambassador Hotel in New York and she in

Hollywood. I didn't try to listen to his words until one night at about 12 o'clock midnight, which was 9 o'clock in Hollywood.

Angry words were spoken and he became quite upset. The last words he ever said to Pola were "Well you can go to hell!" and he slammed down the receiver. He only told me something to the effect that she could go out with that "so called Prince if she wants to, but not with me." These were the last words ever spoken to Pola by Rudy. In June of 1927, Pola married her Prince Serge Mdivani!

Photoplay magazine, through its editor James Quirk, took umbrage with Miss Negri in its July 1927 issue because of her public demonstration of her loves and even went so far as to engage a genealogist to investigate the claims of the Mdivani brothers princely titles. The report showed that it was customary for any young man coming from the Province of Georgia in Russia to assume the label of Prince, but only in the United States.

Hollywood studio executives, forgetting for the time being that a duplicate star can never succeed the original, put out scouts and conducted contests and advertised extensively inviting applicants for an actor to step into Valentino's place as "The Great Lover." Many, many tests were made of men whose photographic likeness even remotely resembled Rudy's. A feature writer for *The Los Angeles Times* had labeled Valentino as nothing more than the product of Hollywood creation. This, of course, is pure nonsense, because there really was something extraordinary that happened when Rudy was photographed in any role. He had magnetism in person, of course, but the camera revealed something deep and mysterious which attracted women primarily, but also many men. It might have been the reflection of his soul!

There were thousands of pictures sent to me and to Edward Small, who was then one of the most successful independent producers of motion pictures. He had declared his intention of producing a motion picture about Valentino's career. One such photograph was sent to Small by Alfred and Lynn Fontaine, the famous actors who had appeared in many Broadway stage successes. They wrote that Anthony Dexter not only resembled Valentino but was also an excellent actor, having appeared in a play with them. Mr.

Small signed Tony Dexter to a long term contract and spared no expense to have Dexter trained in dancing, fencing and horseback riding. He engaged voice teachers to try to get Dexter to simulate Rudy's voice and others to teach him to walk and assume Rudy's screen mannerisms as much as possible.

Other producers, sensing a possible quick buck, also issued announcements that they were preparing screenplays based upon the life of Valentino. Mr. Small announced that he would base his production on my book "Valentino As I Knew Him" and engaged several prominent writers to prepare screenplays. I talked with Mr. Small on several occasions and tried to make him understand that there had to be more to a picture than the bare outline in my volume because there was a spiritual aspect about Rudy that should be an important ingredient. But, even though several very excellent screenplays were presented to him, he and George Bruce, a writer friend of Small's left Hollywood for Palm Springs to write their version of the Valentino screenplay. I read this before production began and vehemently told Small that it was very bad.

But he went ahead anyway and the resulting picture was almost amateurish. The "star" Tony Dexter, tried to emulate Valentino, but the result was rather pitiful. This picture lost a lot of money for Columbia Pictures Corporation who had financed and released it, and caused the almost total oblivion of Tony Dexter, who really was a competent actor.

There were at this time several reports placed by imaginative persons in letters to magazines and newspapers about the activities in the little town, Castellaneta, in Southern Italy where Valentino was born. When Rudy visited the place during one of his trips abroad, the villagers were most abusive to him because he wouldn't dole out sufficient largesse out of the millions he was supposed to have accumulated in the United States!

These published reports of the posthumous honors supposedly being bestowed upon Valentino were just pure fiction. For, from later travelers to that city, I learned that very few natives actually even remembered the Guglielmi family or the Valentino's brief visit!

Mr. Irving Schulman, the eminent author, wrote a book which he called "Valentino." I quote here from his book a part relating to the Italian star, Marcello Mastrioianni, who had announced his intention of appearing in a stage musical in which he would portray the title character in a play entitled "Rudolph Valentino."

"...At a press conference, when asked by me of the attending reporters, why he wanted to do the play he replied, 'As a film actor, I want to do this stage musical as an experiment, just for him.' Asked if the show would be seen on Broadway, Mastroianni replied, 'Perhaps if it is a success in Rome.' "Ciao, Rudy!" (Goodbye, Rudy) opened in Rome on January 6, 1966, and for three hours Mastroianni cavorted about, the only male on stage with a bevy of thirteen leading ladies. It was scorned by even the gentlest of critics. Mastroianni's performance was censored as unskilled, pedestrian and shallow."

Valentino and his wife were seriously interested in occultism and any form of spiritualism that came to their attention. I have already remarked upon the influence of Miss Cora McGeachy, whose letters she said were written while she was in a trance and conveyed messages purportedly from souls, old and new, in the beyond.

The Valentinos, and my wife and I, frequently attended séances in New York at the residence of Victor Miller, an antique dealer who sold Rudy very many antique pieces of armor and jewelry at high prices. There, Mr. Miller assembled a number of other psychics and spiritualists and as a group they were called upon spirits to manifest themselves. Frequently one or more of these "believers" urgently and loudly claimed that they had seen a spirit known to them. I cannot dispute this, but neither Rudy, Natacha or my wife nor I ever saw or heard anything beyond the heavy breathing of the assembled guests.

We frequently attended gatherings of endowed persons but, excepting for the automatic writings by Miss McGeachy, we were not fortunate enough to "see" or hear any persons from beyond the grave!

After Rudy died and while administering his estate, I made valiant efforts to sell Rudy's last unhappy home. I had to engage a caretaker to keep the curious and vandals away. On one occasion early one morning a tenant phoned me at my home to tell me that he hadn't been able to sleep since he came there because of various ethereal sounds in the house. He pleaded with me to come up at once and hear these sounds myself.

I drove to Falcon Lair that rather windy, cold night and soon he called my attention to sounds one could imagine were groans and other sounds somewhat like the soft music of a harp. I cannot say why, but I had no fear or apprehension and slowly prowled around the house until I located where the sounds originated. They were caused by some loose wiring near the partly open door leading to the tunnel which connected the main house to the servant's quarters. So the caretaker remained in the house. Later, however, he became a "believer" in spiritual communication, and persuaded my wife and I to attend another séance in Hollywood where, the talented medium told him, Rudy was certain to appear, but only if I was present.

We attended a séance there one night. There were about twenty people present and the manifestation began in a dimly lighted room. The voices came from behind a curtain and a wraith like figure in white gauze appeared for a moment, breathing the name of one of the persons present. Some of these people believed entirely because they wanted to believe and several times one would cry out for forgiveness or blessings or enlightenment.

I noticed that all of the wraiths were about the same height and build and that the voices were almost alike. The great moment arrived when the voice said, "I am here, George. I am Rudy." And the same figure stepped out from behind the curtain, this time dressed in her version of a Sheik! It was quite difficult to withstand the impulse to approach the figure but it disappeared behind the curtain in a few seconds. Later I spoke to the Medium and complimented her upon her histrionic ability and gave her a five dollar bill.

No purpose would be served if I were to write about the many persons who by the court's permission and upon the payment of a few dollars, lived in the Falcon Lair house for short periods. Spiritualistic Social Clubs, a man who had acquired some of the armor from the bank which had become the administrator of the estate, by paying a fraction of its value and hoped to attract buyers to the house, and many others. There is no truth whatever in statements I have read that any of the transient tenants had spent their own money to repair or redecorate Falcon Lair.

Falcon Lair was later actually bought by Doris Duke, a very wealthy woman. The purchase price was not very much but Miss Duke, an ardent music lover, wanted the house occupied by musicians. As far as I know, Miss Duke still owns what is left of Falcon Lair.

Natacha, who outlived Rudy by several years, tried, without any success, to become involved in some branch of the theatrical field. I believe that picture executives recalled her behavior when she was Rudy's wife and, at that time, more than now, did not welcome any female into the motion picture field. But as far as possible she did capitalize upon her relationship with Rudy. Several books, magazine stories and paid interviews by Natacha appeared for more than two years after Rudy died.

❧

After Rudy's death I received thousands of letters from people in every walk of life. Some came from prominent people but the majority came from young girls and young women and were written only to express their loss upon his passing. I received no less than thirty-five letters, some in great detail, from women who claimed that Rudy was the father of one or more of their children. He must have had these brief but wild affairs in several cities at the same time! Some of these good ladies sent pictures of their child and tried to point out the resemblance to Rudy.

Letters from all over the world addressed to me continued to pour into my office. Many were from women who said that Rudy, even though dead, visited them often in their homes and spent the night with them. Many contained messages reportedly given to the writer through spiritual automatic writings from Rudy. Some of these stated that Rudy wanted to "talk" to me, that he wanted to come "home"!

It is impossible to segregate the "true believers" from the great number of men and women who, through these many years have reported conversations and writings directly from Valentino to them, but I do know that several of these people have made a business of sorts by sharing their communications with gullible followers.

A lady came to my office many years after Valentino's passing. She had with her a bulky manuscript of a book allegedly dictated to her over a period of time by Valentino. She identified herself as Reverend Carol McKinstry and pleaded with me to read the manuscript, so that I could confirm the authenticity of these spiritual

99

words from Rudy. Reluctantly, I promised to read her book and then get in touch with her.

I read the book with care but I couldn't detect one sentence that had any of Rudy's philosophy or any phraseology that could be identified as his. I had to tell Mrs. McKinstry the truth, but that didn't disturb her one bit. She later frequently attended psychic meetings and read portions of her book to the assembled believers.

Shortly after Rudy had been entombed, a young lady named Marian Benda made annual pilgrimages to the crypt in the Hollywood cemetery. She was in direct conflict with others who also appeared on the anniversary of his death, many dressed in deep mourning. But Miss Benda at least had spent an evening with Rudy in New York about a week before he became ill. He told me about this unusually pretty girl and their rendezvous. This was when he came home early one morning feeling, he said, just great.

Unfortunately, Miss Benda began to have hallucinations which included her statement that she and Rudy were married in New Jersey in 1925, and that she bore his child just before he died. The unfeeling Eastern newspaper reporters investigated her assertions and, of course, found no records anywhere that such a marriage had taken place. They discovered that she had come to New York in 1924 from Oklahoma City. She became one of Ziegfeld Follies girls, had married a few times, finally to William Benda, an artist. Marion attempted suicide three times and in 1951 she succeeded.

This did not reduce the number of "Ladies in Black" who visited Rudy's crypt each year. Probably the most faithful of these was a lady named Ditra Flame, who told me that Rudy had been kind to her when she was a little girl and had visited her when she was hospitalized. Although I soon discovered that the dates of her statements were for the purpose of strengthening her position as the head of the Valentino Memorial Club in Hollywood.

Even to this day on the anniversary of Valentino's death, a vast number of visitors arrive to pay homage to Rudy. The last time I went there with a friend we were unhappy because of the demonstrations carried on by some of the regulars—loud cries that they were seeing Rudy there and then; yodeling and loud praying all to attract attention to themselves. I asked the man in charge of the cemetery whether he could do anything to prevent these demonstrations but he said that he could not.

During these lush years there were a few successful actors who mistook their national recognition as a sign of their own abilities, entirely discounting the contribution of their producers, directors and writers.

One such was a fine comedian, Charles Ray. He was discovered by an astute producer who cast him in simple, small town American boy stories which endeared him to the public. He acquired a great amount of money and wisely purchased a small studio and several houses and land.

But unfortunately he wasn't content with his quick success and longed for the day when he could use his own judgment as to the subjects he wanted to appear in, and to become one of the only actors who tried to produce his own pictures.

He wanted to portray historical and dramatic figures and chose that of Captain Miles Standish as his initial production. He alone passed judgment on the scenario and the sets and the cast. He mortgaged all of his holdings to obtain funds to start the picture, but soon exhausted the money and had to turn the production over to a major production company. They tried to rescue the picture but could not without pouring much money into it.

It is difficult to prove, but the rumors at the time were to the effect that the major producing companies decided to teach a lesson to other revolutionary stars by ruining one who stepped out of line.

At any rate poor Charles Ray lost his entire investments as did his mother who contributed all of her assets in the attempt to salvage the picture Charles had undertaken to produce. Furthermore, he couldn't get an acting assignment.

The next star to attempt to produce her own pictures was Alla Nazimova, who, under contract to Metro-Goldwyn-Mayer Company, achieved immense fame because of her successes, determined to appear in a classic picture "Salome", despite the studio's advice that such subjects were not good box office. But they agreed to release the picture when it was completed, providing that Nazimova would finance the production costs, which she did with the expected results. Her money was lost.

Natacha was Nazimova's confidant and had much to do with all aspects of the filming of "Salome"; sets, clothes, script and general supervision because of Nazimova's faith in her. This is where Natacha got her first taste of power which, unfortunately, ruined Nazimova's film career and, later, almost did the same to Rudy's career.

One of the myths frequently circulated was the one about Rudy's desire to become a farmer. He never said this and I am positive that he had no such inclination because he disliked physical labor unless it had something to do with machinery or automobiles. He actually spent many days entirely dismantling his Voisin automobile, cleaning and oiling all parts before reassembling and replacing the entire structure of the car. Never had I seen a person so absorbed in any work.

After we were more or less settled in Hollywood for about six months, I felt the need of a larger home for my little family and talked to Rudy about this. He was all for the idea of my building a house in Beverly Hills, but I knew that I didn't have the time or the money to start such a project at that time. Nothing could deter him from going with me to inspect the various houses referred to me by agents, and we finally found one that pleased him immensely. It was a modern home but the builder and owner had been in the ornamental tile and marble business and there was much travatine marble and black marble fireplaces and beautiful tile in the bathrooms.

The house was really somewhat out of my financial reach, but his enthusiasm overcame my usual restraint and I bought the house. Sadly enough, I lost the house during the panic of 1929-30, but Rudy had already been dead for three years.

Because we had an orderly and well managed home, Rudy spent a great deal of time with us during the months that he and Natacha were separated. The children began to regard him as a member of the family.

During our travels and at their homes in New York and Hollywood, I had ample opportunity to observe Natacha and Rudy's behavior towards each other. They were not particularly demonstrative in kissing and hugging as young married people do. I concluded that they were both shy, even in my presence, to which they seemed to be accustomed. I believe this was a natural reticence on Natacha's part and the fear of appearing enthusiastic about any phase of her behavior excepting only her great ambition to become a power in motion picture production.

In this area she was most daring and unnecessarily verbose in her attempts to project her knowledge and to gain her dominance over people and situations. Rudy, on the other hand, seldom expressed an opinion unless it was instilled in his mind by Natacha. It was entirely her fault that Rudy lost any initiative that he might have exercised had she not, by various tactics, taken control over all of his impulses. I believe that he became mentally lazy.

I never heard Natacha and Rudy discuss money or the lack of it. Probably this was because they so entirely believed in their future affluence, or that neither of them had any conception of the value of money, even though they had had experiences when, at times, they had to borrow to obtain necessities. I doubt that Rudy ever knew what his earnings were until the time that Natacha demanded the right to produce her own picture "What Price Beauty." Of course I had a certified public accountant audit the books of The Rudolph Valentino Production Company and to prepare the annual tax return. This was as much for my protection as it was for Rudy's. But he would only go through the motions of examining the monthly report and then return it to me.

103

One result of Mrs. Montgomery's broadcast actually occurred to me. During or about December 10, 1972, my phone rang and a man's voice asked whether I was the George Ullman identified with Rudolph Valentino. When I answered affirmatively, he said, "I'm back! This is Rudy!" I asked him which Rudy and he said "Rudy Valentino!" Of course I scoffed at this but he insisted that he wanted to see me.

I told him that I was too ill to talk to him and for him to not annoy me. But he did find his way to our apartment and when my wife answered the door, there was the tall young man who said to her, "Don't you recognize me? I'm Rudy" He asked for me, but she told him that I was ill and in bed. She closed the door and when another visitor came he said, "Someone left you a present."

There, on the carpet of our landing was an opened raw egg spilled there. This fellow has phoned several times, once at 7 a.m.! He wrote an angry letter to me, but I haven't heard from him in about two months.

This isn't the only time men have believed themselves the reincarnation of Valentino, but this one was the most persistent and annoying.

The Chateau

Rudy spoke frequently to me of his first impression of Mr. & Mrs. Hudnut's chateau in Juan les Pins. He and Natacha had driven from Paris –a particularly rough and dangerous automobile journey– and in order to arrive at the chateau before dark, Rudy had driven too fast to test his new Voison car. Neither Natacha or Rudy had seen the house before and they were overwhelmed by its size and grandeur. He described some of the furnishings, almost entirely in the 18th century, with an apartment especially furnished in ultra modern style for them.

They only remained at the chateau for ten days, he said, when he decided to drive to Italy to again see the home and surroundings where he grew into manhood. He didn't have many nice things to say about his treatment by the officials, either upon his entry through customs where they put an enormous tax on the cigarettes he had in his luggage, nor of the officials and people in other parts of Italy where his name was known. All had their hands out for some of the great sums of money he was presumed to have with him. This was especially true in his birthplace, the southern-most part of Italy, the little city of Castellaneta where he met his brother and family.

Another of his favorite monologues was when he felt like talking to me of some of his adventures in Madrid, Spain. There he first saw dozens of pieces of armor, many of which he purchased then and there and at great length told me the history of many in his collection. This visit to Madrid was very costly, because, while Rudy was buying swords and old guns, daggers, and other armor, Natacha was purchasing a great many pieces of ivory and her mother was buying jade. All of this accounts for the constant shortage of funds here, because these purchases were all charged to our production company.

On several occasions Rudy told me of the tremendous thrill he experienced while watching the bull fights in Seville. He demonstrated the toreador's art and his grace and enthusiasm was a sight to behold. I don't believe that he seriously meant it, but he did say to me that he would like to get out of motion pictures and begin to seriously take up the art of bull fighting!

Valentino as I Knew Him

By

S. George Ullman

WITH DEEP APPRECIATION TO

LILLIAN BELL

AND

RAYMOND FAGER

1926

An Introduction to this Book

By

O.O. McIntyre

I was one of those who confused Rudolph Valentino with the vaselined dancing world of Broadway's meandering mile, until I met him. I was not alone. Many did this while Valentino, frightened and questioning, swept on until he became the most amazing figure of our time.

Valentino was never sure of himself. True genius never is. He was constantly lifting his eyes to the hills. I have sat with him in the curtained box of a theater while first showings of his films evoked laughter and tears; and always he sat motionless, moist-eyed and pale.

No man I have ever known was quite so humble in success. It is trite for the artist to say he wants to do better things. Valentino would never say it, but he felt it to the very depths.

Next to George Ullman, I suppose I shared as many of his serious confidences as any man. He came to me many times, perplexed, harassed and soul-spent – but never defeated. His courage was boundless.

During those dark days when he broke off relations with the Famous Players and dropped like a plummet from the movie pinnacles to the semi-obscurity of "barnstorming", I ran across him in Chicago. His future was uncertain and already there were murmurings of a fickle public: "Valentino is through!"...adrift on the shoreless sea.

He was never gayer, for responsibility crushed him, and he had cast off the fetters. "When I pay off my debts barnstorming" he said joyously, "I am going to live"; and he was like an eagle poised for flight.

No apologia is needed for Rudolph Valentino, despite the fact I doubt if ever a man in the public eye was so misunderstood. He became involved in that senseless abracadabra that singled him out as "a sheik"-and how he despised that appellation!

He once attended a little dinner party of mine at which Meredith Nicholson, the distinguished Indiana novelist, was the guest

111

of honor. In recounting the list of guests to Nicholson before the dinner I mentioned Valentino. He said nothing, but I could see he was rather surprised.

And yet, five days after Valentino's passing came this note from that kindly and learned man: "Poor Valentino! I could not reconcile the press agent stuff about him with the lad himself after meeting him at your party. He was splendid."

Valentino impressed himself in that manner upon every one with whom he came in contact. He was always appealingly shy, but when he spoke you listened, for his words were surcharged with an eager vitality. He was a scholar, indeed a poet; and had he used his pen as an Alpenstock he would have scaled up the Matterhorn.

But he was not always the dreamer knocking his head against the stars. His vision was more practical than not, as is shown by his "come back" when the betting was 100 to 1 in astute cinema circles that he wouldn't.

He had an extremely human side which was displayed in his appreciation of the ridiculous. He often plagued me about my propensity for loud clothes. From here and there he would send me ties that hooked and snapped on, the color of poisonous wall paper.

Once, when we talked on the telephone, I said: "Drop around, I have a new tie." An hour later, on this warm summer day, he came in gravely wearing fur ear-muffs as though to muffle the din.

Another time, from Spain, he sent me a postcard of himself taken with a goat. A slight imperial graced Valentino's chin. He wrote "The one with whiskers is the goat."

Still another time he said to me: "It sometimes worries me that you might think that, because I invite you to the first showing of my films with me, I am seeking a little publicity through the things you write. It would please me if you would never mention me in any of your articles. I would like to think our friendship transcends that." He was tremendously sincere and, until he died, I never mentioned him after that until his passing.

Valentino was particularly abstemious as to liquor. He had been reared in a land where a goblet of wine was an essential with meals, and this he enjoyed; but that was all. He smoked innumerable cigarettes, but his was a strong physique and, outside of smoking, he took excellent care of himself.

He was totally and sincerely oblivious to the gaping of the curious. Mrs. McIntyre and I once stepped out of his automobile in front of our hotel after a drive with him and Natacha Rambova. He preceded us and stood to chat for a few moments. The sidewalk soon overflowed with curious. He suddenly saw them and exclaimed: "I think something has happened in your hotel." He did not realize until a few seconds later he was the object of the attention. Then he sheepishly lifted his hat, blushed and rode away.

One night in St. Louis, when he was making personal appearances, I happened to be in the city. A mutual friend invited us to dinner at a pleasure resort on the outskirts. Downstairs some factory employees were giving a dinner to relieve the tedium of rather humdrum lives. It became noised about that Valentino was upstairs.

Timid faces began shyly to peep in the door to gaze at Valentino. A message finally came up that these workers would like to see him. He was touched. "Why, I'll dance for them!" he said, and he went down and, looking over the crowd, selected, I am sure, the most poorly dressed girl in the gathering, bowed to her in the courtly manner of a true gallant, and swung off into a waltz.

Valentino loved the author of this book in the manner of a devoted brother. He did nothing of importance without "discussing it with George". And no one was so grievously stricken by his passing as Ullman. It was a heart-wrench that will be with him always.

I last saw Valentino in Paris, a few months before he died. He called on me at the apartment in which I was living on Avenue Henri Martin. Gray dusk was sifting through the delightful pink of Paris twilight. We went for a walk out beyond the Trocadero and sat on a bench. In the distance the Eiffel Tower was scissoring its network of starry squares against the plush of night. We talked of many things; I do not recall them now, but I do remember walking on later to the Arc de Triomphe, where I bade him good-by and saw him swing down the brilliantly-lighted Champs Elysee, his head held high. And it has pleased me that Valentino justified my faith in him in that adventure called death just as he had in the adventure of life. Not once did he falter. Not even in that black moment when, ghostly pale and weak, he said to his doctor, with a wan smile, "Doctor, I guess we won't go on that fishing trip after all."

So he turned his face to the wall and his indomitable spirit burst from dull clay, free.

And as I write these concluding lines to my friend, I think of those far worthier lines of Edna St.Vincent Millay:

My candle burns at both ends;
It will not last the night;
But ah, my foes, and oh, my friends-
It gives a lovely light!

Valentino as I Knew Him

Chapter 1

With the death of Rudolph Valentino, at the very height of his career, came a demand from the public for an intimate story of his life.

In attempting to construct such a story, I am confronted by the problem of sifting chaff from wheat, of separating those colorful stories in newspapers and magazines from the real Valentino, who was known only to his intimates.

Life seldom flows smoothly for any man; but, concerning one who from his earliest youth experienced vicissitudes such as fall to the lot of few, the telling of them becomes a task not to be lightly attempted.

I gather my material, for this last tribute to my friend, from stories he told me here and there, some related in the great bay window of his Hollywood home, some on horseback riding over the desert at Palm Springs, some on our long railway journeys between California and the East.

In writing these memoirs, I can only hope that, in my desire to place a true image of my beloved friend before the public, I have not too intimately delved into the recesses of his private life, or bared secrets of his soul which he, naturally reticent, would have resented.

His whole name was Rodolpho Alfonzo Raffaelo Pierre Filibert Guglielmi di Valentino d'Antonguolla, a big handicap for a helpless child. No matter how poor Italians may be in money, the poorest is rich in adjectives, gestures and names.

When Rudy came to this country he found that no one would listen to him long enough for him to tell the whole of his name. This is a busy country; every one is in a hurry.

Being told frequently to snap out of it and cut it short, Rudy was confronted with the necessity of selecting that part of his name which would best beat translation into Americanese.

He therefore selected Rodolpho Valentino, and at first was insistent on this spelling of his name. But the public insisted upon spelling it Rudolph and pronouncing it Rudolph, so that finally he submitted, and adopted the name Rudolph Valentino as his own.

Now, in telling the story of his life, I find that I cannot relate it in proper sequence. I cannot begin with his birth and go historically on through the changing scenes to his tragic and untimely death.

I must sometimes start with an incident in his childhood and skip to the effect this had upon his later life. Or must I go back, from the years in which I knew him, to the days of his early struggles in New York, long before he and I became friends.

Nor will I attempt to go deeply into that part of his life which was devoted to hard work, to the making of his pictures. Nor will I touch upon that side of him which the public already knows or can imagine.

At the risk of imputing to him the life of a butterfly, the lover or a man interested solely with the glamorous side of life, I shall tell what I knew of him, from long intimate talks in which he, realizing that I was sympathetic, would expound his theories of life, his philosophy, his dreams and ambitions

If it is true that mixed strains of blood produce the unusual, then Valentino's ancestry is partly responsible for his genius. His mother was a French woman, the daughter of a Paris surgeon, Pierre Filibert Barbin. His father, Giovanni Guglielmi, was a Captain in the Italian cavalry.

In her early life, his mother experienced the terrors of the siege of Paris. After she had married his father, the Guglielmi family settled in the little town of Castellaneta, in the southernmost part of Italy.

With flashing eyes, and enacting the scenes which led to the driving of his ancestors thus southward, Rudy told me how it came about.

One ancestor was a brave fellow, according to the story, which undoubtedly grew more picturesque as it passed down the generations. He had the misfortune to get in a quarrel with a member of the Colonna family, one of the finest and oldest in Rome.

And is generally the case in Italian quarrels, it was a matter of caste, a Romeo and Juliet affair. Guglielmi killed the Colonna and was forced to flee from Rome. The men who supported Guglielmi in his quarrel fled into exile with him. They were forced to masquerade as shepherds, and finally settled among the peasants in the province of Leece.

While describing this duel, which doubtless took place on foot, Rudy was on horseback. Thereupon he turned the story into a duel on horseback, so realistic that I asked him if this duel took place in the time of the Crusades! This brought Rudy to, possibly just in time to save my life, as, for the moment, he seemed to imagine that I was the Colonna. But I had no wish to return from an innocent ride on a stretcher.

Brought back to his narrative, he said that in 1850, when Ferdinand di Bourbon ruled over Naples and Sicily, brigands stormed the little town of Martini Franco, where the Guglielmi had settled. In the massacre which ensued, the family was again forced to flee, and this time they settled in Castellaneta, bringing with them only the clothing they wore.

"Ours was a typical farm house," he told me, "built of heavy white stone, flat roofed and square, with its thick walls interspersed by casement windows whose heavy blinds were barred at night. On the main floor was the large living room, dining room, kitchen and my father's study. About a courtyard in the rear were the servants' quarters and stable."

We dismounted and with a stick he drew in the sand the ground plan of this house.

With his arm through the bridle of his horse, standing on the desert sands in the white California moonlight, Rudy harked back to certain things which he remembered. He was a gallant figure, handsome as a centaur, and I could see that he was intensely proud of these early impressions.

"Take my names," he said. "My mother explained very carefully how I came by each of them. You Americans make fun of them, because they are so many, but they were a matter of grave import to her. To my father's house belong the Rodolpho Alfonso Raffaelo. The Pierre Filibert, I inherited from her father. The di Valentina was a papal title, while the d'Antonguolla indicates an obscure right to certain royal property which is now entirely forgotten, because that wretched ancestor of mine fought a duel with the great house of Colonna and so offended them.

"My father died when I was but eleven. He called my older brother, Alberto, and me to his bedside, and said: 'My boys love your mother and above all love your Country!' Even on his death-bed he was true to his calling, a Captain of the cavalry.

"I remember the funeral, too. It was military. There was a coach drawn by six horses, the coachmen wearing a uniform of black and silver, my father's four dearest friends walking beside the hearse, and holding the four large tassels which depended from it. And, in the carriage with my mother, we three children rode, awed by her grief, and hardly knowing what it was all about."

Rudy was then sent to the Dante Alighieri College, which corresponds to one of our grammar schools. He remained here two years and then was sent to a military academy.

One of the greatest mistakes in the world is to ignore the inner life of a talented child. The fact that young Valentino was a dunce at school, badly behaved and impossible of control, should have been warning to his mother that his mind would bear investigating.

While apparently poring over books, in reality the child was a million miles away: a hero, a bandit, a gypsy, a toreador, or a Rajah. He was even then laying the foundation of his ability to enact romantic characters. I have no doubt that he was often cuffed on the ear or switched back to every-day life, from an imaginary gallop over the desert at the head of his faithful band of retainers. Indeed he told me that the books of adventure he read during these troublous periods, in which he attempted to absorb a knowledge of books, where the real beginnings of his ability to act, because he understood the roles from the inside.

When will the time come, I wonder, when educators will attempt to understand unruly children and utilize their impulses toward their chosen work, instead of beating or expelling them!

The reason for which Rudolph Valentino was expelled from the Dante Alighieri College was the very reason for which, thirteen years later, he was able to play Julio in *The Four Horsemen of the Apocalypse*.

The King, the great King Vittorio Emanuele, husband of the lovely queen Elena, was to pass by. And poor Rudy, stripped to his underclothes for a misdemeanor, was left in the dormitory as a punishment.

Knowing where his clothes were concealed, Rudy broke into the locker, dressed and dashed madly down the deserted streets, to find the crowd which marked the King's progress. From a coign of vantage, high above the heads of the people, he watched the procession, the King on his coal-black charger passing so close that the boy was almost able to reach out his hand to touch him. The good children of the school, herded by a professor, were in a position from which they could not see nearly so much as the disobedient adventurer, who, the next day was ignominiously packed home as a punishment.

What did it matter? He had seen the King! And furthermore, in the dormitory that night, with sheets for his uniform, he enacted for the good children what his close up of the King had really signified, embellishing it, no doubt, with details from his own fervid imagination at which the good King would have gasped had he been able to hear.

Thus, in a blaze of glory, the sinner fared forth from the Alighieri College; in the minds of the students, going forth to conquer the world.

His mother did not share his enthusiasm.

Determined to educate this incorrigible, she packed him off to a military academy at Perugia. This was the Collegio della Sapienze, destined for the sons of physicians.

The military atmosphere of this school fired Rudy's youthful imagination. He decided to become a cavalry officer. This is quite excusable, as most of the officers in the Italian cavalry come from noble families, and are the flower of the land. Also, they wear one of the most beautiful uniforms in the world. The women, particularly, admire the long, glorious blue cape of this uniform.

But when Rudy divulged this ambition to his mother, she explained to him the great expense this career entailed and told him that, while his father had left a comfortable little fortune, it was not sufficient to enable him to realize this ambition.

Being enough of a man to realize this, Rudy compromised on the royal Naval Academy, in preparation for which the youth seemed to settle down to real study for the first time in his life. For the physical examination, he trained strenuously and got himself into physical trim, doubtless laying the foundation for that physique which was the marvel of every one when he came into pictures.

When, however, the fateful day arrived for his physical examination, candidate Guglielmi was found to be lacking an inch in chest expansion. After his efforts to achieve the perfection necessary, this deficiency was the most humiliating thing which had ever come to him.

And now was brought out of one of the salient characteristics of Valentino. He never could accept defeat. When confronted with such a short-coming as this, nothing in life was so important as that he should correct it then and there. There was no putting it off to a future time, slurring it over with a shrug or an "Oh, never mind! I'll do better next time." No. On that very instant the work must be begun, to give him a chest expansion which would *more* than fulfill the requirements of any naval academy on the top of the round earth.

This humiliation was like the flick of a whip on the back of a spirited horse. Rudy, of his own accord and with no one to force him, put himself into such marvelous physical shape that never, to the day of his death, did he lose any part of it.

Nevertheless, this failure to enter the Royal Naval Academy marked another milestone in the life of the boy. He was but fifteen yet, in his wounded pride he felt that life was over, that his mother would be forever ashamed of him, and that the best thing he could do would be to end his life.

With a woman's intuition, his mother sensed this, for she took the boy into her arms, assuring him that she never wanted him to be in the Navy anyway, that it was too dangerous a profession and that in her secret heart she was glad that he had not been accepted.

"Better far" said she, "that you go to the Royal Academy of Agriculture and study the science of farming. Italy has need of scientific farmers far more than she has of soldiers and sailors."

Had not his most distinguished ancestors proudly tilled the soil of their estates? Might not he, her son, become a great landed proprietor and recreate the glories of the family?

At these inspiring suggestions, the head of young Valentino went up and again his ambition flamed.

Once more he started forth to school, this time with a high and lofty purpose, and it was with great satisfaction that he finally graduated with the highest honors in his class, showing that he could have succeeded earlier if he had put his mind to it. But he was too full of Romance.

This success seemed to go to his head, for nothing would now do but that he must go to Paris to conquer that metropolis. At first, since he had some money, he was quite successful, for youth and manly good looks he found to be at a premium.

As soon, however, as his money was gone, he found things vastly different and, in a panic, he sent home for more funds. When these came, they were found to be such a modest amount that it would not go far.

Therefore, accepting the advice of the friends he had made in Paris, he rushed off to Monte Carlo to increase his fortunes by gaming. With the usual result.

Penniless, mortified and humiliated, he sat down to take a mental account of stock.

"Certainly I had done nothing to win the title of 'Pride of the Family,'" he told me. "The honors I had achieved at the Agricultural Academy had been entirely wiped out by my escapades in Paris and Monte Carlo. What to do I did not know. The family, including my uncle, who had taken care of my father's estate, met in solemn conclave. They discussed me pro and con, and their conclusions were not flattering. Their decision was to ship me to America. 'For,' said my uncle, 'if he is going to turn out to be a criminal, it is better for him to be in far off America where his disgrace can not touch us."

We both looked at each other and laughed as he repeated these gloomy predictions. George Eliot speaks somewhere of "the brutal candor of a near relation." And certainly Valentino had received an example of this.

"I wonder what would have become of me," he said, "if I had stayed in Castellaneta, bought a piece of land and become a scientific farmer? Can you picture the scene?"

He was wearing the costume of *The Son of the Sheik* when we had this talk, so that his question needed no answer.

With the prospect of America near at hand, his mother raised a sum of money, more possibly than she could afford, and sent him to America on the Hamburg-American liner *Cleveland*, which arrived in New York two days later before Christmas, 1913.

Chapter 2

Young Valentino, when he set sail, knew not a single word of English; on the way over, he made every effort to pick up a few words. As they sailed into the harbor and he caught his first view of the New York skyline, he asked a young Italian friend where to go when he landed, and was told of an Italian place, Giolitto's, in West 49th Street.

The gay life in Paris, along with its many disasters, had taught Rudy the one thing which he now found needful, and that was to dance. From some South American friends of his had learned the tango, so that, when his money gave out in America, and he had tried many forms of work, failing gloriously in most of them, his thoughts turned to the one thing the could do well, namely, dance.

With this in mind, he applied first to the manager of a restaurant where he had formerly appeared as a guest. Here he did so well that it was not long before one of his admirers mentioned him to Bonnie Glass, and brought about an introduction.

She was then in need of a dancing partner to take the place of Clifton Webb. She invited Rudy over to her hotel the next afternoon and, after the first try-out, Miss Glass engaged him at a salary of fifty dollars per week. To him this salary seemed enormous and nothing short of a godsend. With Bonnie Glass as a partner, Valentino's dancing soon took on distinction and the success these two achieved put confidence in the heart which had more than once begun to fail him, causing him to wonder if indeed he had done right to leave his own country.

While Valentino never aspired to be a dancer in the class of Mordkin, yet no one who had ever seen him dance the tango with a suitable partner could ever forget it. He was not dancing the tango, he was the tango. His was the drama of the dance.

His partnership with Bonnie Glass was very fortunate. They danced at the Winter Garden, the Colonial, the Orpheum in Brooklyn, many Keith houses, and even went on tour. In Washington, President Wilson attended their opening and they received sixteen curtain calls for a waltz they had themselves originated.

At the Winter Garden they revived the cake-walk, but under their skillful handling this was turned into a glorified thing which the originators would never have recognized.

Bonnie then opened her Montmarte, in the basement of the old Boulevard Café, and Rudy's salary was raised to the munificent sum of one hundred dollars per week.

As this was the year 1914, Italy had entered the war, and Valentino wanted to volunteer as an aviator, to learn this profession he spent all his spare time at Mineola. But when he offered himself to his country, he was rejected temporarily because of defective vision. Later, in San Francisco, he applied to Major Manchester, Commander of the British Recruiting Station but was told that he could not possibly pass the examination, and would only be sent back at his own expense. He had intended going to Canada to try to make the Royal Flying Corps.

Valentino and Bonnie Glass played their engagement at the Palace Theater and made a tour of the larger eastern cities. Then Bonnie opened the Chez-Fisher on 55th Street, which was very exclusive yet popular with the best people. Here they danced until she married Ben Ali Haggin and retired.

Joan Sawyer then engaged Valentino to dance with her during a vaudeville tour. Afterwards they appeared at Woodmansten Inn.

Although, as the world knows, Valentino was such a success as a dancer that he could have made dancing his career and doubtless a fortune at it, nevertheless he disliked it with his whole soul when it was placed on a commercial basis, and longed to get away from it as a profession.

Deep down in his heart was always the thought that, since he had made his one success in Italy at an agricultural college, he should do something worth-while with the knowledge thus acquired at such cost.

Hearing that California offered great opportunities, the wonders of that golden country being dinned in his ears, he joined a musical comedy called *The Masked Model*, because this was going to the coast. His salary was seventy-five dollars per week and traveling expenses.

In San Francisco he played with Richard Carl in *Nobody Home*.

Shortly after this he met Norman Kerry, who was the business representative for his wealthy father, but who disliked the whole thing so much that he was thinking of going into pictures, and suggested this to Rudy.

Having nothing in particular which appealed to him more, Rudy was agreeable, and set his heart on getting to Los Angeles.

But how? As usual he was out of money. He himself said he never could save, and I, as his business manager, know that was no lie.

The transportation problem to Los Angeles was answered by an invitation from the late Frank Carter, husband of Marilyn Miller, who suggested that Rudy go with *The Passing Show*, in which Al Jolson was starring.

"Join us," he said. "We are doing one night stands to Los Angeles and there is always an extra berth on our train."

Al Jolson, being consulted, was also very friendly and confirmed the invitation, thus giving Valentino his trip to Los Angeles free.

Rudy told me that on this trip Frank Carter would not let him spend a nickel of his little hoard of money, insisting that he would need every penny of it when he got to Hollywood. This generosity on the part of Frank Carter established him as a prince in the estimation of Valentino, for appreciation was certainly one of Rudy's most notable qualities.

He was enormously pleased that Norman Kerry met him at the station, and, in spite of Rudy's protests that he could not afford it, insisted that he put him up at the Hotel Alexandria, then the best in town, and start out by making a good impression.

It is a fortunate thing that the poor boy knew nothing of what awaited him. Having achieved some note as dancer, a little more as an actor, and having made some new and influential friends in the profession, he doubtless felt that all he had to do was to utilize a few introductions and thus be started on his career.

But Hollywood is *terra incognita* to one and all. The profession of motion pictures is strewn with the failures of those great in the professional, theatrical, literary and dramatic world.

Literally scores of artists, great in their own field, have come to Hollywood intent upon cashing in on reputations already secure in the East, and even in Europe, and have crashed to failure because the requirements of motion pictures were such that they could not qualify.

To succeed one must think in pictures, and this many are unable to do. Furthermore, all the large producing companies have an already-filled staff of men and women whose past experience has made them valuable, so that it must indeed be an outstanding figure or presence which can get by the Cerberus who guards the entrance to these studios.

Plainly speaking, it is a case of supply and demand; and there is always an over supply on account of the fact that Hollywood is the Mecca of all artists who hope, through the magic of pictures, to obtain a wider field for their talents.

Valentino's first job in motion pictures was as an extra, for which he received the munificent sum of five dollars a day, when he worked, and this was not continuously. Thus his stay at the Hotel Alexandria was dramatically short.

Valentino was always very grateful to Emmett Flynn who was the first director to employ him. The picture was *Alimony*, starring Josephine Whittel, who was then the wife of Robert Warwick. It is a noteworthy fact that working in this same picture also as an extra was a young girl named Alice Taffe. Later you saw her on the screen as Alice Terry in the *Four Horsemen of the Apocalypse*. Thus these two untried young actors reached fame at a single bound, in and through the same vehicle.

The author of *Alimony* was Hayden Talbot, and one day Norman Kerry introduced Rudy to him. Valentino told me that Talbot had not noticed him among the extras, but immediately upon meeting him said:

"You are a great type for a story I have in mind. If I ever write it and it is produced, you will get the part."

Rudy thanked him, but it was so much like other Hollywood promises that he wisely thought no more about it.

Naturally, after having secured the attention of Emmett Flynn Rudy was very hopeful. He had earned his first real money in pictures. He felt so sure the way had opened that it was difficult for him to understand his inability to get constant work.

In company with thousands of others he tramped from studio to studio, besieging doorkeepers and casting directors, and meeting with an indifference which breaks the heart of all except the stout of soul. He did not realize that, being so unmistakably foreign in type, he did not even fit into the ordinary extra class, which comprised mostly American types. Thus Valentino started with an even greater handicap than most beginners.

His money being gone, Rudy was forced to appeal to the generosity of Norman Kerry who very willingly staked him; and he took a small apartment at Grand Avenue and Fifth Street.

It is interesting to think what might have been the result had Valentino not possessed a friend at this crucial time who was able and willing to give him the necessary financial assistance to keep going. Some are not so fortunate, and fall by the wayside or return home in despair, so that it is in reality largely due to the big-heartedness of Norman Kerry that Valentino reached a fame far surpassing that of his benefactor; who never, however, had the smallness to feel or exhibit the slightest jealousy but openly rejoiced in his friend's success.

About this time Baron Long opened the Watts Tavern, a roadhouse on the outskirts of Los Angeles. He offered Rudy thirty-five dollars a week to dance there. As this meant eating regularly, Valentino was glad to accept this offer, and, as the tavern was a rendezvous for film people, Rudy had the secret hope in some way to attract the attention of a director, and go back to pictures.

His dancing partner was Marjorie Tain, who afterwards was featured in Christie Comedies.

Nothing in pictures came of this engagement, but Rudy did meet some very fine people from Pasadena, who suggested that the Hotel Maryland, one of Pasadena's most exclusive hotels, might be able to utilize his services as a dancer.

He followed up this suggestion, and the Maryland engaged him for one exhibition on Thanksgiving Day, when he danced with Katherine Phelps. They were so well received in their dance that when the proprietor, Mr. Linnard, returned from the east, he offered Valentino a permanent engagement. But the terms were so small that Valentino could not afford to accept them.

By a curious turn of fate, the very day that Rudy turned down the Hotel Maryland offer he accidentally met Emmett Flynn on the street. Flynn seized Rudy by the arm and told him that the story Hayden Talbot had written with Valentino in mind was about to be produced.

Flynn urged Rudy to go at once to see Mr. Maxwell, the supervisor of productions.

Wildly elated, Rudy flew to the studio as on wings. He found the part to be that of a heavy, an Italian Count.

"Will you play the part for fifty dollars a week?" asked Mr. Maxwell.

Would he?

With his usual hopefulness, Valentino imagined that this was the big chance which would lead straight on to fame. But, just here, the jinx blotted out his star momentarily. There was a fight over the negative. The camera men had not been paid and they had obtained a lien on the film, thus tying up the picture.

Later it was released and advertised this wise:

RUDOLPH VALENTINO
IN
THE MARRIED VIRGIN

Chapter 3

Having thus unconsciously starred in his first part, although there was no intention of conferring such honors upon him when the picture was made, he naturally looked for a continuation of his good luck. But there was another long period of inactivity; in spite of his most persistent efforts, he could get nothing.

This astonished Valentino, who was not then inured to the vicissitudes of a movie career. He did not know that he might star in a half a dozen pictures, and then suddenly find his services unnecessary.

Once more Emmett Flynn came to his rescue. Flynn, possessing finer feelings than some, rather hesitated to offer Valentino the part of an extra after he had played a lead. But he finally ventured.

"Would you be willing to play the part of an Italian Bowery tough?" he asked.

"I will play anything!" cried Rudy, who was then only too happy to get the seven-fifty a day to which extras had then been increased.

Rudy afterwards told me, almost with tears in his eyes that Emmett Flynn kept him on the payroll during the entire production, although he did not work every day.

Valentino never forgot a kindness.

About this time, Valentino caught the attention of Henry Otto, a director for Fox, who surprised upon Rudy's face one of those inimitable expressions which were afterwards to make him famous. Otto tried to impress upon the Fox Company the value of his new find, but failed.

Just here Mae Murray, and her then husband, Bob Leonard, whom Valentino had known in New York, came prominently into his life.

One day, on passing through the set, Rudy called out a gay "Hello" to Bob Leonard. His gallant bearing caught the attention of the artistic Mae Murray and, a few hours later, Rudy received by telephone, an offer of the role of leading man in T*he Big Little Person*, to play opposite Miss Murray.

128

It seemed that they had been searching for the right type to play this part, and Rudy had happened to walk on at the crucial moment. This fitted in excellently with Valentino's belief in his star of destiny.

It is impossible to describe the transport of happiness into which this plunged the volatile young Italian. Rudy was almost beside himself with joy, as Mae Murray was then at the height of her youthful fame, and to be selected to play opposite her was like receiving the right hand of fellowship from the gods.

Little did Miss Murray, being a modest person, imagine to what heights she had raised the handsome boy. But this was indeed the first chance that Rudolph Valentino had had in a real picture. That he was afterwards starred in that picture with the horrible name, *The Married Virgin,* was due to the fame he had achieved between the filming of the picture and its release.

But with Mae Murray he was an honest-to-goodness leading man, and that he put his best efforts into her picture goes without saying.

He retained her friendship to the very end, for when, after divorcing Bob Leonard, she married Prince Mdivani, she invited Valentino and Pola Negri to be her attendants at her wedding, which was a secret one.

Bob Leonard remained Valentino's friend, and when he could no longer get Rudy into pictures he was directing, he recommended the young fellow to Paul Powell, who was about to direct Carmel Meyers in *A Society Sensation*. Valentino landed the part in his first interview with the manager, at a salary of one hundred and twenty-five per week. Rudy told me that Paul Powell was the first to say:

"Stick to it, and you will some day make a name for yourself."

Rudy never forgot such words of encouragement.

This munificent salary so went to the head of the youthful leading man that he went out and bought a used Mercer car for seven hundred and fifty dollars, for which he agreed to pay a hundred down and fifty a month. But it cost him about twice that much to keep it in repair, so that, when it was finally taken away from him, because he failed to keep up the payments, he was rather glad to let it go.

Paul Powell liked Valentino so much in *A Society Sensation* that he engaged him for his next production, *All Night,* and was also instrumental in getting Rudy a raise to a hundred and fifty per week.

It was about this time that an epidemic of Spanish influenza broke out, closing all the studios and taking the last chance from Valentino to get work. He resisted the disease for some time, but he finally came down with it and, although he had it in a severe form, he refused to have doctors or to take medicine, because he declared be believed in neither.

Bryan Foy, one of the thirteen Foys, children of the famous Eddie Foy, about this time became Rudy's roommate, and he has told me that even at this time Valentino possessed the aristocratic bearing and grandiloquent manners which later were a part of his fame. Bryan also said that Rudy would starve in order to buy suitable clothes for his parts, being even at that time always meticulously dressed.

Earle Williams, then being at the height of his fame, offered Valentino a part in *The Rouge's Romance*, in which Rudy had to do an Apache dance. James Young was directing, and, since he had the sense to see that Valentino knew what he was about, he allowed the boy to stage the dance just as he pleased with the result that it was a great success.

So much so, in fact, that Valentino got the idea of some day starring in the part of an Apache. This remained with him to such an extent that when he signed his last contract, under which he had a voice in the selection of his players, he asked to have an Apache story written for him, which was done. Since this story was written entirely around Valentino's personality, the idea was very pleasing to him. It had been returned to the authors for some minor changes when he went East on our last trip. When Valentino was taken to the hospital and his recovery was expected by all, the authors planned to send the story east by the hand of Pola Negri, who was to have read it aloud to him during his expected convalescence.

Death put an end to these plans, as to many others.

James Young took a great fancy to Valentino. Having been a well-known actor of Shakespeare, and being a man of vision as well as of artistic ability, he saw the possibilities in this as yet unknown actor. It is my opinion that had not James Young had such tragic experiences in his life, he would now be one of the greatest directors in the motion picture industry. But his sensitiveness led him to take things too much to heart.

Valentino sensed this appreciation and idolized his director. Mr. Young once said to him:

"Rudy, you ought to be a great actor some day for you have more ability than most."

These words put fresh courage into the young man's heart and Rudy told me later that many times, when he was discouraged and was wondering if fame would always remain just beyond his grasp, these words kept coming back to him, and he would say to himself, "I must have the stuff, I must! For Mr. Young is a great artist and knows ability when he sees it."

Thomas Ince was Valentino's next employer. Although his salary was but seventy-five dollars a week, the money was so welcome at the time that it seemed a fortune.

Rudy's next call was from D.W. Griffith, and he owed this to another letter from Paul Powell. Griffith was starring Dorothy Gish in *Out of Luck*, and Valentino was engaged for the heavy.

Again when Mr. Griffith presented *The Greatest Thing in Life* at the Auditorium in Los Angeles, Valentino was engaged to dance with Carol Dempster in the prologue. This, at a hundred dollars a week, occupied Valentino for about three months, and earned him so much recognition from the public that, when *Scarlet Days* was shown at the Grauman Theater, he was also a dancer in that prologue.

It was through Douglas Gerrard that he began to have a part in the social life in Hollywood. Gerrard was a director, and entertained much at the Los Angeles Athletic Club. It was at one of these parties that Valentino met Pauline Frederick, and it was at a party at Pauline Frederick's that Valentino met Jean Acker, his first wife.

It was a case of love at first sight, and they were married almost immediately. Valentino was then working in *Once to Every Woman*, starring Dorothy Phillips.

His marriage to Jean Acker lasted but a short time, yet, in spite of the fact that they were divorced, they remained friends, each always saying kindly and appreciative things about the other. Indeed, I may say that the grief of Jean Acker, when it was known that Valentino was doomed, was one of the most genuine things I ever witnessed. Feeling that the end was so near, and knowing that Rudy's last wishes would have been even more kindly than those which he always manifested, I allowed Jean Acker to come to his bedside. He was unconscious and knew no one.

She had been his companion on many occasions during this last visit to New York, and I realized that there was a growing

131

friendliness between them such as is often remarked with those who are about to die. Thus Jean Acker was the last woman to see Rudolph Valentino in life.

Three other pictures came in rapid succession to Valentino. *Passion's Playground*, starring Katherine MacDonald, in which he played the part of a brother to Norman Kerry, then as a heavy in *The Great Moment*, starring Margaret Namara, and again a heavy in *The Fog*, with Eugene O'Brien.

Imagine the surprise of Valentino when, after he had played these small parts, he was called upon to play the part of Julio in *The Four Horseman of the Apocalypse*.

In my opinion June Mathis should sit forever in the seats of the mighty for having had the vision to see Rudolph Valentino, first as the young South American tango dancer, then as the young soldier in the battle of Armageddon. She visualized him in the part so clearly that she fought for his appointment and won over all her opponents. Too much credit cannot be given to June Mathis for thus drawing back the velvet curtain for Rudolph Valentino in his Great Adventure, his ceaseless quest for undying romance.

To Rex Ingram, super-director whose artistry has just won him international recognition, in the presentation of the Cross of the Legion of Honor for his accuracy and poesy in depicting French history, should go unstinted praise in the handling of that difficult novel of Ibanez. The haunting figure of Rudolph Valentino as Julio, lonely even when among the wheat fields of his South American ranch, lonely even in the drawing rooms of Paris when he struggled with the great problems of where his loyalty and allegiance lay, loneliest of all when in the trenches and on the battle fields of France he was alone with his God, was the one outstanding memory which world audiences carried with them from the countless theaters in which this marvelous picture was displayed.

Fifty years from now those who saw this picture in their youth will tell of it to little children, and old men sitting in their clubs, watching the smoke spiral upwards from their cigars, will hark back to the haunting sweetness and forever loneliness of that wistful young figure, whose beauty they will never have been able to forget.

To say that Rudolph Valentino was made by *The Four Horseman of the Apocalypse* is to state the case too mildly. Rather was Vicente Ibanez made in pictures by Rudolph Valentino. For then, and

132

not till then, was created the vogue for his books, for pictures. And I venture to say that his novel of *The Four Horsemen* later sold by the hundred thousand because of the association of Rudolph Valentino with the character of Julio.

I myself had read the novel before the picture was produced. It made upon me no particular impression, anymore than can be said of any thrilling novel of its style. Yet, when I read it again, after I had seen the picture, I wept over the tragic story of Julio, because to my mind he was Rudolph Valentino.

When the picture was planned, the part of Julio was not intended to outshine the others. Neither was it planned to be an all star production, but merely a super-picture, with every part adequately taken. But when the first rushes of Julio were viewed in the projection room, both June Mathis and Rex Ingram were swept off their feet, and seeing the possibilities which might come from featuring Julio, they began at once to build up the part, literally molding the character of Julio to fit the haunting individuality of Rudolph Valentino.

I think that never before in the history of motion pictures has such a thing been so conspicuously done; a great tribute to the budding genius of Valentino.

After this he played with Alice Lake in *Uncharted Seas*, then Armand with Nazimova in *Camille*.

It is amusing now to realize that Rudy got only three hundred fifty dollars a week during all three of these pictures, and that when, after *The Four Horsemen* was released he asked for a raise of fifty dollars, he was told that Metro did not feel that he was worth it, nor could they afford it.

A peculiar thing about Hollywood is that it does not at once realize the success of its pictures abroad. A preview here, a short run there, is all that Hollywood knows of its greatest successes, so that Valentino was long in discovering the tremendous hit he was making in the East.

Valentino's first work for Famous Players-Lasky Corporation not only marked an increase in salary to five hundred a week. It gave him great satisfaction to work for that firm, which he regarded as among the finest in the modern picture industry.

The filming of *The Sheik*, with Agnes Ayres as his leading woman, gave happiness to all concerned inasmuch as they believed that they were filming a masterpiece.

The sale of this book, by E. M. Hull, an English author, so totally unknown that it was months before the public discovered that its writer was a woman, had reached such proportions that not to have read *The Sheik* placed one in the moron class; and the enormous success of the picture is too well known to need comment.

At an increase to seven hundred a week, Valentino then made *Moran of the Lady Letty,* starring Dorothy Dalton, and, in order to obtain the offer of Famous Players-Lasky of one of thousand dollars a week to play the lead in *Beyond the Rocks,* Valentino gave the company an option on his services.

Trouble began to brew with work on *Blood and Sand.* Rudy understood that he was to have Fitzmaurice for director, and that the picture was to be made in Spain. Whether his contract failed to call for this, or whether he was assured by some one not in authority to know that these conditions would be carried out has never been satisfactorily settled; but there is no doubt in my mind that Rudy was perfectly sincere in thinking that he had been badly treated when, with another director, the picture was made in Hollywood.

It is a strange commentary on the character of Valentino that, notwithstanding the artistic picture which Fred Niblo produced and its box office success, Rudy still clung to the idea that he had cause for grievance.

The fact remains, however, that beyond expressing himself with Italian volubility to all who would lend an ear to his alleged injustice, Valentino was too much of an artist to let his inner dissatisfaction interfere with his work. It is well known that he threw himself into the production of *Blood and Sand* with all the enthusiasm and energy of which he was capable. It was the comment of Charles Chaplin, after the death of Valentino that he considered Valentino's acting in *Blood and Sand* as the greatest achievement of his career.

Blood and Sand was followed by *The Young Rajah,* which, although a vivid and colorful production gorgeously costumed and staged, was lacking in dramatic interest and was, on the whole, an inferior production. This Valentino resented, in the whole-souled manner of the true artist which Valentino undoubtedly was.

Although he was getting a thousand dollars a week, the highest that he had yet received, the habit of some companies, of producing one or two great pictures to be followed by inferior films which Rudy called "cheaters," thus mulcting the public on the reputation of previous successes, was extremely reprehensible to him and filled him with fury. And the mounting trouble between Valentino and Famous Players-Lasky, he always declared, was because they did this, and made him the goat.

In the speeches which Valentino made while on his dancing tour with Natacha Rambova, which I shall explain further in detail a little later along in this narrative, he invariably made the statement that the quarrel with Famous Players-Lasky which resulted in their obtaining an injunction to prevent him from appearing on stage or screen for a long period, was a penalty he gladly paid in order to keep faith with his public. He openly accused Famous Players-Lasky of carrying out the nefarious practice of producing "cheaters" with every star they had under contract.

He also knew that if this practice had been kept up with him, his career would not be that continuously cumulative achievement which he so ardently hoped it would be. And he openly attributed the unnecessarily short-lived careers of other stars in other companies to this dishonest and short-sighted policy.

How much of truth there was in these contentions of Valentino I myself am no judge. I set myself up as no arbiter. I am only trying to outline, in the simplest way possible, the real Valentino as he appeared to me during the all too short years in which I was privileged to know him.

But this I can truly state without fear of contradiction. Rudolph Valentino paid dearly and willingly for his determination to do what he could to elevate stars in the motion picture industry to what he considered was their proper and rightful status. He always declared that no one knew so well as the star himself or herself in what sort of a story he or she could best shine.

Furthermore, he contended most of all for the rights of stars to keep faith with their public, and not to be exploited for the benefit of the producers regardless of the artistic careers of their stars.

In my opinion a grave injustice was done Valentino by his own attorney, who, in filing his answer in the law suit brought by Famous Players against Valentino for alleged breach of contract, laid stress on the lack of proper dressing room accommodations, as if this constituted the main count of his grievance. This gave the Famous Players attorneys a marvelous opening, of which they were swift to avail themselves. They played up what they were pleased to term

135

Valentino's temperamental nature and hysterical demands, thus giving the public an entirely unfair and unjust picture of an earnest young actor whose sacrifices for his heart entailed discomfort, ignominy, poverty and false representation in the press. Whereas I maintain that Rudolph Valentino was the only star in the entire motion picture industry who was willing to starve for an ideal.

His was an isolated example of the determination of all true artists to force justice and to maintain high ideals of dramatic art. These, when called *enmasse*, constituted the actor's strike, famous in history, which resulted in the formation of that tremendous organization called Equity.

Chapter 4

It was previous to this troublous period, in fact, during the production of *Uncharted Seas*, that Rudy first met Natacha Rambova, whom he afterwards married.

She was then the art director for Alla Nazimova, and was designing gorgeous costumes for that eminent artist in Pierre Louys' *Aphrodite*. Rudy told me that he and Natacha did not speak the first time they saw each other, nor were they even introduced. Natacha, in her cool, detached way, calmly went about her business without so much as a glance in the direction of the proud young Valentino.

Possibly this piqued his vanity, for when Nazimova came over to the set where Valentino was working on *Uncharted Seas*, bringing Natacha with her, Rudy sought an introduction. But again he was met with an indifference to which he was not accustomed.

Every strong personality in man or woman will understand that this aloofness could not fail to intrigue so intense an individual as Rudy. Possibly he himself did not realize this, but the fact remains that, from this time on, it was observed that Valentino made persistent efforts to be with Natacha in what was perhaps an unconscious but nevertheless determined attempt to break down her reserve.

But at first Natacha was genuinely disinterested in Valentino. While younger in years, in experience she was much older than the lad. In the beginning her interest in him seemed to be motherly, or rather that of an elder sister.

When Valentino played *Armand*, with Nazimova as *Camille*, Natacha helped Rudy with his costumes, with the arrangement of his hair. In this simple fashion she gave the lonely youth a glimpse of what her sympathy might mean if ever she became his friend.

There is no doubt however, that it was some time before Natacha finally viewed Rudy as a serious aspirant for her hand. And had it not appeared to her that her sympathy was needed, I very much doubt if she ever would have taken Valentino seriously, for he could not fail, on account of his youth and inexperience, to appear somewhat at a disadvantage.

As the acquaintance grew, these two young people discovered that they had much in common. Both were artistic, both possessed towering ambitions and both were very lonely, which last undoubtedly precipitated their romance.

Furthermore, both were interested in distinctive dancing. In this art Natacha possessed the skill which came from a long apprenticeship in interpretive and ballet dancing. But Valentino possessed a dramatic quality in his soul which caused every step in his dances to be forever memorable. Is it not true that his first step in his famous tango rivets the attention and brings, even to the most jaded, a certain retroactive thrill?

I believe that the way each reacted to the other's personality on the subject of dancing finally struck a spark in Natacha and caused her to think favorably of Rudy's suit. Once awakened, however, she began to see the beauties in his character, and this finally caused her to marry him.

Frankly, I say that never in my life have I seen two more beautiful creatures together than Natacha Rambova and Rudolph Valentino during the year in which they were engaged.

That Valentino finally completely won her affections was evidenced by the fact that, disregarding the year which should have elapsed before the decree of his divorce from Jean Acker became final he married Natacha in Mexicali, Mexico.

About this time reelections of politicians high in the legal department of Los Angeles loomed. And, as is always the case, hectic activity was manifest. Anxious for a political scoop, the District Attorney's office pounced upon the marriage of Valentino as marvelous example of the speedy justice it desired to depict.

Valentino was tricked into going to police headquarters on a Saturday afternoon; it was evidently the intention of powers to clap him into jail and keep him there over Sunday. Doubtless other influences were at work. Those having it in for Valentino, for some cause or other, were at the bottom of this *coup de theatre*. It amuses me to recall how ineffective these tactics proved; poor indeed must be the movie actor or actress who cannot call upon personal resources or the resources of their friends for bail in any amount.

In this case, it happened to Douglas Gerrard who heard of Rudy's predicament and forthwith got in touch with his friend Dan O'Brien, Chief of Police of San Francisco, who was sojourning in Los Angeles.

O'Brien, at the telephone, said that much as he sympathized, he did not have the necessary ten thousand dollars, the exorbitant bail imposed upon Valentino; but it so happened that Thomas Meighan was calling on O'Brien at the time and overheard this conversation.

Without knowing the identity of the friend whom O'Brien wished to serve, nor the name of the man at the other end of the wire, Tommy Meighan, with the generosity for which he is famous, got O'Brien's attention, saying:

"Some friend of yours in trouble? How much do you need?"

Out of the corner of his mouth O'Brien replied:

"Ten thousand bucks! Got it?"

"No! But I can get it," said Meighan. "Wait here!"

With that he seized his hat and dashed out, returning in half an hour with a certified check for ten thousand dollars.

O'Brien took the check in his hand, looked at it and, with a quizzical smile, said:

"Do you know Rudolph Valentino?"

"Yes," said Meighan, "I do. Is he the fellow?"

"Yeah," said O'Brien. "What do you think of him?"

"I think he's all right!" said Meighan. "I like him. Regular fellah."

Still holding the check between his fingers, O'Brien said:

"Want to put this up on him, now that you know?"

"You bet!" said Meighan. "He'd do as much for me."

Which is the way that Rudolph Valentino was bailed out of prison on that Saturday afternoon and spent his Sunday at home, as was his custom.

At the first indication of this trouble, Rudy sent Natacha to her parents, at their place, Fox Lair, in the Adirondacks.

When he appeared for a hearing on this charge, he was able to prove that the marriage had never been consummated, and he was thus cleared of the charge of bigamy, but warned that he must not be remarried before Jean Acker's interlocutory decree became final.

Valentino then went east, where he and Natacha set up separate homes.

In the meantime, the suit of Famous Players-Lasky against Rudolph Valentino for alleged breach of contract was dragging its weary length along. The company finally secured a permanent injunction, forbidding Valentino to appear on stage or screen until the terms of his contract were fulfilled.

Chapter 5

I first met Rudolph Valentino in the winter of 1922. I knew that he had a disagreement with Famous Players, and that for some time he would either be at leisure or open to a good business proposition. I knew that he wished very much to marry Winifred Hudnut, or Natacha Rambova, as she now prefers to be called, and that for that some reason he would need money. She was a very beautiful girl, with a marvelous complexion.

I, being essentially a business man, with an eye for advertising, conceived the idea of utilizing the spare time of this young actor, for to me he was not then the movie idol nor the great screen lover which in the last four years he has turned out to be. He was simply a good dancer, well known to the public, and with that magnetic personality which drew the feminine contingent. I knew also, as the whole world knew that there was an injunction against his appearing on the stage or screen. But nothing was to prevent his appearing as a dancer, and this was my plan.

I was at that time connected with a beauty clay company and we needed spectacular advertising. I therefore suggested that we engage Valentino and his bride for a tour of the largest cities, to dance and to recommend our specialty as the reason for the lovely complexion of his bride.

This arrangement having been satisfactorily completed, Valentino and Miss Hudnut were married at Crown Point, Indiana, and came immediately to Chicago, where a special car, luxuriously fitted, awaited them.

I shall never forget my first meeting with Rudolph Valentino. Naturally, I was familiar with his pictures and thought of him as a handsome boy. I had no idea of his magnetism nor of the fine quality of his manhood. To say that I was enveloped by his personality with the first clasp of his sinewy hand and my first glance into his inscrutable eyes, is to state it mildly. I was literally engulfed, swept off my feet, which is unusual between two men. Had he been a beautiful woman and I a bachelor, it would not have been so surprising. I am not an emotional man. I have, in fact, often been referred to as cool-handed; but, in this instance, meeting a real he-man, I found myself moved by the most powerful personality I had ever encountered in man or woman.

This stirring emotion, which was as much a surprise to me as it could have been to any one, was probably the reason for his enormous success upon the screen, for Rudolph Valentino was in the class of those few men and women who possess a tremendous individuality.

The appellation "personality" is too weak. That word may be applied with a propriety to hundreds, even thousands, of men and women in every walk of life. But to sway multitudes by a mere gesture or a glance means much more.

Individuality is possessed by comparatively few. Great military leaders, who have commanded their armies to impossible feats of sacrifice and heroism, which the world has been unable to explain, have doubtless possessed a portion of this magnetic individuality. And therefore I, who greatly loved him, may be excused if I place Rudolph Valentino, after four years of intimate knowledge of his character, in the class of those truly great souls whose individuality was utilized in the cause of humanity, supplying romance to the gray drab lives of those to whom existence was nothing but a daily grind.

No one, privileged to read the pathetic, misspelled and ignorantly written letters which came to Valentino from his myriads of admirers, could fail to be impressed with the pathos of the admiration of these writers for the one who, to them, spelled Romance. It is said that Valentino's fan mail exceeded that of any other screen idol. But it is not fair to leave the impression that only the ignorant wrote to him. Among his letters were those bearing crests, monograms and insignia, giving evidence of the standing and intelligence of their writers, and breathing the most intense admiration of an actor who so passionately adored and represented Beauty.

In this, however, I have been referring to the last years of his life whereas I must now go back to the first few days of my acquaintance with him and emphasize the fact that never for one moment did this man allow his name to be used in connection with the beauty clay. It was part of his contract that it should be exploited always as an adjunct to a woman's toilet, and this fact is only one of the strong indications I constantly had of the intense masculinity of Valentino.

He might wear a slave bracelet or rings, but he would wear them with the fine disregard of a European for what any one might think of his personal tastes. It is only American men who are sensitive to public opinion of their dress. No one who has traveled extensively can but be aware of the sublime confidence of the Britisher, the Continental and the Russian that their clothing is at all times suitable to the occasion and the weather. They feel that it is nobody's business to criticize what they wear, and, if such criticism occurs, their surprise is genuine.

This Continental attitude Valentino shared, and he was constantly amazed that his apparel caused comment, even if favorable; for to him this adornment was but an expression of his moods. This, to him, was perfectly legitimate, and nobody's business but his own. Such an independent habit of mind, being a part of Valentino's confident individuality, was inexplicable to certain newspaper writers, whose comments indicated that they had never been beyond the confines of their home town.

Many of these impressions, which afterward solidified into convictions, were formed during the conversations I had with my friend during the journey from Chicago to Omaha, which was to be the first stop of our tour. Here it was planned that Mr. and Mrs. Valentino appear for their first advertising performance. They were to dance, and afterwards Valentino was to make a little selling talk, attributing the beauty of his wife's complexion to the beauty clay.

Naturally, having conceived this tour, I counted largely on fair weather. But to my horror a fierce blizzard was raging over Nebraska, and I feared that few would dare its violence.

Little did I know the effect of the advertisement that Rudolph Valentino and his bride would appear! To my surprise, the place was packed to the doors, and hundreds turned away. This was the first indication I had of the drawing power he possessed; but in the days to come I was to have it so impressed upon my mind that it ceased to amaze and became a thing to be taken for granted.

The success of our venture in Omaha was but a forerunner of that which attended these two dancers everywhere they appeared. Rambova, naturally graceful, had been taught by Theodore Kosloff, whose pupil she was for several years. So that, when Valentino undertook to complete her education in dancing, there was a little left for her to learn. She was, and is, a rarely beautiful woman, possessing

143

in many ways the inscrutable appearance of the Oriental as well as much of their fascination.

It was a wonderful thing to see these two exotic and graceful creatures dance. Their program consisted of the Argentine tango, which Valentino made famous in *The Four Horsemen of the Apocalypse*; they wore the original costumes. This was followed by another dance, a fiery, tempestuous thing which they originated themselves, and which partook of the qualities of Russia and the Far East. They always appeared to be dancing for and with each other, for the sole joy of being in each other's company. They never seemed to realize that they had an audience, and this increased the thrill the onlookers obtained from watching them. And, if Valentino is credited with introducing a new style of love-making, much of it is due to the fact that he dared to be sincere in public and to allow all who would into the secret of the depth of his devotion.

Many actors spoil excellent love scenes by their self-consciousness. They are unable to forget their audiences; consequently they always appear to be acting. The lack of self-consciousness of the true artist caused Valentino to stand absolutely alone. He dared to express the utmost sincerity, the sublimest passion, without the slightest trace of self-consciousness; and for this reason he could not fail to be called "The Screen's Greatest Lover." But then again, he was supremely gifted in the fine art of being a lover, and this gift he frankly shared with his audiences.

This tour of the United States, in the interest of the beauty clay, consumed about seventeen weeks. It occupied the time which would have been spent on a honeymoon had not the necessity to earn money intervened. In November of the same year, this bride and groom sailed for Europe on a belated honeymoon, which possibly they were the better able to enjoy because of the strenuous time they had spent in earning it.

It was part of our contract that they select in each city a beauty who, for some reason, might be considered outstanding. We early discovered that, if Valentino made the selection, he would make more enemies than friends. So we decided to let the audiences themselves make the decision by their applause. In this way many a girl, by sweetness of disposition or personal magnetism or popularity, obtained the vote, whereas some, possibly more beautiful, but dumb, were obliged to take second place. In this selection we had no hand. In every instance the beauty was selected in accordance with the applause of her own townspeople. It is interesting to note that quite a few of these girls entered the movies or other professions because of publicity resulting from these contests.

I became aware of the tremendous drawing power of Valentino when I saw the crowds which assembled at the stations to greet him. Even at the siding where our train halted to let another train pass, crowds would gather. In Wichita, Kansas, I recall that the town took a holiday appearance. In other towns schools were closed so that the children might see Rudolph Valentino. To me it was a revelation, for I had previously had no conception of his overpowering popularity. I was also surprised at his ability to make extemporaneous speeches. If he attempted a prepared speech he bungled horribly and made a general mess of it, but if allowed to talk as he would he was easy, natural, unaffected and dramatic. In Montreal, I remember that an enormous crowd had gathered to hear him and he made his first speech in English; then, realizing that this was a bilingual town, he repeated practically his entire speech in French, to wild, almost hysterical applause. I have seldom seen him create a more favorable impression or reach the hearts of the people more surely than he did that night through his linguistic ability.

I am also reminded just here of a question I once asked him. He was speaking to me of a Spanish novel which contained a story he thought might be adapted for the screen. I asked him what language he thought in, and he answered, "When reading a Spanish book, I naturally speak in that language, but, since you have asked me, I find that I translate my Spanish thoughts to English when they concern the English making of pictures. In things concerning France or the French, I would naturally think in French. Whereas, of course, concerning Italy and my life there I think in my native Italian. But always in America or England I think in English."

In Salt Lake City, which, by the way, was Natacha's home during her early childhood, one of the inevitable mistakes occurred which are bound to happen in any protracted tour such as ours. An enormous crowd had collected. The dance was to have begun at 8:30, but Valentino failed to appear. During two hours I kept the orchestra playing and made several appearances, assuring the audience that I knew Valentino was on his way; I must admit that I was roundly hissed. It was very hot, there were no seats, and the standing men and women were packed together like sardines. Their tempers grew momentarily more ugly, until they began to mill around in a manner to make me very uneasy. The cries and exclamations were of such a nature that I was afraid that when he did appear they might do him bodily harm. Suddenly, to my relief, at 10:30 he appeared. I warned him that the crowd was in an ugly mood and cautioned him to be careful. I shall never forget how he smiled at me, playfully pushed me aside, and walked out before that crowd, still in his street clothes. He explained to them that for two hours he had been trying to get through their traffic, and reminded them that they knew that this was impossible. This caused a laugh, and cries came from the crowd of, "Do your stuff, Rudy! You're all right!" With a smile and a bow he left them, and came into his little improvised dressing room, leaving the crowd pacified and receptive. Personally, I always thought he would make a good lion-tamer.

Chapter 6

Few would believe, seeing the assured acting of Valentino on the screen, that he was inclined to be shy by nature, almost timid in approaching others. For example, I failed to become very closely acquainted with him until we had been together three or four weeks. I had observed that both Rudy and Natacha were interested in something supernatural. Just what it was I did not know. Afterwards, it turned out to be automatic writing and a form of the psychic. Before making any move, they consulted this power. Not knowing this, I was at first surprised by the quietude with which they received what appeared to me to be startling developments. When surprising things occurred, I naturally expected them to share my own amazement. But this they seldom did. Instead, I would be very likely to hear something to the effect that they had expected it and knew it would come. For example, they had known that they were to go on a long trip, that they were to take a new business manager, and that Valentino would change his attorney. It turned out that these things had come to them through automatic writing.

When Valentino became sufficiently acquainted with me to explain these things, he naturally wished me to share his interest in them. Being open to conviction, I very willingly listened, and, to my surprise, I found that a number of things predicted by this psychic force actually came to pass.

It was in San Antonio, Texas, that Valentino, after many false starts, and some show of nervousness, first broached the subject to me of taking over his affairs and becoming his business manager. I refused. I had a family, whereas Valentino was $50,000 in debt and had an injunction against him which prevented him from appearing on stage or screen; his salary of $7,000 per week he owed many times over. Where, then, would my salary come from? He waved this aside and with a sublime confidence in his guiding star he told me that he would pull out of these, that he would make plenty of money, and that he wanted me to manage his affairs. But I could not see it that way. I needed to know where my income was coming from. Yet when, ten weeks later, I suddenly and without any further assurance decided to become Valentino's business manager, I looked for some expression of surprise at my *volte face*. Both Rambova and Valentino smiled inscrutably, and said it had been predicted before they embarked on the tour that they would change business managers and that I would be the man! These things at first rather gave me the creeps, but later, because of the sublime confidence of the Valentinos in their psychic control, I became less skeptical and more confident.

It must not be thought that Valentino was superstitious in any small and trivial way. He had no objection to spilling salt, walking under a ladder, whistling in dressing rooms, beginning a picture on Friday or sitting down with thirteen at table. These things he ridiculed. The psychic never became a religion to him, but he yielded to its mesmerism more than to any other form. This was entirely due to the influence of his wife who was a firm believer in the occult and initiated him into its mysteries. It was for this reason that she changed her name from Winifred Shaunessy DeWolfe Hudnut to Natacha Rambova. She believed that she would achieve fame under this new name.

When we reached New York, after more than seventeen weeks of continuous but luxurious travel, most of the time in grueling heat, Valentino insisted on my taking immediate charge. He had explained the entire situation to me. I had seen the many leaks and weak spots in his efforts to clear himself of his business difficulties, which were nagging and tormenting him only because he did not in the least understand them. He was as puzzled as a child when things happened, and never knew what it was all about. For example, he was paying an attorney a $2,500 weekly retainer and his affairs were dragging along without any visible signs of improvement. But Valentino was perfectly satisfied until it was pointed out to him that the first thing he must do was to change lawyers and get one who would straighten out his affairs with Famous Players, thus enabling him to get back upon the screen. He was made to realize that no public dancing, however successful, was as dignified as appearance upon the screen. No sooner had this been pointed out to him that he insisted upon my going with him, directly to his house, and writing to the lawyer then and there. He was then living at 57 West 67th Street. I found that the ease with which he made this decision was again due to psychic control.

Just here occurred one of the most remarkable things which Valentino did during the four years of my friendship with him. He had been paid the last of his salary of $7,000 a week, and had deposited it in the Empire Trust Company.

Since he was always lavish in his expenditure, it would have been most natural for this money to fade as quickly as dew before the sun. To my surprise, he told me that before leaving New York to make the tour he had been staked by a friend in the motion picture industry to a drawing account of $750 a week, until it had amounted to $11,500.

"I think I ought to pay this man in full because he was so kind. I want to pay this debt before I pay anything else," said Valentino.

I told him to use his own judgment. We went down to the Empire Trust, and he drew eleven one thousand dollar bills and one for five hundred dollars. Armed with this he telephoned the office of his friend. The secretary, evidently fearing a request for another loan, said that the man was in conference.

"I must see him! I have something to give him! And it is in cash!"

"Come right on up! You can see him!" shrieked the secretary.

That Valentino wished to repay his loan in cash indicated two of his strongest characteristics. One was that he enjoyed the feel of the crisp new bank-notes between his fingers. A check would not have meant nearly so much to him. Another was that he was like a child in his enjoyment of the pleasure of surprising his friend with the entire amount, paid when least expected. Rudy was always a Prince. He loved the *Beau Geste*. While he was not in the least grandiose, nevertheless he got a great deal of pleasure out of parting with almost the whole of his savings, a thing inexplicable to a thrifty or selfish mind. This also indicates his belief in his guiding star, for, when I remonstrated with him, suggesting that he spread the amount over more of his indebtedness and later pay the balance, he said, "Oh, there will always be more."

And, truth to tell, more did come. For immediately the differences with Famous Players were amicably settled, returned to their fold at a marked increase in salary. He made two pictures for them, one *Monsieur Beaucaire* and the other *The Sainted Devil*, thus completing his agreement with Famous Players.

In the meantime, before making these pictures, Mr. and Mrs. Valentino took their belated honeymoon trip and went to Europe in

August 1923. If a motion picture could have been made of this idyllic journey, it would serve as a criterion for other brides and grooms to come.

Without a thought of business or financial complications, these two intensely beauty loving souls drifted leisurely from one capital to another, dividing their time mostly between Paris and Nice, where her mother and stepfather live in a princely style at the Chateau Juan les Pins, overlooking the blue waters of the Mediterranean. Rudy has often told me that some of the happiest hours of his life were spent in this chateau.

Though this is the playground of the aristocracy and close to the gaming center of the world, Monte Carlo, it is a curious fact that neither Mr. nor Mrs. Valentino was a gambler by nature, or found fascination in games of chance. Possibly this was because both, while not offensively so, were supreme egotists. This was less pronounced in Rudy than in Natacha. In fact, it was only by a long association with Valentino that I came to discover that he thought the world was his oyster.

It is true that he frequently took chances so long as to make an ordinary gambler pale, but to his mind this was not gambling. It was simply acting in accordance with his supreme faith in the star of his destiny. He was no weakling. He never faltered. He never lost confidence in himself. It never occurred to him that possibly he would fail or become obscure. He knew without the shadow of a doubt that things would go well with him and that the sun would always shine. And this reminds me to emphasize the fact that, like all Italians, he was preeminently fond of the sun. He could not thrive, nor even live for long, in a country where gray days predominated. The day was made for him by the amount of sunshine it radiated.

He was never so happy as when playing like a boy, with his dogs on the beach. I have often been asked what Valentino did to keep his magnificent body in the pink of condition, and I have always replied, "I do not know that he ever did anything regularly." He had no daily routine religiously to follow. I always observed that his play was work. Instead of tossing sticks into the water for his dogs to fetch, Valentino used the dogs as sparring partners, pitting their strength against in the possession of a stick, or racing with them along the sand.

When, however, he needed extra training for a picture, no one could be more assiduous than Valentino. Up at five o'clock in the morning, he would train with a professional for two hours before breakfast. It may amuse housewives to know that, even to serve so great a star, this habit was not relished by his servants, who growled after the manner of their kind at being compelled to change their habits. Here again the personality of Valentino was apparent. Growls and frowning faces disappeared as if by magic when entered the room, and once again they were the willing servants, devotion itself of his slightest wish.

I do not wish to indicate that the Valentinos were above visiting Monte Carlo for an occasion play. But it was always in the nature of an excursion to please friends. Many were the parties arranged when a dozen or score would go to famous resorts, where they amused themselves with the usual sport of others.

It is rather strange that Rudy did not gamble more, because his luck was proverbial. Again it seems to have been because he did not think it necessary. He did not crave excitement, therefore he found little pleasure in playing for high stakes. It was the wrong kind of exertion. He was dynamic at any form of exercise which disguised itself as a play, for few could play harder than Rudy when he was so minded. Likewise, few could work harder. He possessed an almost uncanny and unbelievable control over his mind, body and nervous system. He could work in a studio for twelve hours. Then if he had an hour and a half in which to rest, he could fling himself down, drop to sleep instantly, and awaken completely refreshed and ready for another siege of work.

I hope that I may be excused for comparing my friend with men to whom the world has granted a far higher place in historical achievement. Nevertheless, it will be recalled that great military leaders, who drained their physical resources by long hours of strenuous and nerve-wracking work, were thus able to sleep. This to me is an indication of a form of greatness, of complete mastery over one's mind.

This naturally leads to mention of another characteristic. He absolutely refused to worry. If things went wrong or the future looked black, what did it matter? The sun would shine if you only gave it time! True, he often became excited; would flare up, into a momentary rage, would say unwise and indiscreet things. But in a moment all was forgotten. With a shrug he would roll the burden from his shoulders. To be sure, it always landed on mine, what was that to Rudy? To his mind, that was what I was for. And again, he knew that the anxiety I could not help suffering was but temporary. His confidence in the idea that things would immediately turn favorable was supreme.

When they returned from their honeymoon, they were still radiant with happiness and, with characteristic energy, both threw themselves into the production of *Monsieur Beaucaire*, the first of the two pictures Rudy was to make for Famous Players. This was filmed at the Long Island studio and during its production the Valentinos lived at the Ritz-Carlton Hotel. I was with them a great deal, and I could not help observing that Valentino so completely threw himself into the part he was playing that he was Beaucaire at home. To his wife his manners were those of the courtly Frenchman; even when talking business with me he was Beaucaire.

Also living at the Ritz-Carlton was Rudy's old friend, O.O. McIntyre, who is said to be paid more for each syndicated word than any other writer. Certainly he was, in Rudy's opinion, the most brilliant.

Valentino admired McIntyre extravagantly, and the two men were much in each other's company, despite the fact that McIntyre was Rudy's severest critic.

During the filming of *Monsieur Beaucaire*, McIntyre's criticisms were so constructive that many of them Rudy gratefully accepted and used.

The friendship of O. O. McIntyre and Rudolph Valentino lasted until death.

I am of two minds about a curious thing I observed in connection with his role of husband. Sometimes I think he was acting, but again, and to this view I incline more frequently, I think it was the inherent quality of Romance in his nature, which prevented him from ever letting down completely in the presence of his wife his self-imposed role of knight. By this I mean that he was always the gallant to his lady. I do not think that his wife ever saw him in a disheveled condition. Nor did I. Always perfectly groomed, dressed for the occasion, down to the smallest detail, whether in dinner clothes or negligee; there was always a fine quality of delicate reserve in him which could not fail to appeal to the fastidious in both men and women. Naturally this would appeal mostly to women possessing the common, or garden, variety of husbands, whose love for grubbing in the garden in disreputable clothes, and hatred of parting with comfortable shoes, often cause clouds to rise on the matrimonial horizon. Valentino never had any old clothes. Everything was new and the last word in fashionable attire. Even his lounging suit of black satin, with red lapels and stripes down the trousers, took an air of distinction from its wearer.

It was during the making of *Monsieur Beaucaire* that Natacha obtained her first real insight into the making of motion pictures. Before this she had been an art director for Nazimova, where her artistic ability was much in evidence; but she was never permitted any hand in the actual production. In the making of *Monsieur Beaucaire* she utilized her prerogatives, as the wife of the star, to the utmost, entering into the smallest details and assisting in an advisory capacity, sometimes to the embarrassment of the director. Rudy, still in the role of bridegroom, and having an over-mastering faith in his bride's ability to do everything perfectly, threw all his influence on her side. If Natacha sometimes presumed too far, all she had to do was to refer the matter in controversy to her husband, who immediately upheld her with a loyalty and a zeal not always wisdom.

Few women, however will cavil at this knightly attitude of Mr. Valentino, the consensus of opinion among wives, I have observed, being that too often husbands slip rapidly, and without visible gradation, from the role of bridegroom into husband, becoming either too masterful or too run down at the heel.

To the very end, when the unhappy divorce of these two wrecked the greatest and most lasting romance which, in my opinion, ever came to Valentino, he maintained his attitude of respectful subservience to his wife's opinions and pronunciamentos. If she said a thing, it became true as by the divine right of the kings. That she accepted this as no more than her due was part of her complex as a supreme egotist. To her, the world was her oyster; in her opinion, there should always, also, be a man standing near, with a sharp knife, to open it for her. That she never evinced either appreciation or gratitude to Valentino when he occupied this role was, again in my opinion, part of her nature, which she could not, and made no effort to, change.

That I thus analyze the character of Natacha Rambova is in no way intended to cast any aspersions on her ability as an artist, which she possessed in a marked degree. I am simply trying to explain to his myriad of admirers why Valentino's romance went on the rocks, to his great disappointment and lasting grief.

It is only fair to say that in my opinion the supreme love of his life was for Natacha. I base this largely upon what he said to me about her after she left California. Also upon the fact that, when in his last illness, he had me telephone from the hospital to her half-sister to ask when Natacha was expected to return from Europe. Had these two met it is my firm conviction that they would have remarried, provided Natacha had consented. Certainly, I believe, Rudy would have asked her, for the greatest happiness in Valentino's tragic existence was during his life with Natacha Rambova. This I know from his own lips. Remember, too, that the title of this book is Valentino as *I* Knew Him.

In the making of *The Sainted Devil*, the second and last picture under the Famous Players contract, a clash occurred between two very beautiful, talented and temperamental women, Natacha Rambova and Jetta Goudal, and it is to correct a false impression caused by idle gossip that I go into this matter at all. It was reported at the time that the clash was caused by Valentino's interest in Miss Goudal, and Natacha's jealousy therefore. But such was not the case.

Jetta Goudal was slated for an important part which required elaborate costuming. The French woman's exotic taste along this line is too well known to need comment. Without hesitation I declare that her imagination is nothing short of remarkable, and for this reason there was bound to be dissension in the ranks. While selecting her costumes, she soared to such heights that two eminent costumers practically washed their hands of her. In all likelihood it was because they were unable to carry out her desires.

On the other hand, the delays thus caused were assuming alarming proportions, so much so, in fact, that since Miss Goudal remained obdurate, the company was forced to substitute an actress who was more amenable to discipline.

Later, when Miss Goudal found herself replaced by another, she publicly expressed great bitterness and wrongfully attributed the cause to Mrs. Valentino, indicating that Rudy's interest in her had caused Mrs. Valentino such jealousy that the French woman was forced out.

If Jetta Goudal really believed this to be the truth of the matter, I can only say that she was very much mistaken. For at this time, and indeed all during his marriage to Natacha Rambova, Valentino had thought for no one but her. His love for her was so great that he never resented her dominance or even her interference in his business career.

In his mind her taste and judgment were perfect and beyond question. It is also to be remembered that at this time the Valentinos had only been married about a year.

Chapter 7

With the release of *Monsieur Beaucaire* and *The Sainted Devil* a most extraordinary fact was forced upon the consciousness of the world, to the effect that upon the absence of Valentino for two years, his return to the screen was heralded by unprecedented popularity. Crowds flocked to see him in these two pictures, and both were enormous box offices successes.

It is unique in the history of motion pictures. Never an actor or actress, having left the screen for such a length of time, returned to such overwhelming ovations. This proved that the hold of Valentino upon his public was never lost, and the truth of the adage, "Absence makes the heart grow fonder," was marvelously evident in his case. For he returned to a more admiring and much larger audience than he had every enjoyed before!

This phenomenon should set at rest forever the tongues of those who claim that Rudolph Valentino was merely a handsome Latin type who enjoyed a vogue, or who had become a temporary fad.

The fact of the matter is that his public loved him and remembered him through sheer inability to forget so engaging a personality. Yet, further than that, he was a very great artist and wonderful actor, for a vogue, no matter how violent, is but temporary at best.

The American public, in spite of certain disparaging statements to the contrary, is fairly discriminating; and, in the long run, its final judgments may safely be depended upon. It may be misled; temporarily it may follow a blind lead; but finally it returns to its true gods. Therefore, any man who establishes a permanent hold upon its affections, such as box office returns and fan mail proved Valentino to have had, presents this truth in a manner never to be gainsaid.

If the proof of the pudding is in the eating, Rudolph Valentino was in a class by himself. No actor, past or present was ever so beloved. I make these statements from a first hand knowledge of the scenes and episodes which took place, not during his life so much as from the moment the news of his sudden illness was flashed over the wires by telegraph and cable to four corners of the earth. From the four corners of the earth messages came winging, to show that those who loved him were the humblest shop girl and the errand boy and also they who sit upon the seats of the mighty.

So great was this love that, although at the time a certain resentment was felt in his native land, when he was forced to renounce his allegiance to his beloved Italy in order to become an American citizen and loyal to the land in which he had found his early and great success, all differences of opinion were erased by death. From the great Mussolini came a giant wreath which was laid upon his casket by reverent and loving hands; while Fascisti and Anti-Fascisti quarreled for the right to maintain an honor guard above the remains of their beloved fellow-countryman.

Tributes such as came to Valentino during his life and after his death could have come from no one reason. They came from the combination which I wish to stress: his ability as artist and actor, his vivid, engaging and heart-gripping personality.

It was always inexplicable to me why Natacha Rambova seemed to feel the indefinable charm of her husband's personality so little. Other women, who were his friends or more, would have yielded to its spell with the generosity of more ardent natures. But Natacha was conspicuously self-centered, and therefore in my opinion she was congenitally unable to feel much enthusiasm for the individuality of anyone except herself. This must not be considered as an aspersion upon her mentality. She was born with this complex, in my opinion, and never seemed, even in her married life, to make any effort to change.

At first, she did indeed appear to be fond of her husband, and to yield somewhat to the glamor of his individuality. But as soon as, through his courtesy, she began to be initiated into the mysteries and complexities of the actual manufacture of an important motion picture, and she began to have a dawning understanding of its methods, this slight knowledge so fed her ambition to be author, artist, producer and sole critic, that her obsession mounted to her brain like the fumes of strong wine. She began then to write day and night a picture in which her husband was intended to star. But that which seemed to be wifely devotion was in reality but the step necessary to be taken to place her in the supreme position she so ardently desired. And, I feel, from that moment dated:

That little rift within the lute,
Which by and by shall make the music mute,
And, ever widening, slowly silence all.

From the moment of Mrs. Valentino's entrance into the motion picture industry she began, it is my opinion, to lose her interest as wife to Valentino and to become more and more occupied with her passion to be a power in the motion picture world. For, when the time came to choose, she chose the solitary path to selfish grandeur, and broke the heart of her husband.

For this I have never blamed her. I felt that she had yielded to her selfish desires. Never having learned the meaning of self-control or self-sacrifice, she could not do otherwise.

Mrs. Valentino became the business manager of her husband as soon as she married him, and her extravagance has wrongfully been considered a contributory cause of the divorce. But this is unfair to her. Rudy was not quite as extravagant as she. His sublime confidence in the star of his destiny caused him to spend money like water, and to incur debts which would have appalled a more conservative man. Had his wife spent ten times the amount she did, he would have applauded her judgment and mortgaged his future to gratify her whims.

It must be remembered that up to the time of the tour advertising the beauty clay, and the completion of his contract with Famous Players, which was followed by a contract with the Ritz Carlton Pictures, Valentino had never earned money in such generous sums. Therefore, his indebtedness of approximately $100,000 in attorney fees and other miscellaneous debts should have withheld him from unbridled extravagance. That it failed to do so did not so much spell failure to realize his financial responsibilities as it stressed his indestructible faith in himself as the captain of his soul and the arbiter of his destiny.

Had he lived, I would share his optimism, for I firmly believe that another ten years of a success which his past achievements would justify us in expecting, would have made him the richest as well as the most successful artist of the screen. I am constrained to believe this from the rapidly increasing value of his estate.

During their dancing tour the Valentinos signed an option on a proposed contract offered them by J. D. Williams. This option Mr. Williams, unknown to Valentino, took to Famous Players and hypothecated the proposed services of Valentino for the financing of those pictures for the production of which a new company was to be formed.

This company was later organized and known as the Ritz Carlton Pictures, Inc. The contract gave the Valentinos that power to select their own stories, which was one of the Valentino's quarrels with Famous Players.

This power gained, it was Natacha's intention to select for the first story *The Scarlet Power*, subsequently called *The Hooded Falcon*, which was her own work. She used for this the pen name of Justice Layne. It was a story of Moors in the early history of Spain. It was estimated that the production would cost between $850,000 and $1,000,000 and at this time all concerned seemed to have been aware that it was the intention of the financial backers to limit each production to a maximum of $500,000.

Armed with permission to browse at will among the art treasures of Europe and to purchase props for the new picture to the extent of $40,000, the Valentinos gaily took ship and sailed for Europe in August, 1924. Their wanderings took them through Spain, where Mrs. Valentino purchased approximately $10,000 worth of Spanish shawls and $10,000 worth of ivories, as well as double this amount in miscellaneous expenditures for their trip. Another $40,000 was spent in props for this new picture, consisting mainly of the original Moorish costumes and jewelry.

Upon their return the Valentinos took a long term lease upon an apartment at 270 Park Avenue, at an enormous rental. Hardly had this transaction been completed and the apartment lavishly furnished, when the hitch in these plans took the startling form of lack of studio space to produce such an elaborate picture in New York. This forced the Valentinos to give up their plan of living in New York.

They retained the apartment, however, for commuting purposes between New York and California, and came to Hollywood, where they occupied the palatial home of Valentino on Whitley Heights.

Soon after their arrival it appeared that the plans for producing the *Hooded Falcon* must be temporarily abandoned, and Mrs. Valentino was given to understand that, for the production of so elaborate a picture as hers, more time must be spent in preparation.

Another story had been selected by Williams, although, by the terms of the contract, this was the prerogative of the Valentinos. This story was *Cobra*, taken from the successful stage play of the same name.

Valentino, with his unerring sense of discrimination, realized immediately that his part in such a picture was not suited to his best efforts, nor to his lasting fame.

Nevertheless, after having registered his disapproval and found it ignored, rather than cause any unpleasantness so early in his association with the company newly formed for him, he yielded, and a picture was made which amply bore out his reaction. While a picture with Valentino in the principal role could not at this time fail to be a box office success, it did not come up to the mark previous Valentino pictures had set.

Those were the days when the Valentinos were the happiest. Not only was their home life idyllic, but Natacha had practically full control at the studio during the making of *Cobra*.

I was production manager and, yielding to what I knew were Rudy's chivalric wishes in the matter, I allowed the reins of control to slip more and more from my own grasp, and to pass into hers, which I must admit reached greedily for them.

To her credit be it said, however, that she exercised to the fullest, in the making of this picture, her remarkable ability as an artist. To be sure, certain explosions occurred, one of which resulted in the changing of camera men right in the middle of the picture, which, even to the lay mind, would appear hazardous, but which did not harm the picture in this instance. This she could not forecast; it simply goes to prove that once in a while the expected does not happen.

To achieve her artistic success, Mrs. Valentino obtained the services of some of the greatest geniuses in the profession; one and all, I saw these men pass under the spell of her personality and yield up to her the greatest treasures of their art. This brings me to the subject of this woman's amazing fascination. Not only was her taste in dress an eye-arresting thing, Oriental, exotic, sometimes bizarre, but her costumes invariably added to the almost sinister fascination she was able to exert whenever she chose.

Those whom she disliked and ignored, very often hated her. But upon anyone on whom she bent her attention for any length of time, or whose allegiance she desired to secure, to serve her own ambition, or to forward any project of her own, she exercised to the fullest her uncanny ability to charm. Men seemed wholly unable to resist her, but yielded to her spell without a struggle. Of women friends she had few. Possibly Nita Naldi and Nazimova were conspicuous exceptions. As an example of the length to which even women would go for Natacha, Nita Naldi, even when a picture contract called for her services in New York, remained in Hollywood to accommodate Natacha Rambova, to play a part in Natacha's famous venture *What Price Beauty*, to which I will return later.

Rudy, although he must have been aware of this pronounced habit his wife had of fascinating her victims, never showed the slightest jealousy, nor seemed really to observe it. This was partly due to the fact that, while Valentino gave no evidences of conceit, his confidence in his ability to fill the picture was such that he never imagined it was necessary to become jealous.

This is also a quality of great egotists which Valentino's charm prevented from ever becoming conspicuous or even noticeable.

Just as in *Monsieur Beaucaire* Valentino took up fencing, so in *Cobra* he took up boxing.

During this time he was in the pink of condition, and seldom arrived on the set later than six o'clock in the morning. He would then box for two hours with his sparring partner, Gene Delmont, who at that time was appearing frequently at the American Legion Stadium in Hollywood.

Rudy's high powered Voisin, a French car, was always in waiting. He would jump in and drive himself home for breakfast, reappearing at the set in less than an hour, eager for work. To these luxurious habits of Valentino is due one thing for which all stars should be eternally grateful, and this is the building of bungalows on the studio lot for their exclusive use. Rudolph Valentino's was the first of these to be constructed, and he was the first to insist that the treatment of a star should be any different from the rest of the cast.

I have so frequently been asked concerning my friend's fine physical condition and tremendous strength, that I am reminded to say that he developed this himself. When he arrived in America, he was only a well-formed boy, with possibly a little more than the ordinary strength. But with this he was not satisfied. It was one of his traits never to be satisfied with mediocrity. In whatever line of effort he was constrained to appear, it was always his ambition to excel. And such was his popularity that even the greatest boxers and gymnasts would freely give him encouragement and instruction.

Jack Dempsey was one of his greatest admirers, and not infrequently the two put on the gloves together.

It was to be expected that Valentino would wish to excel in horsemanship, since his father as a member of one of the crack regiments of Italian cavalry, than which there are no better riders in the world.

Valentino had magnificent horses. Some were gifts, some he himself imported. He was particularly picturesque upon Ramadan, a white Arabian stallion. Though perhaps he looked equally well upon a fiery black charger named, Firefly.

Rudy was an enthusiastic member of the Breakfast Club, that unique organization which entertains distinguished visitors to Hollywood, and which staged a memorial service for Valentino which I will describe later on. The Breakfast Club is largely equestrian, and there was never a more gallant figure than that of Rudolph Valentino, in his immaculate riding clothes, galloping over the hills in the early California sunshine.

He was particularly fond of stunts. He rode a great deal with his friend, Mario Carillo, who was formerly an Italian cavalry officer , and these two would put Rudy's horses through all manner of evolutions, jumping hurdles, rearing, water jumping and descending and ascending steep grades.

A man who is fond of children and animals is generally tender-hearted. Valentino's penchant for dogs, horses and babies is almost too well known to require comment. He was more popular with children that I was myself. They would greet him with screams of joy, rush to his arms, the little one crying out "Swing me up, too, Uncle Rudy!"

On the journey from which he never returned alive, our first stop was in San Francisco, where Mayor Rolph presented him with a beautiful water spaniel, with long silky black hair. Nothing could have pleased Valentino more, and he immediately insisted upon being photographed with the dog. Rudy was very anxious to take this latest acquisition with him to New York, but, fearing that the confinement of a long journey and the intense heat then raging in the east would cause the dog suffering, he unselfishly sent the little fellow to his kennels in Hollywood, where the dog received the best of care, awaiting his new master's return. This dog I personally brought back to Mayor Rolph only recently, and this fine gentleman and his charming wife again brought back to me the wonderful hold Rudy had on the affections of the world, for, with tears in their eyes, these folks assured me that they could never part with this dog, and intended to keep it always in the memory of their dear friend Rudy.

Chapter 8

Upon the completion of *Cobra*, the Valentinos went down to Palm Springs, for a little rest. Palm Springs is about one hundred and fifty miles from Los Angeles, just on the edge of the desert, the San Jacinto mountains rising steeply against the western sky. Although the hotel, the Desert Inn, was a most fascinating place in which to stay, with its bungalows clustered around the main hotel, and the beautiful lawns broken here and there by armadas with their thatched roofs and open fireplaces, the Valentinos preferred to stay with their friend Dr. White, in whose attractive desert home they found sanctuary.

The sandy trails, sage brush and desert loneliness seemed to invite Valentino, and he spent much time riding, either alone or with his wife. When evening came, he always made a point of climbing the mountain in back of the hotel, to watch the changing colors of the sunset on the desert sands.

Gorgeous colors and rich materials always intrigued Valentino's beauty loving soul. Thus he would watch with enthusiasm the colors from the setting sun as they stretched across the sands, turning from gold to crimson and interspersed with those blues and purples which are seen only in the desert.

In these moods the desert was Valentino, and Valentino was the desert. The same look would come into his eyes as I later saw upon the screen in *The Son of the Sheik*. When I saw him he was not acting. He did not even know what I watched, and it was thus that I knew. After once seeing him in what he supposed was a lonely vigil, I realized why it was that he was so great in the roles of the *Sheik* and *the Son of the Sheik*. In my opinion he was more at home in these two pictures, and far greater in them, than in any others in which he appeared, always with the exception of his character of Julio in *The Four Horsemen of the Apocalypse*.

While these two lovers were enjoying themselves at Palm Springs, preparations were going on at the studio for the filming of *The Hooded Falcon*. Valentino, catching the enthusiasm of his wife, was looking forward with keenest anticipation to the performance of his role as a young Moor.

It will be remembered that when Valentino returned from Europe he was wearing a beard. Battles have been fought changing the destiny of a nation which created less excitement than the news that Valentino was wearing a beard. Newspapers everywhere commented upon the fact, and general disapproval was expressed, showing that his public desired to see him as the clean-shaven youth which he had so endeared to his picture public.

Likewise, it is my opinion that being obliged to darken his skin somewhat in order to play the role of Moor would greatly have distressed many of his youthful admirers, so that, when rumbles of disharmony began to reverberate to circulate that a disruption was near, I was perhaps less disturbed than some, feeling as I did that the fame of Rudolph Valentino would not have been the materially increased by the production of *The Hooded Falcon*.

Finally came a letter from J.D. Williams, president of The Ritz Carlton Pictures, Inc., in which he said that he was not willing to go on with the production, fully realizing that in so doing he was breaking his contract with Valentino.

This ultimatum I conveyed to the Valentinos by telephone, whereupon Natacha declared that she would come immediately back to Hollywood, leaving her husband at Palm Springs. Naturally, I expected a storm. To my surprise, she appeared calm, indifferent to the breach, and even content to have eliminated what I afterwards discovered to be what she considered the efforts of the Ritz Carlton to dictate to her and to relieve her of supreme command.

Thus, when I intimated that a new contact with Joseph M. Schenck was under consideration, she welcomed the suggestion, believing that in this new venture she could assume her rightful role of dictator general.

After I had had a conference with Natacha which lasted a day and a half, she returned to Palm Springs, leaving me to complete the negotiations with Mr. Schenck. When the contracts were ready to sign, the Valentinos returned from Palm Springs, and Natacha then discovered that, in order to obtain this contract, Rudy was obliged to promise that she was to have no voice whatsoever in the making of any pictures which it called for.

Naturally, this was a tremendous blow to her ambition. Her plans and aspirations were to produce bigger and better pictures.

165

Under this new contract she could not do so well as under the one which was abrogated.

It must be admitted that Mrs. Valentino possessed a great deal of common sense, for, in spite of the fact that *The Hooded Falcon* was her brainchild, she yielded with considerable grave to the inevitable, fully realizing what it meant to her illustrious husband to be taken into the fold of United Artists.

After the contract was signed, the Valentinos again returned to Palm Springs, while a search was instituted by the Schenck organization for a suitable vehicle for Rudy's next picture.

A story was finally discovered in a novel by Pushkin, the famous Russian novelist, from which the picture, *The Eagle,* was evolved. In the making of this picture Valentino exhibited a splendid cooperative spirit. Gorgeously costumed, he appeared first as a Cossack in the army of the Czarina, Catherine of Russia, then as an outlaw, and, for a disguise in order to meet the girl of his choice, he masqueraded as a French tutor.

Costumes were enormously becoming to Rudy. In ordinary golf clothes, or the habiliments of everyday mortals, he became as near to being commonplace in his looks as it was possible for one of his extraordinary beauty to be. Yet put him in puttees, riding breeches and a silk shirt open at the throat, and he was Valentino of the screen.

To my mind he was less effective as a Frenchman than as a Spaniard, an Italian, a Cossack, or an Arab. The dainty ruffles, laces, and silks of a Beaucaire were less suited to him than the burnoose, the brilliant sashes and the sandals of the desert.

Valentino, at Palm Springs, began to be bombarded by his wife's argumentative questions as to why she should not be allowed to make a picture of her own. At first Rudy demurred, because his finances were not at the that time in a condition to stand so great a drain. But he naturally wished to advertise to the world his wife's ability. He had no more jealousy of her than a child. It never occurred to him that the best that she might do could in the least detract from the radiant sunlight of that public's approval in which he habitually basked.

Even though it may appear to cast aspersions on the sex to which I myself belong, I must admit that so many artists have been jealous of their wives' ability that I must stress Valentino's freedom from this form of self-love. To be sure, it came partly from his own absolute self confidence and the belief that no one could possibly approach him in the perfection of his person and his art, but it likewise eliminated the friction which has wrecked so many other marital barks on the stormy oceans of I and my and thee and thine.

Nevertheless, at this time, I observed that Valentino's nerves were beginning to fray. Always unwilling to quarrel with his wife, unable to answer satisfactorily his wife's arguments, he took to spending whole days riding alone on the desert, galloping over its sands in a mad effort to escape the silky voiced persistence of a woman he still ardently loved.

Finally I received an imperative summons over the telephone to come down to Palm Springs immediately. So urgent was this request of Rudy that I drove the entire distance in a pitiless blinding rainstorm, to find what new trouble had arisen. I must have driven through the rain, for upon my arrival I found Rudy out on the desert somewhere upon his horse, and Natacha confined to the house with a sprained knee.

She was surrounded by books and magazines, drawings and plates, and she immediately took up with me the subject of her making an independent picture at a very small cost, her object in doing so being to show the motion picture world that she could make a commercial picture as well as an artistic success.

Of course I gave her every bit of advice I could concerning pictures, and concurred with her in the thought that inexpensive pictures were commercially practical, if she could make them.

With all the confidence in the world, she assured me that she could. I was still somewhat skeptical, and, when Rudy came in, I referred the matter to him. I, at once saw that the nerves of both were drawn fine. In fact, I may say that they had begun to pull apart, and it was only by his yielding to her in this matter that an immediate catastrophe was averted.

By this time, Valentino had discovered that his wife's determination to achieve a thing was not to be lightly set aside. He knew, as well as I did, that it would be much better if his mind could be concentrated on his own work and not distracted by the anxieties and inevitable problems of an untried venture such as Natacha wished to undertake.

But her insistence, silky and soft voiced though it was, prevailed; a thing which those who know her realize was inevitable. I

167

was distressed to see the signs of nervousness which Rudy displayed, knowing full well that this stay in Palm Springs was intended as a period of rest before the arduous job of portraying *The Eagle*.

Nevertheless we gave up like good little boys, and reached a compromise with the lady by giving her her own way.

I had previously had a long talk with Rudy, during which we discussed the matter pro and con, realizing its inadvisability. But Valentino assured me that, in the cause of peace and of rest for himself, he must give in and do as she wished. I could see that, combined with this desire for a cessation of hostilities, if these bloodless arguments could be called that, there was a very genuine desire, deep down in his heart, to make his wife happy. Likewise a determination to go to any length to achieve this.

Before I left, it was decided to allow Natacha to try her hand at an independent picture, which she declared could be produced for approximately $30,000. That under her unbridled artistry the cost more nearly approached $100,000 caused more friction all around.

Upon our return to Hollywood, plans were at once set in motion for the production of Natacha's picture, *What Price Beauty*. This clever story Mrs. Valentino wrote herself. She was thoroughly familiar with her subject, being the step-daughter of the well-known perfumer and manufacturer of cosmetics, Richard Hudnut. In her picture she made clever fun of the agonies women undergo, the time and money they spend in beauty parlors.

Since she was almost totally devoid of a sense of humor, it was strange to me that Natacha Rambova was able to bring out so much excellent comedy. But this failure in humor was also shared by Rudolph. He was merry, childishly intrigued by simple pleasures. Nevertheless he seldom smiled, and more rarely laughed. It will be remembered that seldom upon the screen has Valentino smiled. This reticence on his part enabled his smile to appear something very choice and precious. One felt flattered when one said or did anything to make him smile. The photographs of these two people almost invariably portray other emotions.

Valentino had not the slightest makings of a comedian. He never did anything funny in private life; he was not a practical joker, nor did he enjoy tricks. When he smiled it was invariably a smile of kindliness, such a smile for instance as one would bestow upon a child or an animal.

When he played with his dogs, or caressed his horses, or romped with children, he seldom laughed. Nor did he indulge in sneers and sarcasms. His temper was volcanic, but its exhibition was soon over; and it was then that he would smile. Invective he used, epithets, foul names and profanity; but among men only. He was punctilious in his language before women. In very truth, his entire intercourse with women was a subtle flattery which seemed to blanket everyone with whom he came in contact.

Chapter 9

It must be admitted that the publicity department of every motion picture is allowed great leeway. It faces the arduous necessity to write readable stuff about the stars, and to see that it is published. For this reason, literally tons of material are published which frequently cause agonized cries from those written about, containing as it does more or less of truth, gawdily embroidered.

In this volume, however, I am endeavoring to depict Rudolph Valentino as he really was, and not to gild the lily, nor to build up, out of my desire, a monument in print of my hero that those who loved him or those who hated, if there truly were any, could complain of.

Stories of Valentino were conspicuously easy to place, so much so as to cause comment. But this only went to show that his picturesque personality made good copy. Newspapers are proverbially hard-boiled, and there is nowhere on record the existence of one easy enough to print of friendship material it neither liked nor wanted. Therefore, it is only fair to suppose that the quantity of publicity concerning Valentino which the press published, and the public absorbed, was considered to be of sufficient interest to give it the place of prominence it unfailingly enjoyed.

For another thing, I observed that whenever Valentino was interviewed, and I read the interview in the paper the next day, I discovered that he had said something of genuine interest. This is truly a mark of great showmanship, for, mark you, he never talked about himself unless directly questioned. Then he would reply with a becoming show of modesty, which possibly he may have felt.

He would generally begin to talk about some one thing in his marvelous collections. He never jumped from one subject to another, like a mental grasshopper nibbling here and there at various subjects, but he exercised the good taste to discourse intelligently upon one thing. Take, for example, his books. He possessed specimens which would grace museums, ancient vellum, marvelous examples of the engraver's art, gorgeous illustrations and beautiful specimens of the book-binder's craft; he had selected judiciously. These books were of a

170

sort to intrigue even a connoisseur, nor were they above the intelligence of the lay mind. They were in Latin, French, German, Spanish, Italian, Old English, Russian, and Greek, and with the exception of the books in these last two languages, Valentino was familiar with the contents of them all. I may misjudge him, he may have known even these.

His library was not large. I should even call it small, but very distinguished. He seldom bought sets of books, no matter how valuable. To be sure he had a few, such as Balzac, Dickens, Tolstoi; but the anthologies, collections of wit and humor, speeches of eminent men, which every *bourgeois* library contains, were conspicuously absent from that of Rudolph Valentino.

He was so keen on costumes of every nationality and every period that many of his most expensive books were on these subjects, gorgeously colored plates. Of almost equal importance to Rudy were books on the customs of nations, their habits and amusements; and with these he was intimately acquainted. It is my belief that you could not open a conversation about any race, even down to nomadic bands, about which Valentino would not know something. And very often his knowledge and marvelous memory would astound you.

As so many of his pictures, both produced and projected, dealt with historical subjects, it was necessary for him to know history, and this he did.

In order to obtain all the information possible, he generally read history in two languages, that of his own country, and English. In this way it became so impressed upon his mind that he was not obliged to memorize. Two readings in two languages were sufficient.

This would frequently amaze reporters, who generally expected to find movie stars beautiful but dumb.

If a reporter showed any interest in the armor or firearms of which the Valentino collection is *sui generis*, here once more his showmanship came into evidence. Not only did he possess specimens of every sort of sword, cuirass, spear, dart, javelin, assegai and what not, but firearms from the most ancient make down to the latest Colt were his. And if you thought that the carving upon an ancient sword-blade was inexplicable or unknown to Rudolph Valentino, all you had to do to correct your impression was to question him.

With a flow of words in the careful English which many foreigners acquire, he would explain to you, not only the carving's

171

significance, but, in all probability, an historical sketch of the man who made it.

And, again, his was no cluttered collection. Small, distinctive, carefully chosen, exquisitely placed, his groups, upon red velvet backgrounds, were restful to the eye and intriguing to the imagination.

He had no large pieces of statuary, but delicate examples of Tanagra, carved ivory, old silver, jade and onyx were scattered not more than one or two in a room, so that each had a dignified space in which to display its beauty.

Knowing the history of each of these bibelots, it can easily be seen that Valentino had plenty with which to interest reporters of both sexes, and one never left his house with a definite story which was very well worth printing. Generally, it may be said that, no matter how prejudiced these feature writers were before meeting Valentino, they invariably left his presence with a very healthy respect for him as a man. If they came to scoff, they remained to praise.

Rudy was always courteous to people of the press, particularly to women. If unable to keep an appointment he would select some unusual way in which to recompense the caller for loss of time. If it were a man, a box of cigars or some of his imported cigarettes made interesting by his monogram, or, if a woman, seldom anything as commonplace as flowers. On one occasion I recall he sent a woman writer a bottle of choice perfume; written on the card were the words, "I will say it with perfume, it lasts longer." His cards, by the way, were of parchment.

Chapter 10

During this period the Valentinos were living in the house on Whitley Heights which Rudy had occupied as a bachelor. This was only about ten minutes' drive from the studio; they were enabled to run back and forth at will.

From its windows you could see the hills which form the Hollywood Bowl, and the flaming cross which marked The Pilgrimage Play.

It was a hillside house. You entered a hall which gave upon a floor with only two bedrooms and two baths. You had to go downstairs to find the living room, with its black marble floor and cerise hangings. The color scheme of the bedrooms was canary and black, the exotic combinations of the entire house being the work of Natacha. It was Oriental in the extreme and its violent contrasts of color were anything but restful. Up a few steps, at one end of the living room, was the dining room, which was quite small, so small indeed that not more than eight persons could sit at table. The furniture was Chinese red lacquer, with black satin upholstery. This room was separated from the living room only by an iron railing covered with black velvet.

Midway in the living room was an enormous bay window on the deeply cushioned seat of which four or five persons could sit with ease. It was here that I had many happy evenings with the Valentinos discussing the homey things of life.

Few people know that Rudolph Valentino was a poet and a philosopher. His book of poems, entitled *Daydreams,* is published both in England and America, and contains such gems of thought that I am constrained to quote one or two of them here:

A BABY'S SKIN

Texture of a butterfly's wing,
Colored like a dawned rose,
Whose perfume is the breath of God.
Such is the web wherein is held
The treasure of the treasure chest,
The priceless gift – the Child of Love.

THREE GENERATIONS OF KISSES

A Mother's kisses
Are blessed with love
Straight from the heart
Of Heaven above.
Love's benediction
Her dear caress,
The sum of all our happiness.

Til we kiss the lips
Of the mate of our soul
We never know Love
Has reached its goal.
Caress divine,
You reign until
A baby's kiss seems sweeter still.

That beloved blossom
A baby's face
Seems to be
Love's resting place.
And a million kisses
Tenderly
Linger there in ecstasy.

Were I told to select
Just one kiss a day,

Oh, what a puzzle!
I would say.
Still a baby's kiss
I'd choose, you see,
For in that wise choice
I'd gain all three.

These two seem to me to prove the delicacy of Rudolph Valentino's imagination. He crystallizes his love of the children he dreamed of but never possessed. He often spoke of the time when babies would be in their home, and one of the most poignant griefs in my memories of my friend are that he never realized this supreme desire.

Natacha was not opposed to having children, although this calumny has frequently been published about her. She only said that she thought it was wisdom for Rudy to complete his career before they had them, because no one in the motion picture business could be the proper sort of parent while living the abnormal life a star is obliged to live. She always declared that when they ceased making pictures she was perfectly willing and very anxious to have children.

We often discussed these things while sitting in the big window seat. Doubtless here was born many a rhyme which later took form in his book of poems, *Daydreams*.

As I thumb the little volume, I find one more impassioned verse so significant of the great lover of the screen that I am fain to quote it.

If, while reading these lines, you will visualize the scene in the bridal chamber of *The Sainted Devil*, in which he draws near his bride for his nuptial kiss, you will realize the thoughts which were in his mind at that moment:

YOU
You are the History of Love and its Justification.
The Symbol of Devotion.
The Blessedness of Womanhood.
The Incentive of Chivalry.
The Reality of Ideals.
The Verity of Joy.

175

Idolatry's Defense.
The Proof of Goodness.
The Power of Gentleness.
Beauty's Acknowledgment.
Vanity's Excuse.
The Promise of Truth.
The Melody of Life.
The Caress of Romance.
The Dream of Desire.
The Sympathy of Understanding.
My Heart's Home.
The Proof of Faith.
Sanctuary of my Soul.
My Belief in Heaven.
Eternity of all Happiness.
My Prayers.
You.

Considering the brevity of his own tragic life, the following bit of profound philosophy strikes me as prophetic:

DUST TO DUST

I take a bone -I gaze at it in wonder – You, O bit of strength it was. In you today I see the whited sepulcher of nothingness - but you were the shaft that held the wagon of life. Your strength held together the vehicle of Man until God called and the Soul answered.

Flickering glimpses of the finished beauty of these thoughts I frequently discovered in these wonderful discussions on the philosophy of life, its beauty, its sadness, its unclaimed joys, at which time I discovered rare beauties in the souls of both.

Chapter 11

Because of the childlike joy with which the Valentinos threw themselves into preparations for their first Christmas together in California, I almost came to think they believed in Santa Claus.

Naturally I expected each to give a gift to the other, and a very handsome one. But I had no idea that I would be pulled hither and yon, called to confer secretly, first with one and then with the other, until my mind was in a whirl.

Considering the fact that serious differences between these two had begun to manifest themselves, this Christmas enthusiasm gave me great satisfaction. I could not believe that the trouble was basic when both husband and wife were perfectly serious and eager in their desire to please each other supremely.

Receiving an imperative summons from Natacha to come at once because Rudy was out, I dashed up to the house, fearing the worst, only to find that I was to carry out for her an idea which has since caused more comment than any gift from a woman to a man she loved since the days of Cleopatra and Marc Antony.

It was the famous platinum slave bracelet which the world has attributed as the gift of no less than a score of women, but which in reality was a Christmas present from his own wife, and was made to order from a design which she drew herself and gave to me to carry out.

For obvious reasons, I have kept silent when confronted with diverse rumors, but now that the world is learning for the first time the true Valentino in all his weaknesses, his strength, his fascination, and the respect he inspired among the men and women who knew him best, I am telling the truth about the famous slave bracelet.

It was given to Rudy by Natacha.

When newspaper writers, intent upon earning their salaries and space, discovered the innocent fact that Rudolph Valentino wore a slave bracelet, and worried it as a dog worries a bone, dragging its description and their deductions concerning it from paragraph to paragraph, it is worthy of note that their jibes and insults never for one moment tempted Valentino to leave off wearing it. That this shows courage of a supreme order no man can deny, for fear of ridicule is an inherent quality in most mortals. Calamities can be borne with more fortitude than ridicule, and severe pain with more equanimity than continuous gnat bites. But Valentino was superbly indifferent to both. When he set his feet on a certain path, he pursued it calmly to the end, fixing his mind upon his destination and disregarding both rocks and pebbles which might cause him to stumble. A quality of greatness, I call this serene, uplifted attitude.

Nor could a husband's fidelity to the gift of his wife, prepared with such loving care, be attributed to stubbornness. To my mind it is an insult to the quality of Rudy's love for Natacha to suggest such a thing. I am inclined to call it more a quality of faithfulness to memories of the greatest happiness which ever came into his life, that he persisted in wearing this much discussed slave bracelet, and wore it to his death.

The slave bracelet given Rudolph Valentino by Natacha Rambova rests with him still in his tomb.

And the New York reporter who, in commenting upon the unfortunate editorial published in a Chicago newspaper, quoted Rudy as saying, "Yes, I shall continue to wear this bracelet, as it was given to me by someone whom I dearly love," remarked that then Valentino looked thoughtfully down at the bracelet and off into space, caught, to my mind, more nearly the truth of Valentino's feelings in regard to the bracelet, than any other writer who commented upon it. Every time that Rudy's eyes rested upon his slave bracelet I believe that the image of his wife rose before his mental vision.

Rudy's Christmas present to Natacha had a history which can be duplicated in the memories of countless young couples.

This is the story of it.

Several years before, when Rudy and Natacha were engaged; and, by the way, it was the year before his divorce from Jean Acker became final; they were looking at a watch surrounded by diamonds, and embedded in a thinly cut moonstone. It would be worn as a locket or watch; but, at that time, the price of $2000 was more than Rudy could afford.

Natacha had been crazy about it and had always remembered it, once in a while referring to its chaste beauty.

Evidently Valentino had borne this in mind for, on another morning, I was hastily summoned to his bungalow dressing room.

With suppressed excitement, he seized my arm and asked me if I remembered the times when Natacha had described this watch.

I did not, but I lied and said I did, for it seemed impossible to dampen in any way Rudy's ardor. Feverishly he gave me the name of the jeweler, refreshed my mind by a careful and minute description of the bauble, and urged me to go down that very morning and buy it if it was still obtainable.

I went to the bank and drew two thousand dollar bills. One I placed in my wallet, and the other I held in my hand.

I had no difficulty in finding it, for the moment I began describing the watch the salesman interrupted me, saying that he knew exactly which one he meant.

Owing to the fact that it was still on their hands I imagined they might be willing to take less. I therefore laid the thousand dollar bill on the counter and offered to take the watch at that price.

After some demur, a few impassioned arguments, and the statement that at this price it was nothing short of a gift, I succeeded in purchasing the moonstone watch at exactly one-half what had been asked the Valentinos some years before.

Evidently the sight of a thousand dollar bill was too much for them.

On the way home I stopped at the bank, placed the remaining thousand dollar bill to Valentino's account and came home in triumph to my friend, who was delighted with a business ability which he never would have thought of emulating for himself.

While driving along, with this precious jewel, in its white velvet box, safe in my pocket, I could not help thinking of the thousands of young people, either engaged or married, who window-shopped in their spare moments, and selected their heart's desire behind plate glass with an "Oh, I wish we could afford that!" from the girl, followed by an equally impassioned, "Well, darling, just as soon as I get that raise from The Old Man, you shall have it."

Paralleled in ten thousand lesser ways was the window-shopping of the Valentinos. Yet I dare say that just as much love and generosity were in their gifts to each other, as in the humblest lad's selection of a silver plated premium for his sweetheart, to be paid for by coupons.

From this time on, seeing what I was to partake of a Christmas the like of which I had not seen for twenty years, I threw myself into their plans with the enthusiasm of which I was capable. Dark secrets were in the air every moment. Whenever one or the other would be alone I was sure to receive a summons for a conference, and, by their laughter and air of mystery, I rather imagined that I too was due for a surprise.

Now Christmas in California is a feature which I have never encountered elsewhere. What Californians call cold weather is about the climate we Easterners find in autumn, in what we call Indian summer, with the exception that, there having been no frost, autumn colors are lacking. I refer merely to the quality of the atmosphere, for what meets the eye is very different.

The hills, green in summer, have now turned dun. The grass on the lawns is still green, the roses are in bloom, and the flowering splotches of color to a landscape of a beauty to be found nowhere else but the southlands of Europe.

The so-called rainy season has not yet begun, and Christmas may always be counted upon to be a day of fair weather.

Present-giving on Christmas in California over-flows the boundaries of families and spreads itself delightfully among friends and choice acquaintances. It is safe to say that on Christmas morning almost every one goes out for an hour or two to distribute gifts of remembrance in person. It reminded me more of the old-fashioned habit of New Year calls than anything I could remember.

On this particular Christmas, at six-o'clock in the morning I was called from my bed by the frantic ringing of the telephone. Answering it, I found myself commanded, after a cheery "Merry Christmas, " to bring Mrs. Ullman and my little boy Danny, then about six years old, and come immediately to the Valentino home. It was Natacha's voice, and she told me explicitly not to stop for breakfast, but to come at once.

Scrambling into our clothes, we hurriedly obeyed. Our own excitement almost equaled that of our small boy, who was fairly dancing with impatience to get to his beloved "Uncle Rudy."

Upon our arrival there, not later than seven o'clock, we were met on the patio by Natacha, who halted us with a great air of mystery and would not permit us to enter.

When Natacha chose to exert herself, she could be the most entertaining woman I have ever met, and she chose to exert herself that Christmas morning, when, without even a cup of coffee, we had dashed around to obey her summons. It was perhaps half an hour she held us there in the bright California sunshine, curbing our impatience with what grace we could. Then, a wild shout of, "All Ready!" was heard from within the house and, leading the way, Mrs. Valentino hurried us down the stairs into the living room where a sight met our eyes to take the breath of grown-ups, let alone of an impressionable child like Danny.

Covering the entire black marble floor of the great living room was a network of railroad tracks, tunnels, roundhouses, electric switches, freight cars, passengers cars, engines and what not, the whole appearing as a railway terminal in a great city might look to an aviator flying over it.

The cost of this extravagant toy I dared not estimate, and Natacha told us that all night, in fact until dawn, Rudy had spent his time setting up this toy, catching a terrible cold from sitting and crawling around on the cold marble floor for so many hours.

But his joy in seeing the excitement of Danny as the mysterious electricity caused these tiny trains to move forward and back, to switch around, more than compensated Rudy for all his toil and trouble. Natacha jeered at him in a friendly way and declared that Rudy set the toy up as much to enjoy himself as to please the child.

Possibly this was true, as I myself had guilty recollections of doing similar things in taking my small son to a circus I had a sneaking desire to see myself.

I was reminded also of Rudy's passion for machinery and his love for taking thing apart, "To see the wheels go wound," as Helen's babies used to say.

I remember that at one time he overhauled his expensive Voisin car with the help of his chauffeur, who was an expert mechanic, cleaned and oiled every part, and put it back together again. This he did, I am persuaded, from an intense curiosity to see how the thing worked. He could not bear to be in ignorance of the source of its power, yet at the same time he had a mechanic's delight in tinkering and fooling with machinery.

Breakfast was rather a sketchy meal, for over in the corner, shrouded under sheets, stood what even Danny knew to be a Christmas tree. When this was unveiled, it turned out to be a very gorgeous thing, hung with many presents, not only for us, but for the friends who were expected to drop in during the day.

181

The night before, Natacha told us, she and Rudy had a quarrel, and in the early morning they were hardly speaking. But I observed that the good cheer and friendliness engendered by the Christmas season had evidently completely wiped away all differences, and they were as tender and loving to each other as I had ever seen them.

After this, came the presentation of the Valentinos' gifts for each other. With real solemnity I saw Natacha place the now famous bracelet on Rudy's wrist, from which it was never removed, and witnessed the kiss of fervent gratitude for the symbolism it expressed. He declared that he was the slave of her beauty and kindliness, and Natacha seemed to welcome the expressions of fervent gratitude which he uttered.

When she opened the white velvet case and saw the coveted jewel she uttered a cry of genuine pleasure and flung herself into his arms with the abandonment of love.

Rudy was enchanted by Natacha's delight. She immediately put the watch on and continued to admire it all day, and always, and her delight indicated a far greater pleasure than any gift he could have received for himself. Nothing every gave him such pleasure as to make his wife happy, and in this he exercised an ingenuity and persistence which made him one of the great lovers of the earth in real life.

Chapter 12

What Price Beauty ought to be called *The Divorce Picture*, as the difficulties which arose from its inception to its close covered precisely the time of the differences between the Valentinos.

Not that I would have you understand that the difficulties about the picture were the only things that led to their divorce. It is my opinion that, when her dictatorship was taken from her, it was not long before her loyalty to Valentino, not only to his business interests but to him as a wife, began to fail her.

When she ceased to collaborate, she also failed to cooperate with him in more ways than one; and a man as proud and sensitive as Valentino could not fail to detect her failing interest and feel a profound hurt, a hurt so deep and poignant that he carried it with him to his grave.

From a passionate interest in his future and a desire to promote his best interests, Rudy now began to observe that her fancy was straying into other paths and fastening itself to other objects and interests. A natural coldness now began to appear, which threw Natacha more and more upon her own resources. It caused her husband the most profound anguish, not only hurting him, as it did, his natural male vanity, but injuring him in his deepest soul. He felt for the first time that his love was not appreciated, and he began to suspect that he had been married, not for himself alone, but partly as a means to an end. That end was, first and foremost, Natacha's overpowering, unalterable determination to be a figure which the motion picture world could not ignore. That she aspired to take first place as a director and producer of super-pictures is not, in my opinion, too great an ambition to lay at her door.

Cleopatra is her greatest prototype in history. In fact, if I believed in reincarnation, I could very easily imagine that the soul of Natacha Rambova, with all of her physical perfections and her mysterious fascination, had once inhabited the body of Egypt's queen. And that the Nile and its desert sands had once been her natural habitat.

That Natacha yielded to this overpowering urge of ambition must not be held against her by the analyst, for, from her earliest childhood, traits which indicated this desire to be preeminent cropped out whenever the smallest opening appeared. Vital, dynamic, and capable of long stretches of work which were surprising in one of such delicate physique; these were qualities which never could have been entirely stifled without wrecking her. She was the victim of her own ambition, which, in my opinion, was congenital. Nor has the world heard the last of her. Such genius will sooner or later discover its metier, and it would not surprise me in the slightest to discover one day that Natacha Rambova has completed a masterpiece in some line of artistry to compel the attention of a discriminating world.

For one reason, she was never afraid of poverty, nor hardship. She would starve to accomplish an ideal. Her soul was above taking cognizance of bodily discomfort. On the other hand, Rudy, while also an artist, would never have endured rags or dirt, hunger or cold, to win heaven itself. Valentino was a sybarite, a Luccullus, a Brillat-Savarin, and no epicure nor one born with epicurean tastes could ever be also basically a genius as to be willing to go through a hell of deprivation, even to win that preeminence which he most ardently craved. For this reason I do not hesitate to assert that, while Natacha Rambova could never cause a world-worship such as Rudy achieved almost without effort, yet Natacha was the greater soul. And it is only fair to say that her culture, which she painstakingly but subtly communicated to her husband, was one which others recognized and which in my opinion put him forever in her debt. He was truly, and in the highest sense, elevated by his association with Natacha.

Nevertheless, she was sped in her labor of love by the fact that inherently Rudy possessed a fineness and gentleness and chivalry which formed a superb foundation for her superstructure of culture. An example was his regret when the divorce occurred. I remember that he said to me:

" You know I bear Natacha no grudge, and I wish her all the success in the world. She'll get it, too, for she is still young and has her life before her. I am so glad that I did not rob her of the best years of her life. If the separation had to come, I am glad that it came so quickly."

I knew he felt himself deeply injured. I consider this a rather fine thing for him to say, especially as I realize that he meant it, and was not saying it for effect.

In fact, I have no recollection of ever having seen Valentino do anything for effect. All his friends will tell you that he was ever supremely natural. He never posed, nor struck an attitude, nor made an attempt to appear what he was not. He was one man who must have been a hero to his valet.

I take it that this was due to the fact that he could not imagine anyone really disliking him. He had the unfailing confidence of a collie pup, a pretty baby, or a toddling two-year-old, who staggers to your knee and looks up into your eyes with no knowledge of your ability to strike.

To be colloquial, I never in my life saw Rudolph Valentino, "Strut his stuff."

Conceit or egotism as we know it, in other men and women was surprisingly lacking in Rudy. It was more than that. Conceit, I take it, is an attribute of an inferior mind or personality, whereas Rudy's paramount confidence in himself, a quality which has no tangible existence nor name, was individuality raised to the nth power. I have been about a bit, have traveled some and am no longer a callow youth, yet I can say that I never met so engaging and captivating a personality as Valentino's. And the fact that he expected you to see him as he knew he was, and as he wanted you to see him, formed the basis of this amazing form of self-confidence. If I may be allowed a poetic flight in which I seldom indulge, I say that Valentino bloomed like a gorgeous flower, and with no desire to be self-conscious. For example, an American Beauty rose just blooms,which no expectation of being either liked or disliked: it just is, and that's all. So with Valentino.

I do not deny that there was a great deal of secret jealously of Rudy among men who were slightly acquainted with him. I think it never existed among his close friends, although I do not see how so gorgeous a personality, sweeping all before it, could fail to cause an occasional twinge, even among his intimates. But if this occurred, it was instantly dispelled at Rudy's approach, before which everything unkind, resentful or hateful disappeared like magic.

He caused occasional discomfort among his associates in the studio by his preoccupied manner. I have frequently seen him walk about with this eyes fixed on a space, ignoring the morning salutations or the greeting which every one has a right to expect. He never knew that he was thus slighting those admirers who valued his recognition as something very precious. If he had he would have wrenched his mind away from its absorption, even at the risk of the loss of his continuity of thought, in order not to offend. He was truly one of the most courteous and kindly of mortals.

But he was also a dreamer. A bit of blue sky, the flight of a swallow, the iridescence of a butterfly's wing, a strange perfume or a strain of exotic music would snatch at his imagination, which, once loosed, would drench his world in a secret beauty which he confided to no one. And this detachment masqueraded as a self-absorption which certain of his friends resented. For my own part, I rather respected these retreats into himself, for I observed that out of them always came something worth while. Had we ever accused Rudy of these things which I am now writing, and which he never would have admitted to be true, he would have been as shy and sheepish and gauche as a school-boy caught in his first exhibit of puppy love. Certain secrets of his soul Valentino preferred to keep his own. Thus analyzing what I only came to know through close observation of my friend seems in a way to be somewhat indelicate, not to say indecent. For I am probing into the holy of holies of a human soul.

I must be excused, if I do merit blame in this matter, by the necessity to impart to the world the intimate knowledge of Valentino which I shared with few.

Chapter 13

If you visualize the type of woman, gray-haired, motherly, up to date in a sane way, yet one whom one called "Auntie"as soon as acquaintance would permit, you have before you the beautiful character of Mrs. Teresa Werner, whose mention in the will of Valentino as sharing equally with his brother and sister, caused a wave of astonishment to run over the civilized world.

Knowing her and the impartial, tactful, kindly part she played in the growing coolness between these two, which she and I both saw was tending towards a separation, if not a divorce, I was not surprised. In drawing his last will, Rudy instead of remembering her generously, for he experienced a passionate gratitude towards one who, while naturally tending to a defense of her own niece, yet was able to see his side of the question, and to persuade Natacha to a lenience and compassionate patience which, if it had lasted, would have healed the breach.

There are no words to describe the part Mrs. Werner played during this troubled period, it is trite to say that she was like oil on the troubled waters; yet no other simile is so felicitous. When the waves of their discussions ran high and dashed themselves upon the rocks of their their own personalities, along would come Auntie with a healing touch here and tender words there, to smooth the wrinkles from the quarreler's brows, and even, not infrequently, to cause a temporary truce to be signed. After a furious argument, including recrimination of the most biting and personal sort, in an effort to retain that love which we all knew, in our secret hearts, was receding fast.

Sad indeed were those days to all of us. For nothing is more tragic than to be present at the death–bed of love.

Rudy flung himself into the making of *The Eagle* hoping that he would have neither time nor opportunity to think.

Natacha, having completed *What Price Beauty*, took to making long trips with her car, going no one knew where, often staying two days. This we believed an effort to distract her mind from her troubles with Rudy, to make certain decisions and to arrive at final conclusions.

That the decisions she finally arrived at were erroneous and tended only to widen the bridge between the two, is one of those most regrettable things which possibly have occurred at just this time. Arguments and loving remonstrances were of no avail. She had her own codes and standards of life, and this she believed to be nobody's business but her own.

Anyone knowing the situation can imagine how just and righteous were the ministrations of her aunt, Mrs. Werner at this time. She soothed Rudy's just resentment, endeavoring to palliate Natacha's conduct, and the same time endeavoring to bring the young wife back to realization of the beauty and respect which she felt her niece owed to her husband. That she accomplished this without irritating either party, and retained the devotion of both, is ample reason why she occupies today the position of an ambassador whose reward is earned.

For my own part, I do not begrudge her the share in Rudy's estate which she is to enjoy. It was what he wanted to do for the woman who played the part of mother to his soul in its loneliest and most desolate hour.

Had his own mother been at hand, I doubt if she could have proved as efficacious and wise in this crucial period as did Auntie. For having seen the brother, who made an extended visit to Rudy just before his death, and whose return has given me a wider opportunity to analyze his mind and understand his character, I make bold to say that Auntie's understanding heart did what his own mother could not.

The same condition obtained in the Guglielmi family which many of us have observed here in America: into a family of owls an eaglet is born. The owls look wise, but their wisdom will not bear the test. The eaglet longs to soar. The owls have no strength to their wings, and therefore they gossip among themselves as to the strange and inexplicable tendencies of their eagle-child to fly into unknown ways.

Such families are always in desperate fear of what their eagle-child will do to smirch the family name of Owls. Newspaper headlines, disapproving comments of neighbors, even the barred gates of jail are forever in the background of their dull and unimaginative minds. From the story of the early life which Rudy has many a time told me, I formed a picture of this *bourgeois* family. His mother has expressed herself as being forever afraid of what Rudolfo would do. To her, it was a never ending shame that he was expelled from school when he played hooky. But it was to see a King! And, to accomplish that, Rudy have risked dismissal from a hundred schools and laughed to realize that he had accomplished what he set out to do.

Kings are interesting folks, and well worth the sacrifice of a common mortal.

Valentino was never sordid. His escapades from his early youth, up to his tragic death, were always of a gay and gallant nature, and he laughed at danger.

Beltram Masses, the famous Spanish court painter, Rudy had known in Europe. He came to Hollywood for the express purpose of painting Valentino, and in the hope that he would obtain other commissions among the movie stars, which he succeeded in doing. Marion Davies was the first and most important of these.

An impressive exhibition of the work of Beltram Masses was given at the Ambassador Hotel in Los Angeles; for two weeks it drew crowds. It was to be observed that the portraits of Marion Davies and Rudolph Valentino attracted more attention than those of the court beauties this famous artist had painted. I think I have never seen a more beautiful portrait of a woman than Beltram Masses succeeded in doing of Miss Davies. He caught that look of innocence which in her picture is one of her greatest assets. In his two portraits of Valentino he caught the air of gay defiance and laughing chivalry of the courtier cavalier. The portrait Beltram Masses did of Valentino as Julio of the *Four Horsemen of the Apocalypse* is the one which Pola Negri so desires that the heirs of the Valentino estate shall give to her.

Beltram Masses, in his character of intimate friend, always endeavored to bridge the trouble between the Valentinos, and prevent the impending separation. For he feared, as we all did, that, if they ever separated, a divorce would follow. Both were proud, difficult to manage, and with that tremendous sense of ego which seems to render compromise well nigh impossible.

But to no avail.

The occurrence which was one of the few of open examples people had of the disharmony between these two, happened in this wise.

Miss Davies and Valentino, feeling that the superb portraits Beltram Masses had painted of them deserved more than the mere financial remuneration, decided to give an elaborate private reception which should introduce the artist to their choicest friends. At this time, also, the three portraits were to be exhibited, and given opportunity for more minute examination.

Unfortunately, however, because the suggestion came from these two, and was later presented to Mrs. Valentino for her cooperation and approval, she of course to be co-hostess at that function, she became so indignant because their idea had not originated with her, that she prevented her husband from appearing at the proper time. She refused to dress. Finally Rudy caused her to appreciate how rude their behavior would be if they continued to absent themselves from their own reception; where upon Natacha yielded, and at the very late hour, the Valentinos appeared, greeted their guests and immediately left for home, abandoning their guests to their resources.

The fact that this breach of etiquette was wholly foreign to Valentino's nature, and also repugnant to him, could not fail to become known to all his friends. But that did not prevent the elite of Los Angeles, who had been bid to the reception, from feeling righteously indignant at being flouted by " mere movie stars", God save the mark.

Beltram Masses, knowing as he did the state of affairs in the Valentino family, was possibly the only one present who knew without any explanation what had caused this apparent neglect.

About this time, the purchase of the handsome new house in Beverly Hills was consummated. For some time it had been Natacha's desire to live in this exclusive and fashionable district; and, even though Rudy knew that a separation was imminent, he concluded the purchase and Falcon Lair became his.

This may have indicated that up to the very last Rudy hoped that the differences could be adjusted, and then Natacha could grace this gorgeous hillside home in which she so ardently desired to shine.

Be that as it may, the fact remains that Natacha never spent one night under its roof.

Despite the effort of both the Valentinos to keep their differences out of the newspapers, the situation had become so tense that news of it began to filter through the guards, and newspaper men began to gather and question for news.

No matter how one tried to throw these persistent news-gathers off the scent, it could not be done. They knew, and we knew that they knew, that something was brewing. And, little by little, those stories crept into print.

Naturally, this caused gossip; and gossip caused more intense irritation to nerves already frayed by the friction of increasing marital differences. Finally Natacha declared her intention of going to New York.

Rudy was agreeable to this, but amended her decision by urging her to go directly to her mother at Nice, hoping not only that a separation from him would be beneficial, but that the good advice he knew she would receive from her mother might influence her.

At any rate, he knew that, away from him, and with time to reflect, she could not fail to find herself; and this, no matter which way it cut, what was Rudy chivalrously desired.

I being called East on business about this time, and Natacha being determined to go at once, Rudy decided to send Auntie with her, knowing well that in her he was sending an envoy and ambassador upon whose wisdom he depended with wholehearted favor.

These plans were thrown open to the press, and on the morning that we left a great crowd assembled at the station to see the travelers off. Rudolph and Natacha were driven down in their big Isotta Fraschini town car, and well greeted by the clicks of countless cameras.

It was part of our program of endeavoring to conceal the fact that we feared a divorce, to have Rudy and Natacha pose for that final kiss which appeared in so many newspapers. I am not aware how Natacha felt, whether she was genuinely sorry to part from her husband, or whether at this time it was a genuine relief. As for the feelings of Rudy, no one could fail to see that his heart was torn with grief, for despite the prevalent superstition that a man should never watch a beloved woman out of his sight for fear he may never see her again, Rudy either ignored or forgot this stricture, for he clung to the steps of the observation car as long as he dared and then ran along the platform beside the slowly moving train which he feared was bearing her out of his sight forever; which afterwards proved to be true.

As the long train gained momentum and began to move more rapidly, Natacha Rambova had the satisfaction of seeing in the eyes of her husband that expression of love and great yearning which so many times we have seen in his acting upon the screen. This time, being a witness to its reality, I unhesitatingly declare that only because Valentino was so great a lover in real life could he ever have become the greatest lover of screen.

Never have I seen greater anguish, nor more poignant tenderness expressed on a human continence, and this picture of Valentino was constantly coming into my mind during those days when he fought for his life so valiantly, and when I knew his thoughts were turning more and more to Natacha.

Natacha and Auntie occupied the drawing room where their meals were served, and where I joined them, often spending part of the afternoon in their company.

At all times, when it was feasible, Mrs. Werner used her gentle arguments to persuade her niece to that compromise without which no married couples can hope to live harmoniously.

Natacha, always diplomatic, put up no counter arguments; but her iron determination to carry out her own career became known when we arrived in New York and she flatly refused to go to her mother, even though we urged upon her that her husband would join her there as soon as his picture was finished.

The deaf ear Natacha turned upon us, is spite of our best efforts, proved to my mind that from the first she had had no intentions of leaving New York. At once she began to besiege me with requests to find an opening for her pictures.

Pursuant to these plans she took an apartment at 9 West 81st Street, and set about making a home for herself, with Auntie as chaperone.

I do not mean to imply that Natacha had definitely given up all hope of reconciliation, for I recall that one morning when I went out to see her, about ten o'clock, she appeared in a white negligee gorgeously embroidered in gold, with her luxuriant hair braided in two long loose braids, down her back, her face pale, her eyes delicately ringed from a sleepless night, and her whole attitude one of wan dejection.

I determined to question her definitively, to see if I could find out what she really thought, and what she purposed to do.

" Do you love Rudy?" I asked her.

Twisting her hands together, in a small voice she replied;

"I – I don't know!"

"Do you want to go back to him?"

"I – I don't know!"

"Do you want to get a divorce and lose Rudy out of your life forever?"

She paused at this, and stared at me with her great eyes full of woe.

"I – I don't – know!" she faltered. And then burst into a flood of tears. Whereupon I knew no more than when I began to question her. Nor, I am convinced, did she.

All during this time letters of more or less bitterness, recrimination and accusation, had been flying back and forth between Hollywood and New York, until finally one particular telegram was sent by Natacha which forever ended any possibility of any reconciliation.

Business now urgently calling me back to California, I turned Mrs. Valentino's interests over to a friend of mine, with instructions to serve her to the best of his ability.

That he did so, we have ample proof in the fact that he secured for her a contract to star in a picture called, *When Love Grows Cold,* a most fitting title considering the circumstances.

With the excuse of the necessity to purchase a wardrobe for this picture, Natacha went abroad, took the preliminary steps of establishing her residence in Paris in order to obtain a divorce, then paid a visit to her mother in Nice.

Then began caustic cables from Mrs. Hudnut, who, since she had heard but one side of the story, and did not possess her sister's breadth of character, keen imagination and vision, gave scant consideration to the story Valentino might possibly have to tell.

These messages cut Rudy to the heart, their tenor being so contrary to the oft-repeated statement that he was regarded more as an own son than as an in-law.

As soon as Natacha had left California, Rudy, in order to give himself no time to think, began to take painting lessons from Beltram Masses, his friend; who, discovering a real talent in Valentino, did his best to develop it. They spent many hours in serious study; which, together with his work at the studio, gave him little time to himself.

Nevertheless, he began to take up once more the friends from whom he had been alienated by his marriage. Natacha was one of those women who could brook no interest in the heart of a man she loved but her own. She wished to reign supreme, and to this end she slowly but surely separated her husband from all his old companions.

Had it not been for these absorptions, it is my opinion that Valentino would have taken the first train possible and followed his wife to New York. But, after the reaction which that fatal telegram caused, his attitude changed, and he began to seek the society of those to whom he was attracted.

During the filming of *The Eagle*, the beautiful little Hungarian actress, Vilma Banky, played opposite him; and it was observed that her delicate blonde beauty, her innate refinement, added to her shy demure admiration of the great artist, began to take effect.

It is significant that so many of those who win recognition on the screen come of humble parentage. Vilma Banky, who was reported to have been a stenographer in Budapest, found herself raised by her great beauty to the position of star, almost over-night.

She was one of Samuel Goldwyn's remarkable finds. This man possesses an almost uncanny ability to select sure-fire box-office successes, as witness his discoveries of Ronald Coleman and Lois Moran.

The world has chosen to attribute a love affair to Rudolph Valentino and Vilma Banky: such, in my opinion, was not the case.

Propinquity is responsible for more marriages than love, and it was propinquity in this case, added possibly to a sincere admiration on Valentino's part for Vilma's budding ability as an actress, as well as for her undeniable beauty.

It might be interesting to describe the bungalow dressing room which was built for Valentino on the United Studio's lot.

This consisted of a dining room and reception room, in which were bookcases, an open fireplace, davenport and a combination dining room-library table, with easy chairs, a Brunswick cabinet phonograph and plain one-tone velvet rugs upon the floor. Adjoining this was Rudy's dressing room and bath. His dressing table was equipped with Cooper-Hewitt lights beneath which he could don make-up and get the same effect he did under the Kleigs. The walls of both rooms were made interesting by groups of armor and firearms, swords and spears. Pictures of friends in the motion picture industry, framed and autographed, were also here in great profusion.

A hall divided these rooms from Valentino's private office, the walls of which were filled with bookcases, containing countless volumes on costumes and history. Next to this was the office of his secretary, and adjoining that a kitchenette.

During the filming of *The Eagle* , Rudy's time was so limited that he adopted the custom of having his luncheons brought down from his home in containers and served in this bungalow. Here Beltram Masses and Vilma Banky generally joined him. I am persuaded that the atmosphere of good-fellowship and camaraderie which obtained at these intimate informal luncheons did much to foster a natural friendship between the star and his leading woman. And Beltram Masses in the role of chaperon!

By this time Auntie had returned from New York. She was living in her own home on Sycamore Street, but not a day passed in which she was not in the house on Whitley Heights. Not in the capacity of housekeeper, for so well was Valentino's house run that there remained nothing for her to do along this line. She was there in the capacity of welcome guest, so that, when Vilma Banky was asked to dine and spend the evening, they were chaperoned by Mrs. Werner.

Rudy and Vilma frequently appeared in society together at parties and openings of plays, so that it is no wonder that a world avid for gossip should link their names. In my opinion it was more a community of interests than a love affair; but possibly in this I am mistaken.

At the conclusion of Valentino's work in *The Eagle,* he began deliberately to seek the society of Pola Negri, who had previously given evidences of her interest in him.

Well he knew the effect that this would have upon Natacha, as Pola Negri was the one woman whose fascinations Natacha Rambova feared.

The Polish beauty is the antithesis of the Rambova type. Natacha is cold, mysterious, Oriental, languorous and beguiling. Pola is passionate, hot-blooded, hot-tempered, tempestuous and volcanic. Both are equally fascinating. And both are so supremely beautiful in their different types that it just depends upon one's individual taste which is preferred.

Just as Rudolph was more in love with Natacha, so Pola, in my opinion, was more in love than Rudy. But Valentino was always gentle and yielding where a beautiful woman was concerned.

Pola Negri knows very well what she wants. None better. And from this time on Pola and Rudy were as continuously in each other's company as their arduous work would permit.

Valentino had a small yacht, a cabin cruiser, and aboard this boat he made frequent trips to Catalina for the week-end and sometimes longer.

Every new amusement captured Rudy's imagination, and he pursued it with all the enthusiasm he possessed. Thus the purchase of this small craft only fired him to greater length. It was his intention either to build or buy a yacht large enough to enter it in the long-distance races, so that he could compete in such events as the Los Angeles to Honolulu annual race.

Once aboard his boat, nothing would do but he must perform every bit of labor possible, cleaning, polishing, even cooking the meals. Valentino was a marvelous cook, and, in my opinion, held the diamond belt at cooking spaghetti.

It may seem from this narrative that Valentino did nothing but play. The entire world must realize how long and severe the strain of working on his tremendous pictures must have been, so I am deliberately avoiding the description of that side of his life. But what with the ability of the European to enjoy life as he goes along, what with giving proper time to amusement, and not confining himself too strenuously to business, Valentino's life was evenly balanced and distributed.

No matter how many pictures may have been made by a company, it is always a time of tense excitement when the hour comes in which a new picture must be cut and edited. Every one connected with the making, from the production manager down, is interested to see what retakes may be necessary, if any.

As soon as the picture is in as perfect form as seems possible, it is then previewed at one or two outlying theaters, with the public's being notified of this fact. Thus is obtained the reaction from an audience not necessarily composed of devoted fans. Members of the production staff are scattered through the audience, carefully watching the picture's reception. If at any part the audience seems restive, as the tempo of the picture lags, a note is made, and the next day the picture is again cut at these places, thus tightening the tension and increasing the interest. Then, again, a title may be added, to elucidate the meaning of a scene which to that audience seemed obscure.

Until a picture is in its final form, it is impossible for a star, or other important members of the cast, to leave town, for fear retakes may be necessary.

When, however, all these things had been done to *The Eagle,* and it was in a finished state of perfection, Valentino went to New York to be present at its premiere.

196

Seldom has a premiere attracted such a throng. People stood in line all day at the Mark Strand Theater, and in the evening the crowds of well-dressed people thronged the theater to its capacity. These crowds continued all during the showing of *The Eagle,* making it one of the most successful of Valentino's career.

It is interesting to note that *The Eagle,* in the directing of which Natacha had no hand, was more successful than the two previous ones, *Cobra* and *The Sainted Devil,* in both of which she had almost a free hand.

After a short stay in New York, Rudy left for London, to be present at the English premiere.

Lady Curzon was his devoted friend, and she had assured Valentino that arrangements would be made for the royal family to be present.

But the death of the beloved Queen Mother, Alexandra, had cast such a gloom over the whole of England that the entire court went in the deepest mourning and canceled all social engagements.

Seldom has an entire nation been so deeply moved at the passing of one who sat upon its throne as was Great Britain when there passed, at a ripe old age, the Danish princess whose arrival as a slip of a girl, to become the bride of the Prince of Wales, and had aroused all England to such enthusiasm. Her popularity with the British people never waned; even with her difficult mother-in-law, Queen Victoria, she was always a favorite.

But in spite of the absence of the Court, the opening of the Valentino picture was a great social success. Lady Curzon made it her personal business to see that as many of her friends as possible were present.

Rudy remained in London as long as he could; but, faced with the necessity to establish his residence in Paris, in order to complete the legal arrangements whereby Natacha could obtain her divorce, Valentino left for France.

Many of Valentino's friends hoped that he would meet Natacha in Paris, and possibly patch the thing up so that there would be no divorce. But here Fate seemed to take a hand, for, without waiting for Rudy's arrival, Natacha had returned to New York.

During his stay in Paris he lived at the Plaza-Atheneé, and it is well known that he appeared much in the company of Jean Nash, the Dolly Sisters and others equally well known to the night life of Paris.

It was also here he met Prince Habible-Lotfallah. This Egyptian Prince, a man of great wealth and learning, was enormously taken with Rudy, and urged him to come to Cairo to make a picture. He promised Rudy every cooperation in his power, with the added inducement of the gift of a pure-bred Arabian horse which Rudy was to select from the Prince's stables.

Since nothing would have pleased Valentino more than to make a desert picture upon the Great Sahara, it is not saying too much to say that, had he lived, Rudy would have arranged to do this.

Rumors now began to sift through into the press concerning the elaborate parties which were staged in Paris for, and by, Valentino. But when I questioned him later (I was rather suspicious of the bounty of some of his friends), I discovered that he had invariably been obliged to pay the bills, his coterie of acquaintances having been most obliging in their willingness to help him spend his money.

I did not blame them so much, however, knowing as I did how easily Rudy could be imposed upon, and how open-handed he always was with his money.

Having now complied with all the requirements of the law in order that Natacha might obtain her divorce, Rudy invited his sister Maria, his brother Alberto Guglielmi, his sister-in-law, and their eleven-year-old boy to travel with him to London, where he took them about with him generously, showing them the sights of the English capital and opening up to them a world which had existed hitherto only in their imaginations.

While in London, Rudy endeavored to provide his sister Maria with a profession by which she could be self-supporting. He induced her to take a course in interior decorating, for which course he gladly furnished the money. But, finding the work not to her taste, Maria gave it up, and later returned to Paris to live.

Rudy was very anxious to place his family in professions whereby they could become independent. And, to this end, he arranged later for his brother to go into the office of United Artists in Paris, hoping that there he would learn the business of distribution and might thus become the firm's representative in Italy.

That Christmas which the Guglielmi family spent in London was the first in which brothers and sisters had been united since the death of their parents, and was for this reason one which they never forgot.

To satisfy the curiosity of the public as to any possible resemblance between Alberto, several years older, and Rudolph, let me say that never were two men more unlike, either in physiognomy or character.

Having such a gorgeous time in London, meeting many persons of title, and being entertained at princely homes, Valentino joyously sent me a cable saying he could not possibly leave London until the middle of February. To which I replied saying that, on the contrary, he would be in Hollywood not later than the first of February. Whereupon Valentino, seeing that his bluff had failed to work, gave in graciously, as usual, and returned on the *Berengeria*, bringing Alberto and his family with him and arriving in Hollywood the last of January.

Mrs. Ullman and I met them in Pasadena, where they left the train in order to avoid publicity. It is difficult for a star of any magnitude to arrive in Hollywood without assembling crowds who crave to catch a glimpse of their favorite. In spite of the glorious time he had had in Europe, Rudy was childishly glad to be at home again, and assured me, almost in his first breath, not only that everything was paid for, but that he had a balance in the bank. Very cautiously and totally without belief, I questioned as to the amount of this mysterious reserve fund, whereupon Rudy told me it was thirty thousand – I held my breath until he said the fatal words -francs.

Yet even this was cause for congratulations until bills began to seep in for the thirty-two suits of clothes, the forty pairs of shoes, the scores of neckties, shirts without number, and other purchases which he had neglected to tabulate in his first enthusiasm at returning with money in the bank.

Afterwards it turned out that almost all the money he spent in Europe had been to pay for the glorious time he had there, while he left most of his purchases to be paid for at this end.

Not that it made any material difference, for at this time his affairs were in such a state that he could allow himself any moderate extravagance without harm. I only mention this to show the little-boy attitude of Rudy, one of his most endearing characteristics.

Before leaving for Europe, the purchase of the Beverly Hills house, which Rudy named *Falcon Lair*, had been completed. It clings to the top of a mountainside, overlooking Beverly Hills, the City of Los Angeles, and, on clear days, Catalina Island.

199

Perched on the surrounding hills, and easily visible from the broad windows of *Falcon Lair* , lie the palatial estates of Harold Lloyd, the late Thomas Ince and Charles Chaplin, *Pickfair*, and just the chimneys of Marion Davies' beautiful English country place.

On the hillside to the left, and equally as high, lies the estate of John Gilbert, and, highest of all, on a hilltop back of *Falcon Lair*, rises the gorgeous Spanish home of Fred Thompson and his famous wife, Frances Marion.

Although Rudy had seen many of the medieval castles of England, France and Spain, to say nothing of his beloved Italy, he was thrilled when he returned to his home in Beverly Hills and saw the picturesque beauty of the panorama which spread itself before his eyes. Nowhere in all the world are grouped together such magnificent estates so ideally situated as those owned by the movie colony surrounding *Falcon Lair* in Beverly Hills. The Valentino estate, although comprising eight and one half acres, is situated in the choicest part of Beverly Hills, with a view excelled by none.

While in Europe Rudy had, at various times, made exclusive purchases for the home he sometime hoped to have. These were now assembled at *Falcon Lair*, together with the choicest pieces from his apartment in New York, and the house on Whitley Heights. Many of these he caused to be reupholstered in colors he himself selected. He adored rich materials and splendid colors, all shades of dark red being his favorite. Brocades, velvets, and satins which would stand alone, gorgeous embroideries in gold and silver, wrought iron, carvings in ivory and jade, gorgeously bound books with priceless colored plates, china and porcelain worth its weight in gold, Venetian and Bohemian glass, and distinctive bibelots from many lands, all these were included in the furnishings of *Falcon Lair*.

He seemed to care little for the rich Oriental rugs which adorn many of the homes of his friends, priceless though they were. With the exception of the dining room rug in *Falcon Lair,* which was many-hued, the rugs were of neutral tinted one-toned velvet, which, like the plain walls, formed an artistic background for his many treasures.

From the reception hall to the servants' quarters, I have never been in a house which was so essentially masculine. Luxurious in the extreme and most artistic, it nevertheless reflected the colorful dominant personality of a man accustomed to express himself in his surroundings.

Nevertheless, living in a house, even though it was built by one's self, is certain to bring out the defects of that house, and those of *Falcon Lair* were discernible to Valentino. With characteristic energy, at once he set about eliminating them, and making certain improvements which he felt would add to the comfort, not only of himself, but of those guests with whom he intended to surround himself.

Rudy loved nothing so well as entertaining. Yet, during the stay of his family at *Falcon Lair*, he was limited in this line both by the illness of his sister-in-law and by the torn-up condition of the house.

Possibly these conditions may have contributed to throwing him into the society of Pola Negri more than otherwise. At any rate, it is certain that these two began to be together on all occasions, Rudy frequently a guest at Pola's handsome colonial home on Beverly Drive, and Pola frequently a guest at *Falcon Lair*.

Chapter 14

Ever since the filming of *The Sheik,* with lovely Agnes Ayres as his leading woman, Rudy's fans had been asking, by the thousands, when he was going to do another Sheik picture, so that when Mrs. Hull wrote *Son of the Sheik,* it went without saying that the only person who could play the young Sheik was Valentino.

It was therefore purchased for him; the twin brother in the novel eliminated, it went into production under its now famous title, *The Son of the Sheik.*

Nothing could be happier than the circumstances surrounding the making of this picture. For the first time, Rudy felt that the world was with him. He was freed from the unhappy belief, instilled in his mind by Natacha, that everyone was trying to get the best of him. His own sunshiny belief in the honor of his friends and associates once again asserted itself.

Conditions were indeed most favorable. He was once again in the role made famous by his former great success, which not only established him in a niche all his own but added a word to the English language, a word so potent that is became noun and verb and adjective.

Again he had for his leading woman one who never failed to portray her part, Vilma Banky, whose youthful blonde beauty was an excellent foil for the dashing, gallant Son of the Sheik.

Notwithstanding the selection of Miss Banky to be his leading woman, the suitability of the story purchased for him, and the cooperation of the entire staff, the outstanding joy in the making of this picture was the fact that Rudy had, for the first time, the services of George Fitzmaurice as director.

It is to be recalled that one of the things contributing to the split between Valentino and Famous Players/Lasky was the fact that Rudy wanted Fitzmaurice to direct *Blood and Sand,* and really never got over his disappointment in not having him. He was like a child. Disappoint him and he would remember it for years. Now, when a fortuitous circumstance gave him Fitzmaurice as director, he was supremely happy.

There is no gainsaying the fact that Fitzmaurice had a marvelous understanding of Valentino. An artist to his fingertips, Fitzmaurice understood the volatile Italian, knew how to handle him, to get the best out of him, to thrill him with an enthusiasm which brought Rudy to his toes, and how to develop to its highest point the peculiar genius of Valentino as an actor.

Both spoke French and, when the limits of the English language were reached, they dropped into French to indicate to each other those delicate *nuances* which are often elusive to the English tongue.

I remember the long discussions which would take place between these two over a trifle which some would have ignored, or possibly never would have seen. But, to Fitzmaurice and Valentino, they were important, as indicating the fine line between a mere performance and an artistic interpretation. They worked together so harmoniously that all finally agreed with Rudy in his contention that Fitzmaurice was indeed the outstanding director for him.

I think that Rudy had a better time during the filming of *The Son of the Sheik* than in any other of his pictures. He used to have his lunches brought down from his home, and there gathered in the dining room of his suite at the studio, Constance Talmadge, Ronald Coleman, Vilma Banky, George Fitzmaurice, Pola Negri, Allistair MacIntosh, Louella Parsons, Marion Davies, Lady Loughborough, Eugene Brewster, Corliss Palmer and many others. All these I met at different times at Rudy's famous luncheons. Brilliant conversation was the order of the day.

The costumes worn in *The Son of the Sheik* Rudy had bought abroad. Most of them originals and absolutely authentic. Some people would consider a fortune the amount of money he had tied up in costumes and props, for nothing less than the best suited his fastidious taste.

As I have said before, when Valentino was filming a picture he enacted his role at all times. Once, when we were on the train going to New York, he read *The Sea Hawk*, which afterwards Frank Lloyd produced with Milton Sills in the leading roll. Rudy went wild about this part, and declared it was made for him. Under its spell he was indeed *The Sea Hawk*. His manners were rough. When he wanted to move me aside, he shoved me out of his way with his elbow. He ate like a pig. Considering Valentino's fastidious table manners, this ability to get inside the skin of a character greatly interested me.

Valentino begged J.D. Williams to buy the picture for him, as at that time Rudy was under contract to Ritz-Carlton Pictures. It was only when Williams lacked the foresight to accede to Valentino's request that Rudy gave over being *The Sea Hawk*, and again began to use a fork.

Again, when he was filming *The Sainted Devil*, his habitual courtesy left him entirely, and he was rough and swaggering. I shudder to think what would have happened if he had ever been called upon to play a cut-throat Apache. His friends would have had to run for their lives!

Another ambition of Valentino's was to play *Ben Hur*, and I imagine that there are a few who would not agree with me that Rudolph Valentino would have made the greatest *Ben Hur* the world had ever seen. Picture Valentino as the galley slave in the chariot race and then as the idealist forever dreaming of raising his race to its proper place in the history of the world. As the lover of Miriam, he would have made a love story so spiritual, so tender and so appealing that it would have been an idyl to be forgotten never.

One day during the filming of *The Son of the Sheik*, he came into my office, garbed in the striped robe which he wears in the first part of the picture and, seating himself on the corner of my desk, he said, in a calmly dispassionate tone:

"Ullman, I can't forever go on playing such parts as these. On your honor now, how long do you give me to play the romantic lover?"

I looked at him in astonishment, wondering if he were in earnest.

He nodded his head at me.

"I'm serious. I really want to know."

After thinking a moment, I said:

"Well, I should say about five years."

Rudy smiled one of his rare smiles and said:

"That is about what I think. And long enough, too! After that I want to do great characters like Cesare Borgia, Christopher Columbus; men who have accomplished great things. Then, of course, there is the American Indian. I would very much like to play a young Chief; and, before I finish, I want most of all to play a Gypsy and an Apache."

Alas! That he did not live to carry out these dreams! Every reader can visualize what he would have made of these roles.

In a limited way his portrayal of the father, the old Sheik in *The Son of the Sheik*, gives us an idea of how well Valentino would have handled these character parts. It gave him no end of pleasure when, with his marvelous make-up for the old Sheik on, he walked around on the lot and not one of his associates recognized him.

Concerning the character of The Sheik, which, as all the world knows, Valentino created, he had peculiar ideas. He loathed utterly the application of the word Sheik to himself, except as to his portrayal of the part in his two pictures. To call him a Sheik in real life offended him to the soul; he deplored the lowering of the majestic title of an Arab chieftain to describe the common street flirtations of the morons to whom it became generally applied.

He endeavored to give a dignified portrayal of the character in both the pictures in which he played the young Sheik. And I believe I am right in saying that, if viewed intelligently and without bias, Valentino gave to both characters a dignity proper to the original. To be sure, he idealized the part, a thing which Valentino could not fail to do with any role he essayed. Personally, I recall the Arabic salutation of respect which he pays to his father as a gesture of as great a dignity as I have ever seen.

There is no disguising the fact that Valentino actually loved the desert. The long stretches of sand dunes which appear in the first part of *The Son of the Sheik* were filmed near Yuma, Arizona, and there Rudy exhibited such joy in the desert scenes that others in the cast came to share his enthusiasm. His favorite music, played during the filming of this part of the picture, was Homer Grunn's *Desert Suite*.

Later, scenes were filmed near Guadalupe, California, and still others on the set at the Pickford-Fairbanks Studios, where tons and carloads of sand were dumped to simulate the desert. But the sandstorm during which Valentino sets out to find Yasmin was filmed near Yuma, the storm being precipitated by wind machines.

No actual sand storm on the Sahara could have been more violent and blinding in velocity than the one stirred by those terrific wind demons which drove the particles of sand against the faces and bodies of the actors in a way to cause actual suffering.

The women, Vilma Banky and Agnes Ayres, disliked these sand storms, but Rudolph actually enjoyed them. They seem to exhilarate him so that I used to wonder if at any time in his previous career he had been a son of the desert.

It is only another instance of the way in which Valentino's personality could perform wonders, that Agnes Ayres was induced to return to the screen for the short scenes in which she portrayed the mother of the young Sheik. It was considered among the impossibilities to secure her services, and others were under consideration for the role when Rudy performed the miracle.

Lest the public underestimate the quality of her sacrifice, let it be remembered that it required great courage for a young and beautiful woman deliberately to don make-up which would cause her to appear matronly, despite the fact that for many years to come she will be able to play youthful leads. However, she did this gladly for Valentino, so that the beauty of the picture was enhanced by the actual appearances of the same character which graced the earlier romance.

Another great concession was that of W. K. Kellogg of Battle Creek, Michigan, and Pomona, California, owner and breeder of the finest Arabian horses on this continent. The beautiful white Arabian stallion, Jadan, used in the filming of *The Sheik*, was necessary in that sequence in *The Son of the Sheik*, wherein the father rides to his son's rescue. Of course, another horse could have been substituted; but, with Valentino's passion for accuracy, he greatly desired Jadan, and Mr. Kellogg, appreciating this, allowed the horse to be used.

I shall never forget Rudy's joy when he discovered he could have Jadan. It was one of those small things, unimportant to some, which delights the soul of the artist.

Work on this picture was so arduous that Valentino took more time off than was his custom. He was seen in the company of Pola Negri, with whom he took long horseback rides Sunday mornings,and whom he escorted to various premieres.

At the Charlot Revue, which fairly swept Los Angeles off its feet by its brilliance and cleverness, Rudy gave a large party which included Pola Negri and other screen celebrities.

Rudy and Pola were seen often at the dances of the Sixty Club, which were always given at the Biltmore Hotel; on one occasion these two won first price in costume dance at which Pola appeared as a Spanish dancer and Rudy as a toreador, in the costume he wore in *Blood and Sand*.

It was a joyous day when the picture was finished. Rudy supervised the cutting, which was so competently done by Hal Kern that few suggestions were necessary.

Notwithstanding this supervision, Rudy attended the preview at Santa Monica, where we sat together and, for the first time with an audience, watched the scenes of his last masterpiece unroll before our eyes. It was then that we realized, from the enthusiasm displayed, the great appeal which this picture would have upon the public at large.

To me it seemed well nigh perfect. I could pick no flaws in it. But at least a dozen times Rudy nudged me with his elbow and whispered:

"If I could only do that bit over, I could do it better."

This ceaseless ambition to improve his work, this gnawing dissatisfaction with his best efforts, were to my mind indications that Valentino belonged to that great company of artists who possess genius of a high order, for it is only the mediocre who boast and brag of their prowess.

It touches me deeply to recall how, in the last few weeks of his life, Rudy bridged the discord which had separated him from many of his old friends. It was as if he gathered up the raveled ends of friendships he had cherished, and knit them together into a more enduring fabric.

On the occasion of this preview he saw Cora Macy, famous character actress of stage and screen, and her equally well-known daughter Cora McGeachy, whose genius in costuming is almost too well know to need comment. For the most important revues on the New York stage, for Hollywood studios where she designed the gorgeous costumes for Colleen Moore's production of *Irene* and other First National Pictures, Cora McGeachy's work is in constant demand. Rudy had formerly been friendly with these two distinguished women, but during his married life, he had not seen much of them. The same was true of June Mathis, to whom he was more indebted than to any other one person in the world. On account of the quarrel between Natacha Rambova and June Mathis, Valentino had become somewhat estranged from her, also.

When he saw these three old friends coming out of the theater after the preview, he stopped them, and then and there showed by his cordiality that the old Rudy was again in evidence and at heart had never changed.

Cora McGeachy was in tears, seeing which Rudy inquired what the matter was.

"Oh, I am so happy," she sobbed, "at seeing you back in your old place on the screen."

Rudy was very much touched by this evidence of friendship and sincere interest in his career.

I have often thought since his death of what satisfaction it must have given his old friends to realize that before he went away he gave them so much evidence of his affection.

I know that Rudy had no premonition of his approaching death. Yet as I look back I can see that the last few weeks of his life were almost entirely given over to the smoothing out of old misunderstandings. Notable among them were those with Jean Acker and Natacha Rambova.

After announcing previews at Santa Monica and Burbank, *The Son of the Sheik* had a special preview showing at Grauman's Million Dollar Theater in Los Angeles.

The opening night was a veritable triumph. All day long crowds had attended the continuous showing and, at the evening performance, every notable of the screen was present, pausing under the Kleigs to be photographed, as is the custom at premieres.

In the richly decorated foyer of the theater stood the most imposing floral piece I had ever seen. It was about eight feet high and ten feet wide, the background composed of red gladioli diagonally across which was written, in white carnations, Valentino's name.

When this huge structure met his eyes Rudy halted, almost overcome by tribute. When I whispered in his ear that this was from Pola, a slow smile crept over his face.

The manager of the theater had previously informed me that he hoped Mr. Valentino would be willing to rise in his place in the audience when his name was called and take a bow. When I told Rudy this he said:

"Very well. But no speeches."

Man proposes, but God disposes.

As usual there were two evening showings, one at seven, and one at nine. Valentino had as his guests a party of twelve, among whom were Pola Negri, Prince Mdivani and his wife Mae Murray, Louella Parsons, Charles Chaplin, others equally noted. With these friends Rudy was chatting pleasantly, when, to his surprised, instead of being asked to rise in his place in the audience, he was called to the stage by the manager just before the prologue of the second showing. As he made his appearance, such a tumult of applause broke forth that Rudy was confused. When the manager spoke up, saying that so long as Valentino was before his audience, doubtless he would not object to saying a few words, Rudy saw that he was caught.

Game as usual, he made a short impromptu speech which was a masterpiece of cryptic utterance.

Had Valentino ever attempted public speaking for such worthy objects as a Community Chest or a Liberty Loan, for anything in which his emotions were engaged, I venture to say that few could have equaled him in the ability to move audiences. On this occasion, when he faced a Million Dollar Theater audience filled to capacity with his fans, little did he or any one of them imagine that this was his last appearance in public on the Pacific Coast, and that never again would any of them face him in life. But so it was, for soon after this it was decided that it would be wise for him to make personal appearances in certain of the larger cities where *The Son of the Sheik* was to be shown, and Rudy, filled with his periodical wanderlust and desirous also of seeing his brother and family safely on board the ship which was to take them home, willingly agreed to make the arduous trip East, although this proved to be in the midst of such grueling heat that I doubt he would have attempted it had he known what was before him.

However, the future is mercifully hidden from us all.

We thereupon set out upon what was to be his last journey in this life.

He left for San Francisco, while a few days later his brother Alberto and family went by the southerly route to New York, where we expected to meet them.

A large group of people came to the station to see Rudy off, among whom was Pola Negri, who again violated the superstition of the danger of watching a beloved one out of sight.

She stood on the platform watching Rudy, who hung out the door of the observation car, disregarding the efforts of the trainman to close the door, and waving a hand until a curve in the track whisked him out of sight. This also was the last time Pola Negri saw Rudolph Valentino in life.

We arrived in San Francisco on Thursday, July 15, being met by Mayor Rolph and a host of notables and newspaper men and camera men.

A luncheon had been arranged at the Fairmont Hotel, at which Mayor Rolph presided. This lasted until four o'clock in the afternoon, when the Mayor took us out to his home, where we met Mrs. Rolph, a gracious and charming woman.

We were shown about the spacious grounds, and when we reached the kennels Rudy's delight burst all bounds. An ardent lover of animals, particularly horses and dogs, he expressed so much appreciation of the Mayor's finely bred animals that Mr. Rolph made him a present of the beautiful black water spaniel to which I have alluded previously.

Both Mr. and Mrs. Rolph were extremely fond of Valentino and received him almost as a beloved son. He was lonely at all times for the family love which he continuously seemed to miss and long for. The homelike atmosphere of the Rolphs, and the sincere affection they expressed, felt like a balm upon Rudy's soul.

The next morning we left for the East, in the midst of such terrific heat that, as soon as we boarded the train, Rudy donned a Chinese lounging suit and, after a weak attempt to read a book which only lasted about ten minutes, turned over and went to sleep.

The trip was uneventful until we reached Chicago, where we found the heat to be sufficiently eventful to rouse even the dullest to take notice of it.

Although we were in Chicago only between trains, we went to the Blackstone. Here I was handed the now famous editorial which originally appeared in *The Chicago Tribune*. Since this scurrilous attack embittered the last days of Rudolph Valentino, killing his usual joy in living and causing him more mental anguish than any other article ever written about him, I quote in full the infamous anonymous attack, which I recognized as coming from the same poison pen which earlier in the year had, without cause and without reason, attacked my friend.

"PINK POWDER PUFFS

A new public ballroom was opened on the north side a few days ago, a truly handsome place and apparently well run. The pleasant impression lasts until one steps into the men's washroom and finds there on the wall a contraption of glass tubes and levers and a slot for the insertion of a coin. The glass tubes contain a fluffy pink solid, and beneath them one reads an amazing legend which runs something like this: "Insert coin. Hold personal puff beneath the tube. Then pull the lever."

A powder vending machine! In a men's washroom! Homo Americanus! Why didn't some one quietly drown Rudolph Guglielmi, alias Valentino, years ago?

And was the pink powder machine pulled from the wall or ignored? It was not. It was used. We personally saw two "men" - as young lady contributors to the Voice of the People are wont to describe the breed – step up, insert coin, hold kerchief beneath the spout, pull the lever, then take the pretty pink stuff and put it on their cheeks in front of the mirror.

Anther member of this department, one of the most benevolent men on earth, burst raging into the office the other day because he had seen a young "man" combing his pomaded hair in the elevator. But we claim our pink powder story beats all this hollow.

It is time for a matriarchy if the male of the species allows such things to persist. Better a rule by masculine women than by effeminate men. Man began to slip, we are beginning to believe, when he discarded the straight razor for the safety pattern. We shall not be surprised when we hear that the safety razor has given way to the depilatory.

Who or what is to blame is what puzzles us. Is this degeneration into effeminacy a cognate reaction with pacifism to the virilities and realities of war? Are pink powder and parlor pinks in any way related? How does one reconcile masculine costumes, sheiks, floppy pants, and slave bracelets with a disregard for law and an aptitude for crime more in keeping with the frontier of half a century ago than a twentieth-century metropolis?

Do women like the type of "men" who pats pink powder on his face in a public washroom and arranges his coiffure in a public elevator? Do women at heart belong to the Wilsonian era of "I Didn't Raise My Boy to Be a Soldier?" What has become of the old "caveman" line?

It is a strange social phenomenon and one that is running its course not only here in America but in Europe as well. Chicago may have its powder puffs; London has its dancing men and Paris its gigolos. Down with Decatur; up with Elinor Glyn. Hollywood is the national school of masculinity. Rudy, the beautiful gardener's boy, is the prototype of the American male.

Hell's Bells. Oh, Sugar."

As I read this cowardly and yellow attack my countenance must have changed, for Rudy, watching me, immediately asked what was wrong.

If he had not caught me in the act of reading it, I think that I never would have allowed him to see it, so profoundly do I regret the irritating and saddening effect it had upon him. He took the screed from my reluctant fingers, read it; instantly I realized how deeply he was moved. His face paled, his eyes blazed and his muscles stiffened.

I shared his anger, for it seemed to me then, and I have never changed my opinion, that not in all my experiences with anonymous attacks in print had I ever read one in which the name of an honest gentleman had been dragged in the mud in so causeless a manner.

What, I ask you, had the installation of a powdering machine in any public bathroom in Chicago to do with a dignified actor in New York and Hollywood? Had Valentino made dancing his profession, I grant you that there might have been some reason for this envious attack. But I have related in this volume how sincerely Valentino disliked the profession of dancing and what grave sacrifices he made both financially and otherwise in repudiating the career of a dancer and suffering the privations necessary to become an actor in motion pictures.

In running over in my own mind the characters he portrayed on the screen in recent years, I mention *Monsieur Beaucaire, Cobra, The Sainted Devil, The Four Horsemen, The Sheik* and *The Son of the Sheik*. And I ask the public to tell me if in any of these super-pictures Valentino assumed a character which would connect him in any way with the sort of effeminate man who would resort to a pink powder puff.

For myself, I answer emphatically that there is no connection whatsoever; and I agreed with my friend that no one, unless he were animated by personal jealousy of the exalted position of Valentino enjoyed in the estimation of the American public, could have written so impudent an attack upon a gentleman. I purposely made use of the term impudent, because an inferior can be impudent only to his superior.

Wounded to the soul by the implication that his ancestry had been common, whereas the world knows that marriage between the daughter of a surgeon and a Italian cavalry officer constitute honorable parentage for offspring, to say the least, Valentino prepared at once to avenge the insult offered.

Summoning the representative of *The Tribune's* powerful and greatly feared rival, *The Chicago Herald-Examiner,* Valentino handed to him for publication the following:

"July 19ᵗʰ, 1926

To The Man (?) Who Wrote The Editorial Headed "Pink Powder Puffs" in Sunday's "Tribune" :

The above mentioned editorial is at least the second scurrilous attack you have made upon me, my race, and my father's name.

You slur my Italian ancestry; you cast ridicule upon my Italian name; you cast doubt upon my manhood.

I call you, in return, a contemptible coward and to prove which of us is a better man, I challenge you to a personal test. This is not a challenge to a duel in the generally accepted sense — that would be illegal. But in Illinois boxing is legal, so is wrestling. I, therefore, defy you to meet me in the boxing or wrestling arena to prove, in typically American fashion (for I am an American citizen) , which of us is more a man. I prefer this test of honor to be private, so I may give you the beating you deserve, and because I want to make it absolutely plain that this challenge is not for purposes of publicity. I am handing copies of this to the newspapers simply because I doubt that any one so cowardly as to write about me as you have would respond to a defy unless forced by the press to do so. I do not know who you are or how big you are but this challenge stands if you are as big as Jack Dempsey.

I will meet you immediately or give you a reasonable time in which to prepare, for I assume that your muscles must be flabby and weak, judging by your cowardly mentality and that you will have to replace the vitriol in your veins for red blood — if there be a place in such a body as yours for red blood and manly muscle.

I want to make it plain that I hold no grievance against the Chicago Tribune, although it seems a mistake to let a cowardly writer use its valuable columns as this "man" does. My fight is personal — with the poison-pen writer of editorials that stoops to racial and personal prejudice. The Tribune through Miss Mae Tinee, has treated me and my work kindly and at times very favorably. I welcome criticism of my work as an actor — but I will resent with every muscle of my body attacks upon my manhood and ancestry.

Hoping I will have the opportunity to demonstrate to you that the wrist under a slave bracelet may snap a real fist into your sagging jaw and that I may teach you respect of a man even though he happens to prefer to keep his face clean, I remain with

Utter Contempt,
RUDOLPH VALENTINO

P.S. I will return to Chicago within ten days. You may send your answer to me in New York, care of United Artists Corp., 729 - 7th Ave. "

The publication of this challenge, which was originally in *The Herald-Examiner*, was flashed immediately over wires and cables to the four corners of the earth, and the furious discussion which resulted is of too recent date to need comment.

While we were on the train going from Chicago to New York I asked Rudy, as soon as he had time to cool down and think coherently, for this attack had thrown him into a rage so abysmal that his whole being was disorganized:

"What are you going to do if you find this editor is seven feet tall and twice your weight?"

To which he replied:

"What would be the difference? If I am licked by a more powerful man that will be no disgrace and at any rate I'll show him that I am no pink powder puff."

That unhappy epithet, pink powder puff, stuck in Rudy's craw. During the few short weeks between the time it was applied to him by this antagonist who was too cowardly to make himself known, and Valentino's untimely death, Rudy repeated the words more times than I heard him utter any other phrase in all the years that I knew him.

He would repeat them seemingly in agony of soul, as if fearful that, in the minds of some who did not know him, the thought of effeminacy might stick. Whereas I, his friend, make the statement that no cowboy on the Western plains nor athlete from the Marines could boast a more powerful physique than that of Valentino, nor more truly possess the right to the title of he-man.

What if he did wear a slave bracelet? It was given to him by his wife, whom he still adored, and no power on earth could have

214

persuaded him to remove it. Would God there were more men as faithful!

When we arrived in New York we were met by the usual crowd of fans, reporters and cameramen, who followed Rudy to the Ambassador Hotel as if he were a visiting potentate.

Rudy was so naïve that he got a great kick out of the acclaim which followed him after he became famous. The sight of motorcycle traffic officers clearing the way for his triumphal car always thrilled him.

Arriving at the Ambassador, he good-naturedly posed again for the many stills which have now become so valuable.

The press at this time was much exercised as to Valentino's reputed strength, and many were the conjectures as to what would happen when we went back to Chicago should the unknown dare to emerge from his editorial incognito and face Rudy in a fistic encounter.

So much was said on this subject that I was not at all surprised one day to receive a call from Mr. Frank O'Neil, known in sporting circles as "Buck" O'Neil, who is the boxing expert on *The New York Evening Journal*. Buck told me that, privately, he very much doubted Valentino's reputed ability as an athlete; and that, just for his own satisfaction, he would like to stage a little friendly bout.

He assured me very confidentially that he would not hurt Rudy, whereupon I rather bumptiously told him that he would be so much better to look out for himself, as Rudy packed a wicked punch. Let me state here that Buck O'Neil in his gym clothes weighed approximately one hundred and ninety-five pounds and was six feet one inch in height, while Rudy at that time weighed one hundred and sixty-seven pounds and was five feet eleven in height.

So confident was I of the outcome that, without consulting Rudy, I gave my consent to this plan, and we arranged to have the bout on the roof of the Ambassador Hotel the following afternoon.

When I told Rudy of this plan his only comment was:

"That's great!"

Not one word had been said about the difference in size and weight and not one question had Rudy asked about his antagonist. Just a single, "That's great!": this was that lad's spirit.

Accordingly, at the appointed hour, they met on the roof of the Ambassador; both posed obligingly for the usual stills. Then, to the accompaniment of the grinding of motion picture cameras, the two pugilist fell to.

At first they boxed very lightly, until Buck curled a beautiful left to Rudy's chin, his first intimation that the thing was serious.

With that, Rudy pulled himself together and began to fight. He aimed a short jab at Buck's jaw, but O'Neil ducked and caught it on the side of his head and went down to the gravel of the roof. Instantly Rudy was beside him, helping him up and apologizing profusely for letting that one slip.

Buck was game. He just laughed it off and said that that was what he had tried to do to Rudy, but failed.

They went at it again for a while, and Buck's tactics were confined to what is known as turtle shell covering; he was protecting himself and occasionally lashing out with either hand.

I recall at one time that he landed one on Rudy's nose, and I can truthfully say that the blow hurt me more than it did him, fearing as I did that some damage might be done to that important screen asset.

Later, when Buck O'Neil was taking a shower in my bathroom, he turned to me and said:

"Don't make any mistake! That boy has a punch like a mule's kick. I'd sure hate to have him sore at me!"

When we went down to dinner that night, O'Neil was enthusiastically urging upon Valentino to the possibilities of a pugilistic career, should he ever care to give up pictures.

The next day Rudy saw his brother and family off to Paris on the S.S. France.

Not waiting to see the ship sail, we jumped into a taxi and drove post haste to another pier, where General Nobile was sailing on an Italian liner. Rudy said good-by to him and congratulated him again on his successful flight over the North Pole.

The next day his picture, *The Son of the Sheik,* was to open at the Mark Strand Theater.

From early morning the crowds had begun to gather for the eleven o'clock performance. The double line stretched two blocks in each direction, and, when we arrived with a small party about two o'clock, to attend the afternoon performance, traffic was blocked.

The heat was terrific, the thermometer registering around ninety-eight degrees; yet that huge aggregation of people was standing quietly, neither pushing nor crowding, waiting patiently their turn to be admitted. They fanned themselves and wiped perspiring faces. I distinctly remember that there was no laughing nor apparent lightness of thought. It seems rather that earnestness and respect animated the crowd, as if a desire to see a great artist rather than a popular movie star motivated them.

Inside the theater there was hardly standing room. The picture was received with acclaim and, at the close, Rudy made his appearance and gave one of his gracious charming speeches, extemporaneous as usual, and captivated his hearers.

To quote one of those little speeches of Valentino in cold print probably would not convey to the reader anything of its charm which came mostly from Rudy's gallant presence, his flashing eyes, and his all too rare smiles. I myself, well as I knew him, invariably yielded to his fascination as a speaker and felt myself carried along as inevitably as he swayed his unknown friends in his great audiences.

I do not say that the enthusiasm of his fans was not sufficient in itself to create the scenes which followed, but I think that his little speeches increased their ardor considerably.

When we reached the stage door on our way out, such a sight met our eyes that we were in despair. Between three and four thousand people were jammed around the entrance, against whose volume the ten policemen detailed to clear a pathway for us were of no avail. They simply added ten more to the number.

Milling and pushing, the crowd choked every foot of space up to the door itself. Our automobile was only a little black spot, like an oasis in a desert. We sent ahead of us the other members of our little party, Aileen Pringle, Jimmie Quirk and Major McCutcheon, who reached the car in safety.

The people were waiting for *Valentino.*

Then I started, with Rudy behind me, his hands on my shoulders. In this fashion we plowed our way though the crowd, as if we were carrying a football to the goal.

I was safe, but the crowds snatched at Rudy, tearing off his tie, grabbing his pocket handkerchief, ripping buttons from his coat and even tearing the cuff links from his shirt. Somebody, somewhere, has a hat belonging to Rudolph Valentino.

The poor boy was almost torn to bits, but he was laughing at his predicament until a woman fan, more frenzied than the others,

217

jumped on the running board of our car just as it started to move and was torn off by the crowd. She fell to the pavement with a thud which startled all of us, but Rudy was most concerned. He endeavored to have the chauffeur stop the car, but before it could be done the woman had been swallowed up in the crowd and could not be found.

Valentino's anxiety, however, was not sufficiently allayed; upon our arrival at the hotel, he had me telephone all the police stations to see if a woman victim of an automobile accident had been reported. Upon receiving a negative answer, he was greatly relieved.

Strange to say, Rudy seemed rather quiet after his ovation at the Mark Strand, whereas the rest of us were very much excited.

We separated soon after this. Aileen Pringle, Jimmie Quirk and Major McCutcheon went to their homes to dress, with the agreement to meet later for dinner.

Rudy's quiet mood continued, so much so that we fell into a most serious conversation. In moments like these I most appreciated the quality of the boy's friendship for me. He trusted me as a son might trust a beloved father, and he confided to me his reactions to every occurrence in his life, both physical and mental, insofar as a gentleman might.

At this particular time he talked to me of his ambitions. One thing in particular, I remember, was his plan, immediately upon his return to Hollywood, to go in seriously for piano lessons, for which instrument he had a natural aptitude. He said that he intended to let no one, not even his closest friends, know of his work until he was prepared to be able to play commendably, regardless of the amount of time this would take.

In this I realized two things. One was his love of the dramatic, and the other his boyish desire to spring a surprise on his friends.

He talked to me of marriage. He asked me if I thought it would ever be wise for him to marry a girl who was not in pictures. My answer is irrelevant. I only quote his words to show his mind was not made up even at this late hour, and that questionings as to the propriety of marrying this or that woman who had taken his fancy for the moment were bubbling in the back of his mind.

Just here it might be well to answer, once and for all, the question which was hurled at me by reporters and feature writers every time the train stopped on our transcontinental journeys or upon our arrival at theater or hotels. And that was: were Pola Negri and Valentino engaged?

I repeat that, although I was entirely in his confidence, he never told me so, and I never asked him.

When reporters put the question directly to Rudy, his gallant reply was, invariably:

"Ask the lady!"

He did tell me, however, that until he had completed his career he had no intention of marrying anybody.

After this we dressed for the evening, and Rudy gave his disheveled suit to Frank, his valet, for much needed repairs.

We started out, first picking up Jean Acker at her home and later meeting the rest of the party, which had then been augmented by Donald Freeman, Hal Fyfe and Ben Ali Haggin.

We had dinner together and then went to Texas Guinan's, where an incident occurred which I thought rather remarkable.

Texas, who, by the way, is an attractive woman and a marvelous hostess, brought over to our table the fakir Rahmin Bey, then at the height of his fame as an exponent of magic.

Rudy, as usual, was much interested; again his overpowering curiosity to get at the secrets of a puzzle animated him. Rahmin Bey told Valentino that, if he would permit, he, Rahmin, would thrust a needle through Valentino's cheek without pain and without drawing blood.

Rudy was game and would have allowed this had I not intervened, whereupon Rudy offered to allow the test to be made upon his arm.

Rahmin Bey being agreeable, Rudy then stood up, stripped off his coat and rolled up his shirt sleeve.

With the eyes of every one in the night club upon him, Rudy submitted to the thrusting of the needle through the flesh of his forearm, and gazed upon it with amazement. The needle being withdrawn, without blood and without pain, as Rahmin promised, Rudy laughed, pulled down his shirt sleeve and resumed his supper as if nothing happened. But I, fearing an infection, sent for alcohol and thoroughly cleansed his arm with the antiseptic.

During the time we were in New York, Rudy revived the acquaintance of Mal St. Clair, Sigrid Holmquist, Greta Nissen, Ann

Pennington, Barclay Warburton and his sister Mary Brown Warburton, Schuyler Parsons, and many others of social and theatrical renown.

He spent several very happy week-ends with Mr. Parsons on his estate at Great Neck.

I was cognizant of his affection for Jean Acker and the quiet happiness he had in her company. The frankness with which he told her of his troubles and his life since they had parted gave further evidence of the understanding which still existed between them.

The following week we left for Chicago, for an appearance at the Roosevelt Theater, where his picture was to be shown. Here we were literally besieged by sporting editors, feature writers and reporters, who camped on our trail wanting to know if there was to be a fight with the *Tribune* editor, until Rudy consented to go to a gymnasium to demonstrate his prowess.

Although he was always willing to wrestle or box, at this time he was particularly glad to give publicity to anything which would throw a true light on his ability to hold his own in everything pertaining to manly sports, thus offering his undesirable and undeserved reputation as a dandy, as exploited in the abusive "pink powder puff" editorial.

Having given for two weeks or more, the opportunity to the anonymous writer of the before quoted "Pink Powder Puff" insult, Valentino then issued the following statement, which he gave to the press, the only paper in Chicago which failed to quote it being *The Tribune*, a thing, of course, which it could not very well afford to do, since it had been the source of the attack.

"It is evident you cannot make a coward fight any more than you can draw blood out of a turnip. The heroic silence of the writer who chose to attack me without any provocation in the Chicago Tribune leaves no doubt as to the total absence of manliness in his whole makeup.

I feel I have been vindicated because I consider his silence as a tacit retraction, and an admission which I am forced to accept even though it is not entirely to my liking.

The newspaper men and women whom it has been my privilege to know briefly or for a longer time have been so absolutely fair and so loyal to their profession and their publications, that I need hardly say how conspicuous is this exception to the newspaper profession. "

I want it understood that the vehemence with which I denounce the anonymous writer of this cowardly attack upon my friend is not based so much upon what the article contained as upon the deep hurt it gave Rudy, embittering as it did the last days of his life and, in my opinion, hastening his death.

Who knows but that, in those last days when he was conscious, able to think, and undisturbed by visitors, his mind might not have dwelt on his inability to avenge the insult and that, had his last hours been more free from anxiety, his power to cope with the inroads of the septic poisoning might have been increased, and possibly his life spared.

This will always be a moot question with me. And with others who have not been slow to express a similar opinion. For this reason, to the day of my death, this question will be unanswered.

It is only fair to say that the last paragraph in Valentino's statement, quoted above, is absolutely true. The United Artists as well as Mr. Valentino himself subscribed to the press clipping bureaus, by means of which we were informed of practically everything printed about our stars. And I reiterate that never before has anything come to our attention so bitterly worded, so personal, so far-fetched and entirely uncalled for as *The Chicago Tribune* editorial.

After the opening performance of *The Son of the Sheik*, the huge Roosevelt Theater was packed to suffocation with an audience composed of the literary, dramatic, social and artistic lights of the city. It was said that never before, even at Grand Opera, had such a characteristically cosmopolitan audience been gathered.

The suburbs had emptied themselves, and the hotels were filled with out of town guests who had come to Chicago for this notable occasion. When Valentino made his appearance upon the stage, he was greeted with applause the like of which only Theodore Roosevelt, for whom the theater was named, had known.

The acclaim lasted several minutes, forcing Valentino to stand, smiling and embarrassed, while the enthusiasm spent itself.

Doubtless inspired by his sensational reception, Rudy made what I consider the best speech of his life, receiving upon its conclusion a similarly vociferous acclaim, together with shouts of his name.

That evening after the theater, we were the supper guests of the brilliant young State's attorney, Michael Romano, who was a close personal friend of Valentino.

The next day we left on the Twentieth Century Limited for New York, where we found that the Associated Press dispatch had given wide publicity to Valentino's second defiance of his unknown assailant.

Here we stayed a week, which time Rudy employed in enjoying himself, turning day into night and having, as he expressed, the time of his life.

An amusing incident which occurred during this period comes to my mind. One morning, very early, I was awakened by Rudy, who came to my room. He touched me on the shoulder. There I saw him standing, still in his evening clothes, with a glass of ice cold Vichy in his hand.

"Would you like some water?" he asked.

I rubbed my eyes.

"Why this C.P.R. Service?" I inquired.

"Oh, I thought you might be thirsty!"

"You mean," I said, "that you are bringing me this peace offering, hoping that I will not scold you for getting home at five o'clock in the morning!"

"Well," said Rudy sheepishly, "I did intend to ask you to see that I was not disturbed until noon. I'm going to lunch with Jean at one."

The glass of ice cold Vichy I found refreshing after all, as New York is no summer resort; so I let Rudy laugh that one off.

When we went down to Atlantic City we motored, leaving New York at noon and arriving at five o'clock. We were halted on the outskirts by an escort consisting of the Acting Mayor, ten motorcycle policemen, and hundreds of fans in automobiles, which fell in behind our car, and made quite a triumphal procession.

Valentino's appearance had been well advertised. An enormous crowd greeted him at the Ritz-Carlton. Here he found his old friend Gus Edwards, who was then running one of his famous reviews at the hotel, and who begged Rudy to come down as his guest, as soon as he had finished making his appearance at the Virginia Theater, where the picture was to open.

In spite of the heat, Rudy promised.

Our attempt to get from the Ritz-Carlton to the Virginia was the most riotous thing I ever experienced. The crowds were suffocating, the largest and most insistent we had ever seen. The ten policemen who attempted to clear a path so that we could get to the waiting car were of no avail whatsoever. They were simply in the way.

When we finally plowed our way to the automobile and got in, both of us had to settle our disordered clothing. The car crawled at a snail's pace, being blocked before and at each side by the crowds of men and women who leaped upon the running boards and thrust their hands in at the open windows. Rudy shook hands with as many as he could reach, quite pleased with these expressions of interest.

When we reached the theater some fifteen minutes later, we had the same trouble in gaining the entrance. As we entered, we could hear the shouts of the audience attempting to silence the announcer, who was vainly endeavoring to quiet their impatience by telling them that Valentino was on the way.

Very quietly Rudy walked on stage and tapped the announcer on the shoulder. The latter turned with a start.

The great audience was so instantly silenced that you could have heard a pin drop. Then a roar of welcoming applause burst forth which lasted at least three minutes.

It gives me the greatest satisfaction to recall that picture of Rudolph Valentino, as he stood before that vast audience, radiant with health and happiness, smiling boyishly at the sincerity of his welcome. If I had known that death stalked so near, I could not have wished him any greater joy than came to him during the last five public appearances at the showing of *The Son of the Sheik*. It proved to me, beyond any doubt, that Valentino was indeed the outstanding idol of the screen.

Again he made one of his delightful impromptu speeches, thanking the audiences for its appreciation of his efforts and impressing them and me anew with his charm and dignity. At the risk of being considered a bore I repeat that, had Valentino been making a request for contributions for a worthy philanthropy, it is my opinion that he could have turned people's pockets wrong side out.

Then we made our way through the crowds to the broadcasting station on the Steel Pier. While we were waiting for Rudy's scheduled time for going on the air, the crowd surged around, climbing on each other's shoulders and almost breaking the windows in their attempt to see the star.

If the fan letters which poured into the station after this speech of Rudy's are any criterion, he must have been as much of a success on the air as ever he was on the screen.

Back at the hotel later, Rudy kept his promise of going to Gus Edward's Revue. Just as we were entering I saw him rush up to a man, seize him by both hands and pour forth a torrent of voluble Italian, to which the other responded with equal excitement.

I asked what the trouble was, fearing the worst, but Rudy reassured me saying that he was not quarreling. That he was a man whom he had asked for a job as bus boy at the Ritz-Carlton in New York when he first came to America, but was refused because the man thought he would be no good.

Gus Edwards seized upon Rudy and introduced him to the audience. He said that, having heard of the bout with Buck O'Neil, he took pleasure in this publicity by presenting him with a pair of boxing gloves. He complimented Rudy upon his fistic ability, of which he had seen samples, and suggested that Rudy use these gloves on the Chicago editor.

Later in the evening, Edwards asked Valentino if he would dance the tango with the professional dancer in his revue. At first Rudy demurred, but finally consented, and danced the tango that he made famous in *The Four Horsemen*.

This was the last time Valentino ever danced the tango.

Chapter 15

Back to New York and a hot drive.

In the ensuing two weeks Rudy had nothing to do except make one public appearance, at the Strand Theater in Brooklyn.

Here the same scenes were enacted. The same heat. The same crowds. The only difference was that in his speech, which he made slightly longer than usual, he paid a fine tribute to Agnes Ayres for the high quality of her sportsmanship in accepting so small a part in *The Son of the Sheik,* since by doing so she had established an important sequence which greatly added to the success of the picture. He also spoke of her in a different role, that of wife and mother, picturing her in her charming Hollywood home and referring to her as the mother of a lovely baby. He spoke with so much tenderness of this home picture of the famous movie star as a mother, and described the baby in words of such sincerity that the audience was touched almost to tears, and again there shone in his eyes that indescribable expression which came into them only when he was speaking of children.

Rudy had promised the Stanley Company to make a personal appearance at their Philadelphia theater, where *The Son of the Sheik* was to be shown, and, although he was by this time getting just a little restive under inaction and anxious to get back to work, he would not break his word. Thus he filled in his time in New York between August second and the sixteenth, which was his Philadelphia date. Only death prevented him from keeping this promise.

On the Saturday evening before his final collapse I noticed that his color was bad, and urged him to come home early and get some rest.

As if summoning all his strength, with fire again in his eyes, he said:

"Why, I feel wonderful! I don't need rest!"

I could not help a feeling of anxiety which remained with me all night. Rudy's color was usually so marvelous that any change in it could not fail to attract my attention.

At the first groan from him the next morning I was at his side, and one look at him was enough. Immediately I summoned physicians who, after a hurried consultation, rushed him to the Polyclinic Hospital, where he was operated on at six o'clock that evening.

At seven the operation was over, and at ten thirty he came from under the influence of the ether.

I want to call attention of the entire world to the first statement Valentino made when he was conscious.

"Well," he said, "did I behave like a pink powder puff or like a man?"

Which goes to prove my contention that the editorial in *The Chicago Tribune* had a distinct bearing on Rudy's life. And if, in future, editors wishing to cast slurs on those with whom they have no personal acquaintance should be restrained by this unfortunate occurrence, Valentino's suffering will not have been in vain.

At first no one, not even the surgeons who operated, the physicians in attendance, or the nurses, had any doubt as to the outcome. We all thought Rudy would recover. And when telegrams from all over the country began to pour in expressing anxiety, our first impulse was to reassure his friends and to communicate our hopefulness by means of the public press.

I once expressed to him the fervent wish that I might be suffering in his place, leaving him to go on with this work without interruption, and his reply was:

"Don't be silly! You have a wife and little children, family responsibilities, whereas I...." And he turned his face to the wall.

Later I asked him whether I should send for his brother, to which he replied:

"By no means. Just cable him that I am a little indisposed and will soon be all right. And wire Pola the same."

These almost deathbed statements of my friend are so sacred to me that I would not willingly distort them by so much as a misplaced word, and I quote those which are necessary to this narrative.

He asked for no one and slept almost all the time. He felt no pain and only expressed himself as being "so tired."

By physicians' orders, no one was allowed to see him nor even to go near his room, for the purpose of enforcing which, I stationed a detective at his door to see that even nurses not on his case could not gain admittance. Notwithstanding the broadcasting of these orders, people continuously tried, by every known ruse, to gain admittance to the hospital and even to storm the corridor in which Valentino was fighting for his life.

Telegrams now began to arrive in such numbers that I was obliged to summon my secretary to handle them. To say that flowers arrived by the truck-load is not to exaggerate.

When he was able to bear a little conversation, I told Rudy about the telegrams and flowers, as well as the special delivery letters and notes sent by hand or by messenger, and explained to him that, owing to the necessity of keeping the air in his room pure, he could only have a few flowers in his room at a time.

Without waiting for me to suggest it, he told me to see that the free wards in the hospital were supplied with his flowers every day.

It was typical of Valentino that he invariably wished to share whatever happiness he had with others.

One day he surprised me be asking for a mirror. I was loath to humor him, as his illness had left marks upon his face I did not wish him to see. He seemed to read my thoughts for he said:

"Oh, let me have it! I just want to see how I look when I am sick, so that if I ever have to play the part in pictures I will know how to put on my make-up!"

Thus he, too, had no premonition of the short time he had to live.

He was certainly on the road to recovery and, as late as Saturday morning at one-thirty, when Mrs. Ullman and I left him, no one had expressed any anxiety as to the outcome.

Nevertheless I was uneasy. I do not say that I had a premonition. I only know that after I had taken Mrs. Ullman to the hotel and bathed, instead of going to bed I dressed myself again and went back to the hospital, arriving there before five o'clock in the morning.

It was still dark, and the night shift of nurses was still on. Rudy was asleep; but I got his chart from the night nurse and saw, to my consternation, that both his pulse and respiration had increased. Whereupon I immediately telephoned the four physicians to come at once, which they did.

A little before seven Rudy wakened, smiled at me and said:

"I feel fine now. The pain is all gone and I can feel the place where they made the incision. By Monday I think we can have Joe and

227

Norma in, and by Wednesday I will go back to the hotel, taking the nurses, of course."

The doctors then made a thorough examination, and afterwards held a consultation lasting almost an hour. There was the most complete discussion of the symptoms, in which they frankly stated that the sudden cessation of pain was an exceedingly bad sign.

I was by this time so much alarmed that I asked the doctors to cancel all other engagements, put substitutes on their cases and never be beyond call, as the case of Valentino was too important for us to run even the slightest risk.

From this time on, Rudy waged courageously his failing fight with death.

Unwilling to leave any stone unturned, I called in another specialist, in the hope that he might have new ideas or be able to suggest something which had not occurred to the others. Every possible method was discussed, even to blood transfusion, but all were discarded one after another as being impracticable.

That night no one slept, and a dreadful air of suspense hung over the entire hospital. The doctors were again forced to issue bulletins and in silence crowds slowly began to gather in the streets, eager for the word of hope which never came.

Early Sunday morning I went again to his bedside and even my unpracticed eyes saw that he was sinking rapidly. His fever had increased, and his pulse more rapid.

Realizing that were he able to think clearly he would probably wish to see a confessor, I sent for Father Leonard, who had frequently called up during his illness to ask how he was.

The priest came at my summons and was alone with the dying man for some time. When he came out his face was uplifted and I saw the interview had been satisfactory. Later when I saw that Rudy was calmer, I felt that I had done right.

Knowing that what was to be done must be done quickly, I telephoned to Mr. Schenck and his wife Norma Talmadge, who were visiting Adolph Zukor in his home in New York City. Also to Frank Mennillo, one of Rudy's dearest Italian friends.

About half past four, Mr. and Mrs. Schenck arrived and Norma waited in another room while I took Mr. Schenck into the sick room.

At first we thought Rudy was asleep; but, sensing our presence, he opened his eyes and said, in a weak voice:

"Mighty nice of you to come to see me. How is Norma? How is Connie?"

Totally unable to control his feelings despite his best efforts, Mr. Schenck stood there, holding Rudy's hand, tears running down his cheeks. Finally he pulled himself together enough to say:

"Everybody's fine! And-and you must get well, too!"

Rudy forced a smile so wan that it belied his brave words, and said:

"I'll be all right."

Nothing more was said, and we went out to where Norma was anxiously waiting, so deeply moved that she was almost on the verge of a collapse.

Early in the evening Frank Mennillo arrived, and, after I broke the news to him of Rudy's serious condition, we went in and he spoke to Rudy in Italian. But Rudy answered, in English:

"Thank you, Frank. I'm going to be well soon."

All during the night the doctors, Frank Mennillo and I kept watch. I went into Rudy's room at least every hour, but found that he was sleeping quietly, until about four o'clock Monday morning, when I observed that he was tossing about and in great pain.

At once I called the doctors, who came hurriedly and did everything they could to revive him.

About six o'clock,when I was again in the room, Rudy recognized me and called me by name in a voice much stronger that I felt encouraged, until he went on to say:

"Wasn't it an awful thing that we were lost in the woods last night?"

Too shocked to reply, I simply stroked his hair. He looked up at me and said:

"On the one hand you don't appreciate the humor of that do you?"

I tried to smile and said:

"Sure I do, Rudy. Sure, I do."

A quizzical look came into his eyes and he said again:

"On the other hand, you don't seem to appreciate the seriousness of it either."

Fearing to excite him further, I turned away, hoping that he would drop off to sleep, I went to the window to pull down the blinds, since the sun was just rising and the room was growing light.

I turned at the sound of his voice. He waved a feeble hand and, with a wistful smile just touching his lips, he said:

"Don't pull down the blinds! I feel fine. I want the sunlight to greet me."

I turned with a start, for I could not fail to sense that the light he referred to was that of another world.

These were the last intelligible words he ever spoke.

Hurriedly I summoned an Italian priest, thinking that possibly Rudy might wish to say something in his native tongue to a confessor, but when he arrived Rudy was too far gone to answer, and only muttered one Italian word, which no one could understand.

So died Rudolph Valentino. Gallantly, as he had lived.

The End.

The Life of S. George Ullman

Although S. George Ullman was a classically trained violinist he is not remembered today for his mastery of the violin. It would be his affiliation with silent movie icon, Rudolph Valentino that would grant him distinction in Hollywood history. As of this writing it has been eighty-eight years since Valentino's untimely death in 1926, yet George Ullman continues to command a dominant role in any film production, publication or discussion on the subject of Rudolph Valentino. Although little has been known about this pioneer in celebrity management, George Ullman has been portrayed on screen and written about for decades.

His professional and personal relationship with Valentino was complex and involved. Consequently, for Valentino's fans and film history buffs the mere mention of the name George Ullman still generates controversy. One fact, however, is indisputable; during the dawn of Hollywood's Golden Age, S. George Ullman gained international recognition as Rudolph Valentino's trusted mentor, best friend and business manager. Yet Ullman's fierce devotion to his friend "Rudy" would ultimately result in a descent from this pinnacle of prestige and professional power and cast him into a thirty year legal morass. His extraordinary story began just before the turn of the twentieth century.

George Ullman was born on September 19, 1893, to Joseph and Anna Ullmann. Perhaps the midwife filing the report of his birth was in err or his parents neglected to record their change of heart. For the name on Ullman's birth certificate reads, Simon Joseph Ullmann. In later years, George eliminated the second "n" in his surname and was known as, Simon, or "S." George Ullman.

George Ullman's parents were immigrants; his father from Hungary and his mother from Germany. Father Joseph earned his living as a master tailor with his clientele including some of New York's wealthiest and finely dressed gentlemen. When their son George was born, Joseph and Anna resided at 1606 Avenue B in New York City.

George Ullman was the third born of the Ullmann's four sons

and a bright and scholarly child demonstrating an early passion for classical music and an aptitude for writing. The precocious boy became such an accomplished violinist he was soon giving lessons to other aspiring young virtuosos in the neighborhood. This inspired George Ullman's dream of one day conducting a symphonic orchestra.

Joseph and Anna Ullmann never tired of listening to their son practicing the violin and were confident his promising future was guaranteed. They never imagined his life and legacy would be defined instead by a chance meeting with movie star Rudolph Valentino.

On December 8, 1915, a twenty-two year old George Ullman enlisted for a brief but eventful stint in the National Guard in New York City. The ledgers of the National Guard's New York Field Artillery's Battery D of the First Regiment list two Ullman brothers as privates first class. George Ullman's younger brother Leo was also included on the First Regiment's roster.

Ullman's National Guard record cites his horsemanship as "fair," his character as "excellent," his hair black, complexion dark, height at five feet seven inches and his occupation as "advertising solicitor." In June of 1916, Battery D's First Regiment was mustered into federal service and dispatched to Texas and New Mexico to join the Pancho Villa Expedition. President Woodrow Wilson summoned some 12,000 troops in a campaign to suppress the invasion of U.S. territory by the rebel general of the Mexican Revolution, Pancho Villa. For a few months during the summer of 1916, George Ullman and his brother Leo rode the Texas plains with the provisional cavalry division in an effort to bring Pancho Villa to justice.

In May of 1917, George Ullman received an Honorable Discharge from the National Guard by reason of, "dependent relatives." Ullman had just married his eighteen-year old sweetheart, Beatrice Mallet, who preferred her nickname, Bee. After their marriage, Ullman worked for the Federal Reserve Bank during the day and by night he attended law school. He earned additional income pursuing his passion for boxing. His career in the ring was not lengthy and by 1918, he terminated all boxing matches and his law school classes to attend night school at New York University where he studied Industrial Engineering. Ullman devoted three years to this relatively new field of study and was eager to establish himself in this field as by then he was supporting a family. On October 18, 1918, George Ullman and his wife, Bee's first child, Daniel was born.

232

Over the course of the next few years, Ullman was employed as a consultant offering his expertise in industrial engineering to businesses in the New York area. In the fall of 1922, he was hired by the Mineralava Beauty Clay Company to troubleshoot the company's flagging profits. Ullman proposed a cross-country celebrity promotional tour to boost the company's sales and he was hired to act as road manager for the three month long journey. The celebrity hired to represent Mineralava Beauty Clay happened to be Rudolph Valentino. From this moment on, Ullman and Valentino's lives would be inexorably involved.

At the time, Valentino was on strike from his employer, Famous Players-Lasky and unable to work as an actor until his existing contract with the studio expired. He and his wife, Natacha Rambova accepted the Mineralava Company's offer to perform as featured stage dancers while extolling the virtues of Mineralava's beauty clay. The tour was Ullman's brainchild, the first of its kind and an unqualified success. By the end of the tour in the spring of 1923, Ullman had not only become Rudolph Valentino's close friend and confidant but also his business manager.

On July 6, 1923, Rudolph Valentino and George Ullman appeared in front of a notary public in New York City and signed a contract naming Ullman as Valentino's sole business manager. One month later, on August 13, 1923, Bee Ullman gave birth to the Ullman's second son, Robert. Rudolph Valentino insisted on becoming baby "Bobby" Ullman's proud godfather.

As soon as Ullman assumed his position as Valentino's business manager, he discovered that neither Valentino nor his wife Natacha Rambova demonstrated any ability in managing their finances. Ullman set out to bring order to the Valentino financial household by clearing their substantial debt and settling many legal collection processes. Ullman also negotiated a swift resolution to Valentino's strike against Famous Players-Lasky by securing a new contract which guaranteed the movie star artistic control over his films and an immediate return to the screen.

As Valentino completed his contractual obligations, Ullman negotiated a new contract with Ritz-Carlton Pictures. As these films would be produced in Los Angeles, the Valentinos left New York to move west. George Ullman joined the Valentinos and relocated his family to Southern California. On November 24, 1924 the Ullman's arrived in Hollywood with their sons, six-year old Daniel and one-year old Bobby. They rented their first home in Los Angeles but soon purchased a home at 701 Foothill Drive in Beverly Hills. The backyard of their Foothill Road home would be the site of many fond childhood memories for Dan and Bob Ullman. It was there that their father sparred with his sons and where "Uncle Rudy" would become a frequent and favored visitor.

Today Ullman's multifaceted position would be filled by a full staff including not only a business manager but a publicist, a bodyguard, a personal assistant, an accountant and press agent. While fulfilling all of these roles, Ullman continued to secure lucrative screen contracts for Valentino. The movie star quickly grew so dependent upon his stalwart friend and manager he rarely made a move without his advice.

At the time, holding the position of Rudolph Valentino's business manager granted Ullman considerable caché in Hollywood. By 1926, Valentino's popularity was at its peak and George and Bee Ullman enjoyed a comfortable lifestyle and counted the Valentino's and film industry's elite among their closest friends.

George and Bee Ullman's glamorous life in Hollywood would be short-lived. Less than two years after their move to California, Rudolph Valentino's sudden death on August 23, 1926, devastated Ullman both personally and professionally. The strain of managing the international response to the movie star's death, including the ensuing riots in New York outside of Campbell's Funeral Home, overwhelmed George Ullman. He would later write that this was one of the most difficult times in his life.

His work for and involvement with Valentino did not cease with his friend's death. This came about due to Rudolph Valentino's vague Last Will and Testament which left few of his affairs in order. As Valentino's executor, George Ullman was charged to negotiate the settlement of the star's heavily-involved estate. Complicating matters in this regard, Valentino's older brother, Alberto, arrived from Italy to contest his deceased brother's will and petition the court to have George Ullman removed as executor.

As Ullman responded to this legal challenge from Alberto Valentino, he endeavored to generate income for Valentino's debt-ridden estate. By promoting the star's last two movies, *The Eagle* and *The Son of the Sheik*, Ullman was able to keep Valentino's production company, Rudolph Valentino Productions profitable. He also organized a memorial gathering before Valentino's crypt in Hollywood to commemorate the day of his death and founded many memorial guilds across the country with the purpose of promoting the showings of Valentino's movies. In this manner, George Ullman strategically broadened Rudolph Valentino's post-mortem commercial appeal.

The court rejected Alberto Valentino's petition to have Ullman removed as executor and this permitted Ullman to fulfill his dual role as executor of Valentino's estate and as head of Rudolph Valentino Productions. This would not be the last time Alberto Valentino challenged George Ullman in court. For Ullman's dual role and his very authority as executor became the crux of what would become a prolonged legal exchange between the two men.

Ullman asserted that his authority to act in this dual role was explained to him personally by Rudolph Valentino. He remained adamant Valentino imparted oral instructions to him as to how he wished his estate to be dispersed. Ullman stated these instructions were to have been attached as a second page to Valentino's original will. Unfortunately for Ullman, when Valentino's will was filed with the Los Angeles Probate Court, it consisted of a single page document. With no copy of this critical document of instructions in hand, Ullman's defense against Alberto Valentino's charges was considerably weakened.

The existing one page, Last Will and Testament of Rudolph Valentino appointed George Ullman as executor and appeared to specify estate funds be dispersed to Valentino's brother Alberto Valentino, his sister Maria Strada and his ex-wife Natacha Rambova's aunt, Teresa Werner. Ullman recalled that the instructions contained within the missing second page of Valentino's will, clarified specific amounts be disbursed to these three heirs apparent.

Ullman was under great pressure to generate profits and bring the Valentino estate into solvency. He continued in his role as head of Rudolph Valentino Productions and aggressively promoted Valentino's last two films, investing all profits and dispersing money as weekly stipends in specific amounts to Alberto Valentino, Maria Strada and Teresa Werner. In this effort, Ullman was successful in generating sufficient income for the estate, clear the nearly $200,000.00 debt and show a profit.

However, Alberto Valentino remained adamant he was entitled

to more than a weekly stipend and protested to the court claiming Ullman was basing his actions as executor upon a second page of the will which he claimed never existed. When no copy of these instructions could be found to support Ullman's memory of Valentino's oral instructions, he had no other option but to accommodate Alberto Valentino's requests and disburse cash advances from Rudolph Valentino Production accounts to the heirs apparent.

While Ullman responded to the continued legal petitions from Alberto Valentino, he also continued to manage Rudolph Valentino's post-mortem business and do so from the office of his own talent agency on Sunset Boulevard, The S. George Ullman Agency. Ullman founded his business in 1928, in anticipation of the final settlement of the Valentino estate. On April 4, of that same year, the Ullman's celebrated the arrival of their third child, a baby girl. At the time, silent screen vamp, Theda Bara, lived across the street from the Ullmans. As she was immersed in the study of numerology and astrology, her gift to her friends upon the birth of her daughter was the divination of their baby's perfect name, Brenda. As the baby happened to be born at Easter time, baby Brenda's five-year old brother Bobby renamed his sister, Bunny.

Before baby Bunny was a year old, Bee Ullman fell gravely ill with tuberculosis. In a desperate surgical maneuver to save the young woman's life, doctors collapsed and removed one of her lungs. Bee Ullman's recovery was lengthy and required several subsequent surgeries over the next ten years. In one procedure, several of her ribs were removed.

As George Ullman cared for his ailing wife, he devoted as many hours as possible to rebuilding his career as an artist representative. Although George would never again represent a star with the earning power of Rudolph Valentino, he did represent some stars of note, including John Carradine, Francis Lederer, Constantine Shane and character actor, Jack Kruschen. A few of Ullman's clients became his personal friends and visited as guests in his home. When he represented actor Frank Orth, he and his wife, vaudeville star, Ann Codee, spent many Saturday nights in the Ullman's home. Ann Codee was a virtuoso pianist and often accompanied Ullman on his violin. George Ullman also became a life-long friend of a young radio host, Jack Paar.

During one evening soireé in the Ullman home, one of

Ullman's clients, Erich Von Stroheim, tumbled into the backyard fish pond after one too many cocktails. Outfitted in one of Ullman's suits, Von Stroheim stumbled back to the garden party and to the howls of laughter from the other party guests, he toppled a second time into the shallow pond.

Throughout this time, Ullman struggled to find the time and resources to operate his talent agency as he was also required to spend a great deal of his time and money responding to Alberto Valentino's legal challenges. While awaiting the court's approval of his executor's accounts and consequently the final settlement of the Valentino estate, Ullman continued dispersing funds to the three people he believed to be Rudy's rightful heirs. He also invested a portion of Rudolph Valentino Production's profits as secured loans. Although a few of these investments failed to turn a profit, by 1929, Ullman managed to increase the value of Valentino's previously bankrupt estate to nearly $300,000.00. Accomplishing this during the early days of the Great Depression was an impressive achievement by any standard. Nevertheless, Alberto Valentino continued his campaign to impugn Ullman's integrity and have him removed from any position of authority over his brother's business affairs.

In 1930, Alberto Valentino filed a lawsuit against George Ullman charging him with fraud and mismanagement of the Valentino estate. He also petitioned the court to dissolve his deceased brother's production company. It was then Ullman resigned as executor and informed the press he did so to avoid discord clouding the memory of his dear friend, Rudolph Valentino.

This court hearing continued into 1931, with Ullman taking the witness stand many times in his own defense. During these proceedings, a carbon copy of the missing second page of Valentino's will was found and presented to the court by the attorney who originally drew up Valentino's will. This document was declared by the court to be a valid portion of Valentino's will.

Ullman was vindicated by the appearance of the smudged paper which proved he was correct in claiming Rudolph Valentino appointed him to the dual role of managing Rudolph Valentino Productions and executor of the estate. The document also revealed critical information which Ullman failed to recall from Rudolph Valentino's oral version of the instructions. According to the newly discovered portion of the will, Valentino did not leave his estate in a three-way split between his siblings and Teresa Werner. Instead, he left his estate to his sole heir, his "nephew", Jean Valentino. This meant that George Ullman had unknowingly advanced estate funds to the wrong heirs for years.

According to the second page of Rudolph Valentino's will, as sole heir, Jean Valentino held the only legal right to borrow against a future share in the estate. Consequently, executor Ullman was held responsible to reimburse the estate the entire amount he dispensed to the three people he believed to have been the rightful heirs.

Despite the fact Ullman had no access to this missing page of the will and despite the fact a court-ordered audit found no evidence of fraud or mismanagement in his book keeping, early in 1932 the court ruled against him. The judge appeared to deny the reappearance of the long-missing second page of the will and levied a judgment against Ullman totaling $183,754.00 plus 7% interest. By today's standard, this was a judgment of nearly two million dollars. Ullman was ordered to reimburse the estate all money lost from several failed investments made from the profits of Rudolph Valentino Productions, to reimburse the estate a portion of his salary drawn as executor, as well as all of the Rudolph Valentino Production company office and business expenses. He was also ordered to reimburse the estate for all monies advanced to Alberto Valentino, Maria Strada and Teresa Werner. Ullman filed his appeal of the court's ruling.

As a result of this crushing legal decision, Ullman sold his home on Foothill Drive and moved his family into a rented house on Canon Drive in Los Angeles. His real property was then subject to seizure by Jean Valentino and his wages subject to garnishment by the Los Angeles County Sheriff. While Ullman awaited the Appeals Court decision, he supported his family with income from his talent agency and focused his professional efforts on protecting his family and home. Throughout these lean financial times, he found the means to take his wife Bee and their children to summer evening concerts at the Hollywood Bowl.

In 1934, the Appeals Court decision was handed down. Based upon the instructions contained in Rudolph Valentino's revised two page will, the Appeals Court dismissed portions of the lower court's previous ruling by stating that executor George Ullman had correctly maintained his dual role of head of Rudolph Valentino Productions and as executor of the estate. The Appeals Court found no evidence of fraud or mismanagement and ruled Ullman should not be held responsible for losses incurred from his legitimate investments of the production company's profits nor held responsible for any expenses incurred within the course of carrying on the business of Rudolph Valentino Productions. To quote the Appeal Decision document:

" ..when the appellant (George Ullman) resigned after having received a practically bankrupt estate, and having thereafter paid all creditors' claims in excess of $190,000.00 and other expenses, and having advanced some $66,000.00 to the heirs, he (George Ullman) turned over to the petitioner as successor (Alberto Valentino), assets in an appraised value in excess of $300,000.00 and in actual value, as conceded by petitioner (Alberto Valentino) in excess of $100,000.00. With these facts..the District Court of Appeal very naturally and reasonably holds that there was no mismanagement."

The Appeals Court decision allowed Ullman to retain a portion of his salary as executor but held him financially responsible for all of the money he advanced as executor to Alberto Valentino, Maria Strada and Teresa Werner. These disbursements totaled nearly $70,000.00. The Appeals Court recognized the "unusual circumstance" of the missing second page of the will by saying it was unclear to the court how it came to be missing or whether George Ullman had ever had a copy in his possession or ever read the original document.

The Appeals Court decision reaffirmed the disappearance of the second page of the will and explained the fact that George Ullman had not personally benefited from the cash disbursements to the people he rightfully believed to be heirs to the estate. The Appeals Court's recommendation was that a fair and appropriate lien be established against the estate to cover the total amount of the advances. The Appeals Court then deferred any final decision on the subject of the establishment of this lien to Jean Valentino when he turned twenty-five and inherited the estate. With the $70,000.00 worth of disbursements by Ullman temporarily set aside, the Appeals Court reduced the judgment against him to $26,000.00 by stating,

" ..there is not the slightest scintilla of evidence that...he (George Ullman) was not acting in good faith."

On April 18, 1934, a small article appeared in *The Hollywood Reporter* reading,

"Ullman Exonerated in Valentino Estate Row

The District Court of Appeals yesterday exonerated S. George Ullman of charges of mismanagement of the estate of Rudolph Valentino of which he was executor when it reversed an order by the Los Angeles Probate Court. Ullman's management had been objected to by Jean Guglielmi, nephew and heir to the estate who charged Ullman had made too many cash advances to the other heirs. The Appellate Court praised Ullman for his work "

Ullman made his first payment to Jean Valentino of $5600.00, but was unable to immediately pay more against the judgment's principle. Consequently, the interest soared by thousands of dollars. He took solace in the fact that the Appeals Court had found him innocent of any fraud or mismanagement and awaited news as to whether Jean Valentino would hold him responsible for the repayment of the $70,000.00 of advances made to Alberto Valentino, Maria Strada and Teresa Werner.

Upon Ullman's resignation as executor, the Bank of Italy was appointed as administrator of the Valentino estate. Ullman left his position with the estate worth $300,000.00, but less than two years later, it was appraised at only $130,000.00. By the time Jean Valentino inherited the estate from The Bank of Italy on his twenty-fifth birthday, August 14, 1939, the value of the estate had diminished to near insolvency. Jean Valentino's first order of business in assuming his inheritance was to ignore the Appeals Court's recommendation he establish a lien against the estate to recover the monies advanced. Instead, he added the entire $70,000.00 back onto the judgment against Ullman. He then instructed his lawyers to maintain a watchful eye upon George Ullman by offering his legal team a bounty, in the form of a percentage, for whatever amount they could collect on the revised judgment.

By filing notices of wage garnishment and property seizure with the L.A. County Sheriff and issuing subpoenas of the business records of The S. George Ullman Agency, Jean Valentino pursued the collection of the very money Alberto Valentino, Maria Strada and Teresa Werner spent years before. In December of 1952, after years of court scrutiny and garnishment orders failed to uncover any impropriety in Ullman's accounting, Jean Valentino's attorney was asked by the press why his client continued to pursue such a fruitless collection. He replied it was obvious George Ullman could not afford to pay the judgment and admitted Ullman always complied with the court's requests for documentation to prove this fact. The attorney added that Jean Valentino continued to pursue the collection process as he held out hope that perhaps George Ullman would strike it rich one day.

By 1952, the total of the judgment, including interest George Ullman owed Jean Valentino reached $159,949.42. It would be 1956, before Jean Valentino finally dismissed the judgment against Ullman by signing a document titled, "Satisfaction of Judgment" after Ullman made a final payment of $2500.00 .

George Ullman was personally proud of his efforts as executor, especially in regards to his having $61,432.00 of federal tax liens levied against the Rudolph Valentino Production Company abated for over assessment of income taxes and interest. This may be verified by tax records on file as recorded in the L.A. County Library card index number 1-9-4 on October 11, 1931.

George and Bee Ullman lived the last years of their fifty-nine year marriage in their apartment at 8450 DeLongpre Avenue in Hollywood. After Ullman's death in 1975, Bee Ullman moved to Northern California to live with daughter, Bunny and her husband. Despite Bee Ullman's long battle with tuberculosis and surgeries during the 1930's, she lived to be eighty-nine years old.

The Ullman's eldest son, Dan, enjoyed a successful career as a screenplay writer during the 1950's in both television and movies. His work included *A Good Day for a Hanging, The Oklahoman, An Annapolis Story* and *Seven Angry Men*. Dan Ullman died in 1979.

After Rudolph Valentino's godson, Bob Ullman attended Stanford University, he completed a distinguished career as a U.S. Naval Officer and settled in Southern California. He worked as a mortgage banker, fathered two children and was an accomplished tennis player. Due to his father's experiences, Bob Ullman harbored a deep resentment of Hollywood and the motion picture industry. He passed away in August of 2005.

Today, Bunny Ullman and her husband are both retired professionals living in Northern California. They have four children and nine grandchildren.

The facts of George Ullman's story, especially in regards to his tenure as executor of Rudolph Valentino's estate have unfortunately been grossly misrepresented over the years, primarily by the descendents of Alberto and Jean Valentino. Sadly, the truth of his performance and legacy was not publicly available for decades as the case file of Valentino's probate records was stolen from the Los Angeles County Hall of Records. Certified copies of these records verifying Ullman's integrity and history were found only a few years ago and are now publicly available once more. It was due to the recovery of these public records that Ullman has, at along last, been completely exonerated.

The lamentable continuation by some to impugn his legacy defies the evidence filed within the California Appeals Court Library which praise his efforts, high integrity and his life-long loyalty to his friend Rudolph Valentino.

The Photographs

The Ullman brothers – George Ullman on the far right.

George Ullman circa 1910

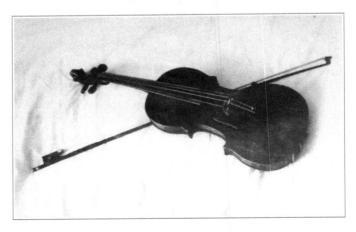

George Ullman's First Violin

George Ullman Circa 1918

George and Bee Ullman

Left to Right – Dan, Bee, Bunny, George and Bobby Ullman

George and Bee Ullman

George Ullman, Bee Ullman and Rudolph Valentino

Left to Right – C. Levee, J.D. Williams, George Ullman Signing the
United Artists Contract

George Ullman with sons Dan and Bobby

George Ullman and sons

George Ullman Circa 1923

Rudolph Valentino with Bobby and Dan Ullman - 1924

Rudolph Valentino and Dan Ullman – 1924

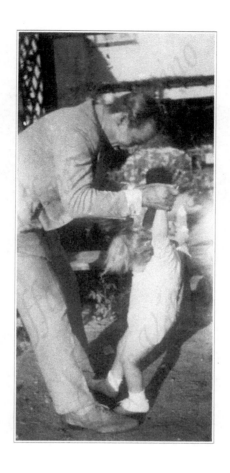

Rudolph Valentino and his Godson, Robert Warren Ullman
1924
"Swing me up too,! Uncle Rudy!"

Bee Ullman

George Ullman, Teresa Werner, Rudolph Valentino and Natacha
Rambova

Bee Ullman and Secretary Clara Trask - Reading Condolences at the
Time of Rudolph Valentino's Death - 1926

Pola Negri and George Ullman Leaving Rudolph Valentino's Funeral
New York City - 1926

Left to Right – E. Carewe, Leroy Mason, George Ullman Negotiate a
Possible Movie on Rudolph Valentino

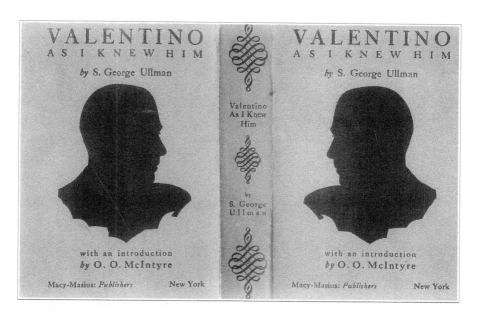

Cover of *Valentino as I Knew Him* by S. George Ullman – 1926

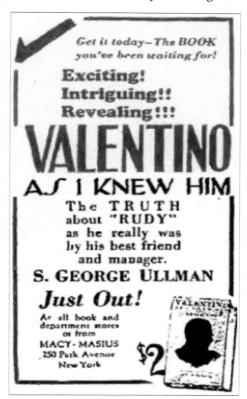

Bee Ullman and Bob Ullman at the Screen Actor's Guild Showing of
The Four Horsemen of the Apocalypse – 1976

The Documents

TO WHOM IT MAY CONCERN:-

MR. S. GEORGE ULLMANN is my sole business
manager. I have none other, and any one other than Mr.
Ullmann representing that he is my business manager
does so entirely without my sanction and authority.
The production of this letter by Mr. Ullmann will
evidence his authority from me to act as my said agent.

Dated, New York, July 6, 1923.

Rudolph Valentino (L.S.)

City, County & State of New York, SS:

On this 6th day of July, 1923, before me personally came RUDOLPH VALENTINO, to me known and known to
me to be the individual described in and who executed the
foregoing authority and he duly acknowledged to me that
he executed the same.

Arthur J. Kremer
Notary Public N.Y. County #93
Comm. Expires Mch 30/1925

Contract Signed Between Rudolph Valentino & George Ullman

September 29, 1926.

Mr. S. George Ullman,
Rudolph Valentino Productions, Inc.
7200 Santa Monica Boulevard,
Los Angeles, California.

Dear Mr. Ullman:

I greatly appreciate your thoughtful courtesy
in sending me the pedigree of "Mission Rudy", following
your kindness in returning the dog to me.

I was very much pleased to greet you and Mrs.
Ullman in my office when you visited San Francisco, and
I too hope that you may both return soon.

With kindest personal regards and again thanking
you for your courtesy, I am

Very sincerely yours,

Mayor.

Letter from San Francisco Mayor Rolph Thanking George Ullman for
the Return of "Mission Rudy"

Mr. S. George Ullman,

Hotel Ambassador.

New York.

Dear Mr. Ullman:

I examined Rudolph Valentino for the first time at 5:15 P.M. August 22nd, 1926 at the Polyclinic Hospital. He was suffering great pain, had a moderate rise of temperature, a very rapid pulse, a board like rigidity of the entire abdominal wall and presented the picture of a rapidly spreading vicious peritonitis. A diagnosis of probably perforated gastric ulcer was made although other possibilities could not be excluded at this advanced stage. I urged immediate operation as his only chance for life.

Operation Findings:

The abdominal cavity contained a large amount of fluid and food particles. All the viscera were coated with a greenish gray film. A round hole 1 cm. in diameter was seen in the anterior wall of the stomach, 3 cm. from the pylorus and 2 cm. below the lesser curvature. There was no walling off by natural processes and fluid was still coming through the opening. The tissue of the stomach for 1 1/2 cm. immediately surrounding the perforation was necrotic. The appendix was acutely inflamed from a secondary infection, turned on itself and so fixed by a plastic exudate at its tip and by an old band at its mid point as to constrict the terminal illeum.

The Medical Report Sent to George Ullman from Rudolph Valentino's Attending Surgeon, Dr. Meeker - Page One

Median vertical incision over right rectus   All possible fluid and foreign particles removed by suction apparatus. Necrotic tissue around mar of ulcer excised, the edges of the opening were approximated by mattress sustures through all coats except the mucosa. A portion of the lesser omentum was stitched with fine linen over this suture line, this was in turn reinforced by a portion of greater omentum over it. A rubber drainage tube was stitched in place with fine catgut. The appendix was removed because it was constricting the gut otherwise it would not have been touched at this time. A second drainage tube was placed in the right illiac fossa and the abdominal wound closed. The patient was placed in bed in position most favorable to gravity drainage. He was in profound shock when put on the operating table with a pulse of 140. This condition did not change appreciably during the operation.

Progress:

    There was a steady improvement up to the 5th day. Abdominal drainage ceased on the 3rd day, pulse and temperature normal on the 5th day. On the morning of the 6th day the patient had a slight chill, complained of severe pain in upper left abdomen and left chest. An area of pleurisy was detected, this rapidly extended, scattered areas of pneumonia developed in the left lung. On the 6th day there was a marked involvment of the valves of the heart. The patient died about noon on the 8th day overwhelmed by the sepsis. The above is a true account of the last illness of Rudolph Valentino as observed by me.

    August 28th, 1926.   (Signed) Harold D. Meeker

Medical Report from Dr. Meeker – Page Two (cont.)

3, North Castle Wynd,
Edinburgh, EH1 2NQ,
March 21, 1975

S. George Ullman, Esq.
8450 De Longpre Avenue,
Los Angeles, Calif 90069,
United State of America.

Dear Mr. Ullman,

Thank you for your great kindness in returning the book on Rudy with your wonderful comment written below your Foreword. I may say this transcends the greatest ambition I ever dreamt when I began the book in 1947. When you wrote the Foreword in 1950, I could scarcely believe the reality that this had happened, so unattainable did I regard this, stamping as it did the book with absolute authority on Valentino second to none throughout the world, that I would never have dared to ask you to write of my own volition.

And now you have affixed your signature upon the book again to bring it up to date and perpetuate the challenge of the truth it contains about Rudy, to vanquish the lies and calumnies that others might say and write about him; as well as bringing enlightenment and nostalgic pleasure to those who will never forget his noble roles upon the screen / and those

Letter from Valentino Biographer, Norman MacKenzie thanking George Ullman for writing the Foreword to his book - Page One

2

of the younger generations who will always find something to admire in the chivalrous example and romantic magic of the hero who thrilled their mothers and grandmothers — and many a grandfather — as the legendary and immortal Rudolph Valentino.

Such is the impact your Foreword and signature has had upon me, and I am humbly and most deeply honoured that my name should appear beside your own upon the book.

The present edition, incidentally, is almost sold out and the publisher is already printing its second impression, to meet continued orders. No fewer than 110 public libraries in Britain now have the book and at least one American books importer ordered 53 copies to be sent to him in the U.S. for his large mail-order business. The book is catalogued in the big public lending and reference library in Edinburgh but is never seen on the shelves — so keen is the demand that it is always out on loan, while there is an increasing number of readers waiting to borrow it on the reserve list.

I am sorry indeed to learn that you have been in hospital and sincerely hope that you will be feeling strong and well again

Norman MacKenzie letter - Page Two

270

3

by the time you get this. Meantime,
thank you for your own good wishes
and please accept mine with my
highest regards and gratitude for the
privilege of knowing you as Rudy's
closest friend.

Yours sincerely,

Norman A. MacKenzie

Letter from Norman MacKenzie – Page Three

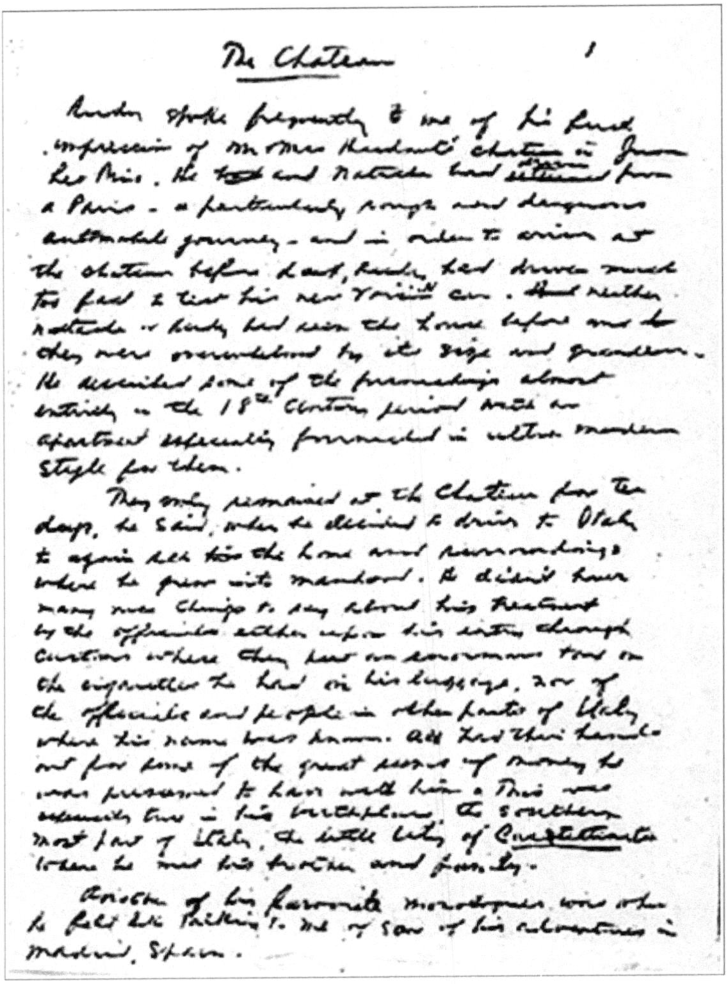

[Handwritten memoir text, largely illegible]

Sample Page of the 1970 Memoir in George Ullman's handwriting

33 A.

The result of Mrs Montgomery's broadcast actually occurred to me.

During on about December 10, 1972 my phone rang and a man's voice asked whether I was the George Ullman identified with Rudolph Valentino. When I answered affirmatively, he said: "I'm ____," "this is Rudy," I asked him which Rudy and he said "Rudy Valentino!" Of course I scoffed at this but he insisted that he wanted to see me. I told him that I was too ill to talk to him and to forbid me not to annoy me. But he did find his way to our apartment and when my wife opened the door, there was the tall young man who said to her, "Don't you recognize me? I'm Rudy". He asked for me but she told him that I was ill and in bed. She closed the door and when another visitor came he said "Someone left you a present. There, on the carpet of our landing, was an opened brown egg shelled there. This fellow has continued phoned several times ___ even at 7 AM! He wrote an abusing letter to me, but I haven't heard from him in about two months.

This was the only time ___ men have believed themselves the reincarnation of Valentino, but this one was the most persistent and annoying.

Sample Page of 1970 Memoir in George Ullman's Handwriting

grind house.

James M. Cain Buys His MGM Contract

James M. Cain has returned $3,330 to MGM and begged out of writing the screen play for "Duchess of Delmonico," on the ground that he had no desire to go through with the assignment and preferred to work on a novel he had already started.

The William Morris office returned its commission on the deal, having set a contract for $10,000 for the writer, one-third of which was paid down.

Sol Rosenblatt Turns Down Vaude Labor Bd.

New York.—Sol Rosenblatt has refused to take any action at this time on the recommendations of the Vaudeville Actors' Labor Committee.

He says that action now would mean the re-opening of the entire code and require open hearings at which all sections of the code would be discussed. This he is unwilling to see happen.

Loretta Young Figures In Double Loan Deal

Due to the postponement of the starting date on "Professional Correspondent," MGM yesterday loaned Loretta Young to Fox. The arrangement

week. The list comprises:

"I Like It That Way" at the Mayfair Monday; "Modern Hero" at the Strand today; "Stand Up and Cheer" at the Music Hall tomorrow; "Wharf Angel," with Gloria Swanson on the stage, at the Paramount; "I'll Tell the World" at the Roxy, and "Tarzan and His Mate," with radio stars on the stage, at the Capitol on Friday.

Ullman Exonerated in Valentino Estate Row

San Francisco.—The District Court of Appeals yesterday exonerated S. George Ullman of charges of mismanagement of the estate of Rudolph Valentino, of which he was executor, when it reversed an order of the Los Angeles Probate Court.

Ullman's management had been objected to by Jean Guglielmi, nephew and heir to the estate, who charged Ullman had made too many cash advances to the other heirs. The Appellate Court praised Ullman for his work.

Twelvetrees Wins Suit

Rebecca and Silton lost their suit for $236 against Helen Twelvetrees yesterday in Superior Court when Judge Thomas C. Gould sustained a demurrer claiming the court had no jurisdiction because of the amount of the suit.

New Universal Title

much so, tha to take him o run around a Austrian Tyrol the boy to ta fast and follov and that, if h all right. So and everyth smoothly whe instructor fre and evidentl Thinking the i vise him of sc he should kn up and finally structor. No very little Eng rushed up ex what he want just grinned ai "Who's afraic

Add to the the torture of a half hours other evening collapse from big brawny ou to the usher a manager, and ger asked hir He claimed t the place, t that the stage a few minut been two hou

George Ullman's Own Copy of the *Hollywood Reporter* Notice of His Complete Exoneration.

Article (Transcribed) Appearing in the
July 12, 1944
Issue of the *Los Angeles Herald-Express*

Dead Valentino Still Hero to His Agent

Real Rudolph is Divulged by Man Who Knew Him Best

By George Ullman
(Film Colony Agent)

Although Rudolph Valentino is almost eighteen years dead, I am still being asked, "What was the real Valentino like?"

Every famous person is more or less the victim of his legend: none more so than the boy born Rodolfo Alfonzo Raffaelo Pierre Filibert Guglielmi d'Valentino d'Antonguolla, who came to be called "The Sheik."

Rudy hated that tag, especially after it became a by-word for what is known as wolfing today. He was never a sheik in the accepted sense of the word; he was a man who sought to love one woman and whose unsatisfied dream was for a real home and children.

Valentino's outstanding characteristic when away from camera was shyness. He hated dance for that reason. His career with Bonnie Glass and later with Joan Sawyer, doing ballroom dances, brought him too close to his audience. He was an eternal boy but understood his capabilities. He knew he registered best in romantic roles. He was a failure when he departed from them, although he was persuaded to do so more than once.

Dodged Book Sets

Valentino was practically a chain smoker. He drank wines, loved good food, ate voraciously, cooked well and liked to cook. He appeared almost ordinary in golf or business clothes, was superb in anything approximating a costume, such as riding clothes, fencing apparel or lounging robes. He kept a large library of books with costume plates which he studied religiously. The remainder of his library was distinguished for rare volumes mostly in foreign

275

languages. He hated sets of books and never bought them.

Al Jolson was instrumental in bringing Valentino to Los Angeles. Norman Kerry, who became a lifelong friend helped him over tough days. Rudy was hopelessly extravagant and died broke. He bought a Mercer with his first permanent salary of $125 a week-spent most of it on repairs. His later cars were Voisons and Isotta Fraschinis. He loved machinery and had a workshop in his garage. Once he took his car apart and put it together again.

Danced for Grauman

Valentino danced in Grauman's Prologues before he made good in movies. Mae Murray gave him his first chance - they were always good friends. He was deeply interested in supernatural things during his marriage to Natacha Rambova - chiefly automatic writing. He had no small superstitions.

He never permitted anyone, even his wife, to see him disheveled. He had no shabby, comfortable old clothes. He spent a fortune on his wardrobe which was always new. He kept himself in superb physical trim, a result of two disappointments. As a boy he was turned down by the Royal Naval Academy because he lacked one inch in chest expansion. The Air Force turned him down in World War One because of his defective vision. His physical routine included sparring with Gene Delmont and Jack Dempsey who was a good friend.

He loved horses; a white Arabian stallion, Ramadan, was his favorite. A harlequin Dane and a Celtic Wolfhound were with him constantly as was a black Cocker Spaniel given to him by Mayor Rolph of San Francisco.

He wore black satin lounging clothes with a scarlet stripe on the trouser leg. His house had a black marble drawing room floor and scarlet velvet drapes. His dining room was in red lacquer and upholstered in black satin. His bedroom was done in black velvet and yellow.

He seldom laughed, rarely smiled, had a volcanic temper, quick and intense. He was often profane, even foul before men; never with women. He hated large statuary but had small figurines of jade, ivory and coral. When on his yacht he cooked, scrubbed, trimmed sail and worked like a navy.

Kidded Odd's Tastes

His intimate friends included O. O. McIntyre whom he kidded about his love of loud colors. Valentino always mailed Odd terrible ties. Beltram-Masses, famous Spanish painter, was an intimate of his. Valentino later studied with him. He was planning to take piano lessons when he died.

Other good friends were Lady Cursan, Cora Macy, Vilma Banky, Pola Negri, Prince Mdivani, Schuyler Parsons, Mario Carillo, Frank Mennillo (who was with him when he died), Ronald Coleman, Lady Loughborough, June Mathis, Cora McGeachy and Prince Habib Lotfallah of Egypt. Had Rudy lived he would have made a picture there.

He was married to and divorced from Jean Acker and Natacha Rambova. He romanced with Vilma Banky and Pola Negri but never confided in me about them. Rambova tired of their marriage first; he loved her deeply and she broke his heart.

I am a firm believer in personality as well as handsomeness being vital on the screen. In this Valentino was a superb showman in his public life and even if he in his private life was as different as the real Valentino was from the Valentino legend.

Valentino

Valentino As I Knew Him. By S. George Ullman. Introduction by
O. O. McIntyre. Illustrated. 213 pp. New York: Macy-Masius. $2.

Business manager, intimate friend, fatherly counselor of the
famous moving picture star, Mr. Ullman, endeavors to make his
biography as interpretation of Valentino's character and an exposition
of the reasons why, because of his qualities, he won fame on the screen
and the devoted affection not only of his friends but of millions who
knew him only by his work in the movies. The author has gathered his
material, he says, for this last tribute to his friend "from stories he told
me here and there, some related in the great bay window of his
Hollywood home, some on horseback riding over the desert at Palm
Springs, some on our long railway journeys between California and the
East."

Valentino had, apparently, told him much about this childhood
and youth, and he reconstructs with considerable completeness all that
period of the star's life before he came to the United States in 1913-sent
hither by his family on a sort of deportation sentence because they
began to fear he was going to be no credit to them and they wanted
him so far away that the disgrace they believed was inevitable would
not touch them. He had a difficult time and many vicissitudes for a
good many years after his arrival before his place in the moving
picture world began to be assured and adequately paid.

Mr. Ullman tells all this in such detail that the story might well
discourage many an aspirant for movie fame. He emphasizes
Valentino's own attitude towards his years as a dancer, saying that
while he enjoyed and loved dancing for its own sake he abhorred
being a professional dancer. He takes pains also to bring out
Valentino's essential masculinity of character and tells how deeply he
resented the slurs that were sometimes cast upon him because of the
parts he played. Mr. Ullman thinks that his life may have been
shortened because of his anger and mental suffering over a reference to
him in an editorial in a Chicago paper not long before his final illness.
The work is written with tender affection and from the viewpoint of
one immersed in the moving picture world.

The Court of Appeals Decision

April 1934

Opinion of the District Court of Appeal.

Civil No. 9321. First Appellate District, Division Two. April 17, 1934.

In the Matter of the Estate of Rodolpho Guglielmi, also known as Rudolph Valentino, deceased. S. George Ullman, executor and appellant, v. Alberto Guglielmi, Maria Guglielmi Strada and Teresa Werner, objectors and respondents. Bank of America National Trust & Savings Association, administrator with the will annexed, objector and respondent. Ray L. Riley, state comptroller, respondent.

Appeal by executor from an order of the Superior Court of Los Angeles county, Albert Lee Stephens, judge, settling account current and report of executor and from an order denying petition for partial distribution. *Reversed.*

For Appellant—Newlin & Ashburn, Gwyn Redwine.

For Respondent Bank of America National Trust & Savings Association, as administrator with will annexed, etc.—Scarborough & Bowen, McGee & Sumner.

Appeals were taken from an order of the probate court settling the account current and report of the executor and from an order denying a petition for partial distribution. Both appeals are presented on the same typewritten transcripts.

Rodolpho Guglielmi, also known as Rudolph Valentino, a motion picture actor, died testate August 23, 1926. On October 13, 1926, the appellant herein was appointed executor and thereupon entered upon the administration of his estate. The pertinent portions of the decedent's will, which was duly admitted to probate, provide: *"First:* I hereby revoke all former wills by me made and I hereby nominate and appoint S. George Ullman of the city of Los Angeles, county of Los Angeles, state of California, the executor of this my LAST WILL AND TESTAMENT, without bonds, either upon qualifying or in any stage of the settlement of my said estate.

"Second: I direct that my Executor pay all of my just debts and funeral expenses, as soon as may be practicable after my death.

"Third: I give, devise and bequeath unto my wife, Natacha Rambova, also known as Natacha Guglielmi, the sum of One Dollar ($1.00), it being my intention, desire and will that she receive this sum and no more.

"Fourth: All the residue and remainder of my estate, both real and personal, I give, devise and bequeath unto S. George Ullman, of the city of Los Angeles, county of Los Angeles, state of California, to have and to hold the same in trust and for the use of Alberto Guglielmi, Maria Guglielmi and Teresa Werner, the purposes of

dear friend Mrs. Werner the sum of $200.00 monthly.

"When my nephew Jean reaches the age of 25 years, I desire that the residue, if any, be given to him. In the event of his death then the residue shall be distributed equally to my sister Maria and my brother Alberto.

"RODOLPHO GUGLIELMI

"RUDOLPH VALENTINO."

In due time the probate court decided that these instructions were made contemporaneously with the will and became a part of the execution of the will, also that the will and the instructions taken together constituted the full terms of the trust created by the will.

Notice to creditors was given and all claims were paid or settled or had become barred when the account was filed. The inventory and appraisal filed April 13, 1927, showed real and personal property amounting to $244,033.15. A supplementary inventory and appraisal filed January 9, 1928, showed additional real and personal property amounting to $244,550 or a total estate of over $488,000.

On February 28, 1928, appellant filed his first account as executor, to which objections were made by Alberto Guglielmi and Maria Guglielmi Strada, the brother and sister of deceased. Proceedings for the settlement of this account were abandoned. On April 5, 1930, appellant filed a new first account to which objections were made by the same parties, but were not heard. On June 7, 1930, appellant filed his resignation as executor, which was accepted and the respondent Bank of America was appointed administrator with the will annexed. On August 18, 1930, appellant filed a supplemental account to which the administrator filed objections, including the objections made by the brother and sister to the former accounts. These accounts, with the objections of the administrator and of these heirs, came on for hearing on November 5, 1930, and on August 8, 1932, the probate court made the decree from which this appeal is taken.

In the course of this hearing the question arose as to the legality of advances made by appellant to the brother and sister of the deceased and to another beneficiary of the will and, on the suggestion of the court, a petition for partial distribution was filed by the administrator. On the hearing of that petition the probate court found that the decedent left surviving him as his only heirs at law Alberto Guglielmi and Maria Guglielmi Strada; that the only persons entitled to benefit from the trust created by the will were said heirs, Teresa Werner, and Jean Guglielmi; that the questions relative to the advances made to three of the above beneficiaries were determined by the decree settling the account entered contemporaneously with this account, and that because of the condition of the estate no partial distribution should be decreed.

During his lifetime the decedent had been engaged in various activities in addition to his work as an actor. He was interested in the production and development of pictures under the corporate name of Rudolph Valentino Productions, Inc., which, however, was but an *alter ego*. He was engaged in the exploitation of chemical discoveries under the corporate name of Cosmic Arts, Inc. He was also sole owner of a cleaning business under the name of Ritz, Inc. In March, 1925, decedent made a contract with a motion picture producer under which he agreed to give his services as a motion picture actor to that producer exclusively. In April, 1925, he assigned his interest in the profits under this contract to Cosmic Arts, Inc. In August, 1925, Cosmic Arts, Inc., assigned its interest in this contract to Rudolph Valentino Productions, Inc. The stockholders in Cosmic Arts, Inc., were the decedent, Natacha Rambova, his wife, and Teresa Werner, his wife's aunt. Though these three corporations were separate entities, the decedent for a long time prior to his death conducted the affairs of all three under the ostensible name of

Rudolph Valentino Productions, Inc., making all expenditures through the latter with little regard for the corporate entity of the other two concerns. During this period the appellant served in the capacity of business manager and personal representative of the decedent; superintendent of Ritz, Inc.; secretary, treasurer and director of Cosmic Arts, Inc.; and manager of Rudolph Valentino Productions, Inc., his compensation for all these services being paid by Rudolph Valentino Productions, Inc.

Immediately upon his qualification as executor and acting upon the asserted authority of the will to continue the Rudolph Valentino Productions, Inc., for the purpose of perpetuating the name of deceased, the appellant entered upon the management of all these concerns in the same manner in which they had been conducted in the lifetime of the decedent. In these transactions the appellant, seemingly acting as the executor of the estate rather than as trustee under the will, paid all claims outstanding against the decedent, personal as well as those incurred by the corporations mentioned. The exact figures covering these expenditures are not material to this inquiry, but the appellant emphasizes the fact that as executor he took an estate which was heavily involved financially and practically bankrupt and through his management all indebtedness was cleared and the property of the estate was increased in value to $890,000.

In the course of the conduct of these activities the appellant borrowed and loaned money, executed mortgages and retired existing liens, purchased new property to be used in the business, and sold property belonging to the estate. To obtain publicity to aid in the display of the decedent's pictures, two spectacular funerals were held—one in New York and one in Los Angeles —and Valentino Memorial Clubs were organized in many different centers. Because of the financial condition of the estate at the time these expenditures were paid largely from money borrowed by the executor on his personal obligations and all or nearly all were made without an order of court. When funds accumulated through the distribution of pictures the appellant made loans, some with security and some without. In September, 1927, he loaned one Mae Murray $22,000 at seven per cent. In March, 1928, he loaned the Pan American Company $50,000 at seven per cent, secured by Pan American Bank stock of the then value of $78,000; at various times during the year 1928 he loaned one Frank Menillo $40,000 at eight per cent. The Murray loan was repaid. The Pan American loan was compromised at a loss of $16,000 to the estate, with which amount appellant was charged to account with interest on the full amount of the loan. The

Menillo loan was unpaid at the time of the entry of the decree herein and appellant was charged to account in full with interest.

The ruling of the probate court on these two items presents the principal ground of attack upon the decree. If appellant was authorized to carry on the business of the decedent, to invest and reinvest the funds in his hands, then any losses arising from these transactions must be borne by the estate. If he was not so authorized the losses are his. The question of the right of an executor to carry on the business of the deceased when so directed by the testator first came directly before our appellate courts in *Estate of Ward,* 127 Cal. App. 347, a case which was decided after the decree herein was entered. In that case Judge Ames, sitting *pro tempore* in the Appellate Court, carefully reviewed the authorities and concluded that, in the absence of fraud or mismanagement, an executor should not be charged with losses while he is following out the instructions of the testator. Numerous authorities from other jurisdictions are cited by Judge Ames, to which reference may be had in that opinion. This distinction between the two cases should be noted—here all these loans were made from profits of the estate accumulated by the executor; in the Ward case the losses were in the principal. The conclusions there reached compel a reversal of the decree as to the Pan

American and Menillo loans because they were attacked on the sole ground that they were made without order of court or without "sufficient" surety, but were not attacked upon any charge of fraud or mismanagement.

The dual capacity of the executor and trustee involved in this appeal is the same as that considered in the Ward estate, where the court, after reviewing authorities on that subject, held that, taking the will as a whole, it could not have been the intention of the testator to suspend operations of the business during the period of time required for the administration of the estate and the appointment of a trustee. The case here is even stronger than the will interpreted in the Ward case, because the instructions of the testator to the trustee are so blended and mingled that they could scarcely be separated the one from the other. The directions to the executor to "perpetuate my name in the picture industry by continuing the Rudolph Valentino Productions, Inc.", and the directions to the trustee "to hold, manage, and control the said trust, property, and estate; to keep the same invested and productive as far as possible", disclose an intention of the testator to treat the executor and trustee without the legal distinction that a court would draw between the two offices.

For these reasons we conclude that the executor was both authorized and directed by the will to carry on the business of the decedent as it had been carried on in his lifetime and that the investments made by him through loans to the Pan American Company and to Menillo were made in the course of the operation of that business and, being without fraud, the appellant should not be charged for the losses occurring therefrom, nor should he be surcharged with interest on account of any investments made in his management of the estate.

The probate court charged appellant with an item of $17,280.19 expended by him in compliance with a contract of Cosmic Arts, Inc. This item presents an issue closely related to that just discussed. Cosmic Arts, Inc., was a family corporation organized by the deceased. Ten shares of stock were issued, all in the name of Natacha Rambova, the then wife of the decedent. One of these shares was transferred to her aunt, another to the decedent, and the three were the directors. Decedent resigned from the directorship and had the appellant appointed in his place. While the latter was acting as director and treasurer of the corporation and under the authority of the by-laws he executed a contract with one Lambert obligating the corporation to bear any and all expenses in connection with the patenting, sale, and exploitation of patents covering a chemical discovery called Lambertite. For a considerable period prior to his death the affairs of this corporation were conducted by the decedent as his *alter ego*, acting through the appellant as his personal manager in very much the same manner as the affairs of the Rudolph Valentino Productions, Inc., were conducted. The contract referred to was apparently ratified by the corporation and the expenses of the corporation were paid by the decedent not only in connection with the patenting of the process, but in the conduct of the laboratory in New York city for the development of the process. Upon his qualification as executor the appellant continued to pay these expenses, amounting to a total of over $19,000 and so accounted to the estate. In the hearing of the objections to this item the appellant contended that the entire stock of the corporation had been transferred to the decedent through a property settlement made at the time of the separation with his wife, but the separation agreement was not produced. The contract with Lambert was received in evidence and from this the probate court found that Cosmic Arts, Inc., was entitled to one-third of the profits resulting from the sale and exploitation of the patents and that therefore it was liable for but one-third of the expenses incurred in the patenting, sale and exploitation of the process. Upon this theory it was concluded that the decedent and his estate were liable for but one-ninth of these expenses, basing this conclusion solely upon the theory that Cosmic Arts, Inc., was a family corporation organized by the decedent, his wife and his wife's aunt, in which the decedent had a one-third interest.

The evidence on this issue is in such an unsatisfactory state that it is impossible at this time to determine the issue. It is manifest that it was tried by the probate court without the benefit of the decision in the Ward case and that if the facts justify the contention of the appellant that Cosmic Arts, Inc., was also an *alter ego* of the decedent, the business of which appellant was authorized by the will to carry on under the will, then such losses incurred by appellant in the operation of that business as may be found to have been incurred without fraud or mismanagement must, under the rule of the Ward case, be held to be the losses of the estate and not of the appellant. For these reasons this issue should be retried.

Appellant complains of the ruling of the probate court surcharging him with interest on the full amount of moneys withdrawn by him on account of his fees for extraordinary services in advance of an order of court authorizing any fee for such services. The evidence discloses that during his period of administration the appellant withdrew from the funds of the estate sums aggregating $22,300, for which he asked credit in the settlement of his account upon the basis of extraordinary services rendered the estate. The probate court disallowed the item and charged appellant to account for interest at the rate of seven per cent from the time of each withdrawal. It then allowed the appellant an additional fee for extraordinary services fixed at $15,000. The appellant now argues that this sum should be subtracted from the total amount withdrawn and that he should be charged to return to the estate the difference, amounting to $7,300 and should be charged interest on that amount only. Authorities cited by the appellant relating to statutory fees to which an executor is entitled as matter of right do not apply to a case of this kind. Extraordinary fees are allowed an executor within the discretion of the probate court and unless and until an order is made there is no obligation on the part of the estate to pay more than the statutory fees. Hence, when an executor upon his own motion withdraws the funds of an estate to pay himself fees in addition to the amount allowed by statute, he is to be charged with the amount thereof with interest thereon from the date of withdrawal. (*Estate of Piercy*, 168 Cal. 755, 757.)

It is next contended that the court erred in holding the appellant liable for the advances to the brother and sister of the decedent and to Teresa Werner on account of what he deemed to be their distributive shares of the estate. The court found in its decree settling the account that the executor improperly and without authority or order of court advanced to decedent's brother over $37,000 out of the funds and property of the estate; to the decedent's sister over $12,000 in cash and personal property; to Teresa Werner over $7,000 in cash and to Frank A. Menillo at various times and in various amounts an aggregate sum of $9,100. Having ruled during the hearing on the settlement of the account that it was not competent for the court in that proceeding to determine questions of heirship, and having directed a special proceeding to be instituted for that purpose, the court, contemporaneously with the entry of its decree in the settlement of the account, entered its decree in the other proceeding wherein it was found that the brother and sister were the only surviving heirs at law of the decedent and that the only persons entitled to benefit under the will were the brother, the sister, Teresa Werner, a stranger, and Jean Guglielmi, a nephew of decedent. It will be recalled that under the terms of the instructions the brother, the sister and Mrs. Werner were each to receive a stipulated sum monthly until the nephew, Jean, reached the age of 25 years when the residue was directed to be given to him; that in the event of the death of the nephew the residue was to be distributed equally between the brother and sister. It is apparent from these provisions of the will that Teresa Werner was entitled to participate in the assets of the estate only to the extent of a monthly payment out of profits which the executor derived from pictures made under his direction and that the brother and sister were entitled to a distributive share in the estate only in the event of the death of the nephew, Jean. It necessarily follows that advancements made to these individuals in excess of the monthly payments directed by the will were improper. The appellant does not question this final result, but does criticize the method by which the court expressed its conclusion. In its decree in the proceeding for partial distribution it declared the issues relative to these advances had been determined by its decree correcting and settling the account of the executor and that by reason of the foregoing decree said advances "are hereby declared to be void and improper and chargeable to said executor herein". It is true, as argued by the appellant, that the issue covering the propriety of advances on distributive shares is not one which may be determined on a hearing of a settlement of the executor's account, but that such issue can be determined only upon a hearing for distribution, partial or final. (12 Cal. Jur. 181.) We are not, however, in accord with appellant's view that the court was in error so far as it went. Though reference is made in its decree to the order settling the account, there is sufficient in the decree denying distribution to constitute a determination that these advances were void and improper and as such chargeable to the executor.

There are certain equities involved in this issue which require comment. In the will proper, which was admitted to probate in October, 1926, the executor was directed to hold all the property in trust "to keep the same invested and productive as far as possible and to pay over the net income derived therefrom" to Alberto and Maria Guglielmi and to Teresa Werner. Four years later, the appellant, in answer to the petition for partial distribution, came into court and for the first time set forth a copy of the written instructions which he alleged had been executed contemporaneously with the execution of the will and which he alleged had been lost, destroyed, or surreptitiously removed from the personal effects and safe of the decedent. In the decree entered in that proceeding the probate court found this to be a true copy of the original instructions executed by the decedent and declared that said instructions should be taken together as the complete terms of the trust created by the will. Under the terms of these instructions the appellant was directed to pay to Alberto Guglielmi $400 a month, to Maria Guglielmi $200 a month and to Mrs. Werner $200 a month out of the "profits from pictures made by the Rudolph Valentino Productions, Inc.". Then for the first time the nephew, Jean, is mentioned and to him is given the entire residue when he reaches the age of 25 years. This is followed by the proviso that in the event of his death the residue should be distributed equally to Alberto and Maria. It will be noted that under the terms of the will proper the appellant was directed to pay over to Alberto and Maria and to Mrs. Werner the net income derived from the estate as a whole, whereas under the terms of the written instructions he was directed to pay stipulated amounts monthly to each of the three from profits from pictures made by the Rudolph Valentino Productions, Inc. It does not appear from the record who was responsible for the loss of the written instructions following the decedent's death nor whether the appellant had any information or knowledge of their terms prior to the advancements he made to these three. It does appear that all these advances were made with the consent and at the solicitation of the three beneficiaries involved. We are in accord with the holding of the probate court that these advances were improperly made if the terms of the written instructions are held to be controlling over the terms of the fourth paragraph of the will proper and if these advances are held to have been made from funds other than the net income derived from the estate as a whole. Under the rule of *Estate of Willey*, 140 Cal. 238, this is an issue which cannot be tried or determined in the proceeding for the settlement of the account, but is one which could have been determined on the proceeding for partial distribution. The proper practice is as outlined in the Willey case to retire from the consideration of the settlement of the account the question of the propriety of advances of distributive shares so that that question can be determined on distribution of the estate. The record on the petition for distribution does not disclose that this question was fully tried and determined. Manifestly, if these three beneficiaries were entitled to the net income derived from the management of the estate as a whole and if the advances made to them by the appellant were from that net income alone he should not be charged to account to the estate in full for those advances or for interest as if he had defaulted or misapplied the funds to his own use. On the other hand, if, upon final distribution, it be found that the nephew is dead and that the brother and sister are then entitled under the will to the entire residue, then the amounts advanced to them by the appellant may be held to have been advanced on account of their distributive shares and appellant would be entitled to a credit accordingly. These considerations were undoubtedly in the contemplation of the probate court when, in rendering its decree denying partial distribution, it found that it was unable to determine whether there would be sufficient funds or property to distribute to the trustee or to permit the trust to be executed and performed and for that reason reserved its determination of the ultimate practicability of the trust until the final distribution of the estate. But in any event, if these advances were made in good faith and at the solicitation of the beneficiaries and appellant is held to be accountable to the estate in full therefor, he should be given an appropriate lien against the beneficial interest of those who participated in the advancement of the property and funds of the estate. (*In re Moore,* 96 Cal. 522; *Finnerty v. Pennie,* 100 Cal. 404, 407; *Estate of Schluter,* 209 Cal. 286, 289.)

Though the appellant has not assigned any special error for the reversal of the order denying partial distribution, the equities herein referred to impel a reversal so that both matters may be before the probate court for new proceedings consistent with the views herein expressed.

The orders appealed from are both reversed.

NOURSE, *P. J.*

We concur:

STURTEVANT, *J.*

SPENCE, *J.*

Lightning Source UK Ltd.
Milton Keynes UK
UKHW021835240621
386102UK00006B/337